# Carole Lombard

## TWENTIETH-CENTURY STAR

# Carole Lombard

## TWENTIETH-CENTURY STAR

MICHELLE MORGAN

The History Press

This book is dedicated with much love and thanks to
Vincent Paterno and Carole Sampeck.

First published 2016

The History Press
The Mill, Brimscombe Port
Stroud, Gloucestershire, GL5 2QG
www.thehistorypress.co.uk

British Library Cataloguing in Publication Data.
A catalogue record for this book is available from the British
Library.

ISBN 978 0 7509 6605 4

Typesetting and origination by The History Press
Printed and bound by TJ InternationaL Ltd

# CONTENTS

# ACKNOWLEDGEMENTS

I first decided to write a book about Carole Lombard nearly ten years ago. Since then, I have received many helpful emails and letters from all around the world. It is impossible to name everyone who has leant their support to this project, but please be assured that everyone who has provided inspiration, help, or both, is very much appreciated. Thank you all!

I would like to thank Christina Rice, who has helped me gain access to rare newspaper articles and stories. I don't know what I'd do without her help.

Vincent Paterno, Carole Sampeck, Debbie Beno, Douglas Cohen, Bruce Calvert, Robert S. Birchard, Dina-Marie Kulzer and Ana Trifescu have all been gracious enough to share their photos, letters, rare documents and other memorabilia with me. Vincent also trawled the archives at the Academy of Motion Picture Arts and Sciences – a kindness I will never forget.

I must also extend thanks to the following: Robert Matzen, Tegan Summer, Stan Taffel, Mary Curry, Karen Zuehlke, Jerry Tucker, Simon Elliott, Ted Okuda, Kay Shackleton, Albert Palacios, Valerie Yaros, David Stenn, Michael B. Druxman, the staff at the Kobal Archive, Jenny Romero, Michael McComb, Matt Vogel, Darrell Rooney, Jay Jacobson, Gregory Moore, Rick and Cora Brandt, Bruce Stier, James Reid, Brian Burton, Creager Smith, Jeffrey Sharpe, L. Thomas Horton, Carole Irene, Dixie Bradley and Evonne Quinn.

Thanks so much to my agent, Robert Smith, and to my editors, Juanita Hall and Mark Beynon, and everyone at The History Press for believing in the book.

I would like to thank my friends, Claire and Helen, for supporting my projects. Claire, I hope this book will join the others in your 'Michelle shrine'!

Thank you to Mum, Dad, Paul, Wendy and Angelina for all the love you continue to give me on an everyday basis. I love you all very much! Finally, my husband Richard and my daughter Daisy … life would be very boring without you two. I love you both to the moon and back!

And to anyone I may have missed, sorry for the oversight, but thanks to you too!

I have never sacrificed myself for another. I am not a martyr. Being a martyr shows lack of courage. There are more lives ruined by so-called martyrdom than are saved. I do not believe in luck. You hear persons speak of his or her bad luck, but it isn't luck they mean. It's judgement – knowing how to take advantage of opportunities, grasping good ones when they present themselves, and rejecting the bad.

Carole Lombard, 1934

# THE HOOSIERS

Throughout her life, Carole Lombard would be reminded by her mother, Elizabeth Knight Peters, that she was the product of excellent breeding. The family was upstanding, she said, and the young woman must never forget that. Stories would be passed down about the men being hardworking entrepreneurs; high achievers in everything they did both personally and professionally. Elizabeth (aka Bessie) wasn't just being overly proud of her relatives, she had good reason to share her tales, particularly on the part of her grandfather, James Cheney.

Cheney was known as the 'wealthiest man in Fort Wayne', with a fortune estimated at $2.5 million by the time of his death. That said, he was a very unassuming man who lived his life in such a quiet way that some of his friends had no idea what he had actually achieved in his lifetime. They knew he was rich, but for the most part he was known only as 'Judge' Cheney, the smartly dressed man who pottered around his garden, admiring the finely pruned hedges and nicely clipped lawn. He waved to passers-by as he raked leaves from the gravelled paths, enjoyed a joke, read the newspaper and always listened with a sensitive ear and words of encouragement.

Despite his unassuming nature, however, James Cheney was an extremely powerful man. Born to a good but relatively poor family, he read obsessively, began working by the age of 11 and continued until his death, over seventy years later. During his career he worked as a dry goods salesman, a builder's supplier, a canal builder, tavern owner, land speculator, farmer, miller, Wall Street financier, stockholder and banker. As well as that, he also had an interest in the Western Union Telegraph Company and the Wabash Railroad, owned shares in several companies including the City National Bank of New York and Fort Wayne Gaslight Company, and became a prominent figure in plans to lay a cable across the Atlantic.

Cheney took great interest in politics, voted Democrat, loaned money to needy causes and frequently fought for justice. While never a member of any church, he donated generously to the First Presbyterian Church because his wife, Nancy, was a member and he wanted to support her interests as well as his own. A dedicated Mason, Cheney even helped out when plans to construct a temple hit blocks. He ensured the project not only got off the ground but took on a new life, too. When asked why he had decided to help, Cheney simply shrugged and said, 'Well I've been a Mason for years but I never did anything much for Masonry, and I thought I had a chance now and would take it'. Such was the simplicity with which he undertook his projects. He may have been a multi-millionaire, but above all he was an honest, quiet and loyal man.

Carole Lombard's grandmother, Alice, was the daughter of James and Nancy, and when she grew up she married Charles Knight. He was successful in a very similar way to James: at one time working as a manager at the Fort Wayne Gas Company and then the Fort Wayne Electric Company. He was also a prominent Mason, and for those reasons alone, he had a lot in common with his father-in-law. In fact, so well did the in-laws get along, that Cheney lived with Alice and Charles for the latter part of his life.

Carole's grandfather on the other side of the family was John C. Peters, also a prominent businessman in Fort Wayne. He had started off as a cabinetmaker before going on to have an interest in various local enterprises and became president of the Horton Manufacturing Company (manufacturer of the Horton washing and ironing machines) and the Peters Hotel Company. His experience of carpentry was put to good use on several occasions. He oversaw the building of the Wayne Hotel in 1887 and also built two houses, one of which was said to be No. 704 Rockhill Street, the house where Carole Lombard was later born.

John C. Peters was described as thin and medium height, with white hair and a Vandyke beard. He and his wife, Mary, had a large family, including son Fred, the man who would go on to become Carole's father. As he grew into a young man, Fred was thrilled to be given a job at the family firm, J.C. Peters and Company. Unfortunately, the experience almost cost the young man his life and would have disastrous results for his future happiness.

On the morning of 2 July 1898, Fred travelled to the shop on East Columbia Street, just as he did every day. He went up to the upper floor to take care of some chores and, once completed, decided to head back downstairs by taking the store's elevator. Tragically, as he stepped in the carriage began to move unexpectedly and within seconds Fred found himself caught between the floor and the lift itself, causing him to be crushed about the head, shoulders, arms, chest, back and right thigh. The accident was horrendous and while Fred was freed quite quickly from the elevator, by that time he was barely conscious and in a terrible state.

Local doctors were called to the store and examined the young man. They ordered him to be moved to his home immediately, where they could examine him in private, away from the eyes of shop staff and customers. Fred was in great pain and distress, but after checking him over thoroughly, the doctors decided that while there were a great many bruises and lacerations, remarkably there were no broken bones and there would be no need for him to be taken to hospital. He was very lucky, they told Fred's parents, but predicted that it would take several days before they would know the full extent of his injuries. It was impossible to rule out the possibility of internal injuries, though after confining him to bed doctors assured his parents that there was no reason why Fred could not make a permanent recovery. Mary and John were considerably relieved.

For the next six days Fred's family fussed around and made him as comfortable as they possibly could. The local press sent reporters to the door, and on the 8 July reported that he remained confined to bed and was 'still suffering much'. However, his mood was lightened somewhat after receiving many visitors. One friend, John Ross McCulloch, had been in hospital having his appendix removed when the accident happened. When he was well enough to leave, John refused to be taken home before he could visit – and cheer up – his friend.

Visits like these helped to spur Fred on to recovery, and he eventually returned to work. Then, on 1 July 1899, almost exactly one year to the day after the accident, the young man was rewarded with a promotion to what the newspapers described as 'a very responsible position'. It was indeed – J.C. Peters & Company had been steadily growing over the years, with much of the success coming from the hard work of Fred Peters. His father John decided to reward him by handing over the day-to-day management of the hardware firm 'as a reward of merit and close attention to business'. The *Fort Wayne Sentinel* wrote, 'The promotion of Mr. Peters will be a source of much gratification to his hundreds of friends, many of whom will undoubtedly take advantage of the opportunity to call at the store and extend sincere congratulations.'

The announcement of the promotion gave great hope to Fred, but it was to last just six months, after which John C. Peters decided to sell the company to Henry Pfeiffer and Son so that he could devote more time to his manufacturing interests. By the time the new owners took charge on 2 January 1900 Fred had decided to leave and rumours went round town that he was about to take over the running of the Wayne Hotel. He did not, however, and instead went to work once again with his father, this time at the Horton Manufacturing Company. By 5 June 1901 he had taken over the prestigious job of secretary and treasurer.

As she grew up, Elizabeth Knight became terribly interested in playing and watching tennis matches. She was also something of a social butterfly, often attending parties and other gatherings with family and friends.

Fred Peters was also a partygoer and enjoyed dances and picnics not only in town, but further afield too. He had known Elizabeth through his circle of friends for many years, but as the two grew into adulthood Fred began to see her in a different light. The two started dating in earnest, though their happiness threatened to come crashing down when it was discovered that Elizabeth was pregnant. It remains unrecorded as to what their families had to say about the matter (though one can imagine that it was not positive) and no time was wasted in trying desperately to hide the unfortunate situation. In late March it was announced in the local newspaper that the two were to be married, 'Mr. and Mrs. C. Knight have issued invitations to the wedding of their daughter, Miss Elizabeth Jayne, to Fred C. Peters. The wedding will occur April 3rd at 8 pm at the home of the bride on Spy Run Avenue.'

Despite it being something of a shotgun affair, the bride's home was a hive of activity during the week of the wedding. Alice Knight fluttered around making sure everything was just right for the upcoming ceremony, bridesmaids practised their bridal march and many friends came and went with good wishes and gifts for the happy couple. Parties and teas were held at various places in the lead up to the wedding, and the big day itself was something of a major event in the town. On that day, the parlour, dining room and living rooms were all lavishly decorated in green and white mignonette, Easter lilies and white tulips. Wild smilax, ferns and daffodils were used in the hall and stairway and in the dining room the tables were arranged in three sides of a square and decorated with sweet peas and maidenhair ferns. The room was romantically lit with candelabras bearing white candles with pink shades.

Elizabeth walked down the aisle in a beautiful gown of lace over white satin and trimmed with duchess lace and tulle, her hair styled beneath a veil fastened with an ostrich tip to match that of the six bridesmaids. After the ceremony, a lavish supper was held, and then the younger members of the family took themselves down to the Wayne Club, where they partied until Fred and his new wife made their excuses and left to prepare for their honeymoon.

The couple were away for two weeks before returning first to the Peters' family home, and then to their new and permanent address of

No. 704 Rockhill Street. Just over five months after their wedding, in September 1902, Elizabeth gave birth to their first child, Frederic (Fritz) Peters Jnr. Considering the couple were still young at the time, this new set of responsibilities could have been terribly difficult and hard going. However, for the most part, their social lives remained unaffected.

In February 1903 Fred was struck with a terrible bout of tonsillitis, but as soon as he recovered the couple continued their regular mix of events and parties. So affluent was their lifestyle that they even made the pages of the *Fort Wayne Journal* and *Columbia City Post* in September 1903, after travelling with friends to a party in a brand new car. 'Their machine attracted considerable attention,' said the *Post*, 'It being one of the latest Wintons and complete in every sense.'

It wasn't all glitz and glamour, however, as just a few months later on 13 December 1903 Elizabeth's grandfather James Cheney passed away after a battle with cancer. The *Fort Wayne Journal Gazette* described the passing:

> The millionaire, who was more widely known in Wall Street circles than in his home, passed away at 11 o'clock yesterday morning, after an illness of only three days. It could scarcely be called an illness, either, for there was no bodily ailment, but only a steady decline of the physical powers. The years had had their way with the mortal frame, the life ebbed away, and James Cheney, the friend and confidant of Jay Gould and Cyrus Field, the modest man who had been a chief factor in some of the greatest movements of modern times, passed from earth. Thus ended one of the strangest and one of the most notable careers in the commercial and social history of the west.

The family was devastated, especially as he had been a constant fixture in Elizabeth's parents' home during the last years of his life. It wasn't the only negative thing to come their way, as not long after they had a break-in at their home on Rockhill Street, when a man by the name of Thomas Vachon entered the property and stole a great deal of food from their larder. The man was caught, though the matter was eventually dropped when the prosecuting witness could not give any intelligent testimony. Strangely the home would be targeted again several years later, when burglars gained entry through a cellar window and made off with a large amount of food and drink, including fruit, eggs, bread, coffee and wine. This time the burglars came prepared, and not only made use of a basket but also a wagon that acted as something of a getaway car.

Still, despite any disappointments that came their way during those first years of marriage, the social interests of Fred and Elizabeth carried on regardless. Fred became a regular fixture at the local golf club, where he not only played in various tournaments, but won many of them too. The accident that almost crippled him some years before had left Fred with blinding headaches at times, but it certainly did not stop him from taking part in his beloved sports activities and tournaments.

On 12 April 1905 the couple welcomed another son: John Stuart Peters (known by his middle name). Not long after, Elizabeth was spotted at several golf club parties and then visited friends and relatives in Chicago, Michigan and Ohio. She also became very interested in playing bridge, and her appearances at parties made the social diary of newspapers during the next year. Her interest in the card game knew no bounds and sometimes Elizabeth would even arrange charity games herself, with entry fees and proceeds from refreshments all going to good causes.

This skill for organising undoubtedly came from her mother, Alice, who consistently made sure that visiting relatives and friends had parties to go to and events to attend. However, Elizabeth's skills went much further than social events, and over time she became involved with many different committees, but particularly the Young Women's Society of the First Presbyterian Church. In February 1907 she became very vocal about her concerns for the nearby Hope Hospital and the various ways they needed help. Along with other members of the church, she organised a charity day which raised money for the hospital, and then afterwards kept a strict eye on what needed to be done in future.

In June 1907, Elizabeth was devastated to learn that her father, Charles, had been taken gravely ill while visiting his mining interests in Kentucky. Leaving the children with Fred she rushed to his side and, together with her brother Willard, managed to nurse the man back to health. In early July, Elizabeth and Willard returned to Fort Wayne with their father, who was described as 'improving rapidly'.

Life got back to normal and continued with Elizabeth's regular parties, weddings and theatre trips, while Fred went on hunting trips with his brother, William. His brother also featured in his golfing activities, and Fred beat him in the finals of the Benson Golf Club. 'Fred Peters played a hard, steady and consistent game throughout,' said the *Fort Wayne Daily News*. 'He was unusually skilful at critical times and won the match on the merit of his work. He was effective in approaching and putting and was driving with accuracy and skill from the first hole to the last.' Fred's interest in golf did not end with just playing it, and before long he was involved with the pastimes committee at the local golf club too.

In early 1908, Elizabeth discovered she was pregnant again, though she continued with her social life in earnest. There seemed to be no stopping her, but on 6 October she was forced to slow down just a little when her daughter, Jane Alice Peters – the future Carole Lombard – was born at No. 704 Rockhill Street. 'Mr. and Mrs. Fred Peters are rejoicing over the birth of a little daughter on Tuesday evening,' said the *Fort Wayne Journal Gazette* on 8 October. The couple fell madly in love with the new child and she quickly became an important and beloved member of the family. Carole, however, didn't ever see herself as particularly beautiful. 'As a child, I not only was a blonde, but worse – a tow-head,' she said. 'I had a round face, wore my hair in a Dutch bob, and was fat.'

Jane fitted straight into her family's social life, and her early childhood was a mix of family weddings, sports and community activities. At the very centre of it all was her mother, Elizabeth, who continued to organise events, win tennis matches and host meetings not only for the Young Women's Society, but for the National Congress of Mothers and Parent Teachers Association too. Many of the meetings were held at the Peters' house, where Elizabeth busied herself with refreshments and entertainment for guests. Jane would entertain the grown-ups by walking around on her tiptoes; a trick that convinced her mother that a dance career was in her future. Fred, meanwhile, won golf tournament after golf tournament while at the same time travelling around the country to oversee various business matters.

When Jane was 10 months old her grandfather, Charles Knight, passed away. His health had been up and down for a while and finally he died after a struggle with chronic Bright's disease. Shortly after, the family went on holiday and then Elizabeth took her mother to Chicago to visit relatives.

The Peters family certainly did not want for anything. They had a servant to help out with general household chores and a washerwoman too. Holidays were spent at a family cottage in Rome City, and the local country club was like a second home. Every Christmas the family home was decorated specifically for the children and their grandmother Alice would arrange for her coachman, George Winburn, to deliver gifts of toys and popcorn. Winburn would also be in charge of driving the children to local parks during big family get-togethers at Alice Knight's home.

Watching the way her mother and grandmother organised family functions and official events was inspiring to Jane and she quickly became a bubbly, confident child. Constantly told that girls could do anything boys could do, she made sure she was in constant competition with her two brothers and became involved in everything they did. Tree climbing, cops and robbers, sports: if it was something her brothers were into, the chances were Jane was too. Luckily, they loved her company and the three got along extremely well together.

In 1931, the Peters' former maid gave a revealing interview to *The New Movie Magazine*. In it she described exactly how Jane spent the early years of her childhood:

> Jane was always sticking up for her brothers, especially when youngsters would kid her by calling for 'Fried Peas' and 'Stewed Peas' meaning Fritz and Stuart, and then the racket would start. She had a little temper and this was developed by her continual contact with the neighbourhood boys, who were more numerous than girls then. Football, baseball, and racing were generally watched by Jane and before the games were over she always figured in the sports some way or other.

In early 1913, Fort Wayne was hit by an almighty flood that rendered many residents homeless. Easter functions were cancelled and those affected were forced to flee their homes and move in with friends and relatives.

Spy Run Avenue, where Alice lived, was hit by the disaster and for a time she moved in with Elizabeth, Fred and the children. Luckily her home was not destroyed and she moved back fairly quickly, but many people were not so lucky and the flood ruined their properties and threatened the lives of their animals. Police were installed to stop residents returning to feed their pets, but this did not stop everyone. Children built rafts and tried to paddle along the streets, but soon found themselves stranded or, even worse, thrown into the water. The police labelled small boys as one of the biggest nuisances and newspapers begged children to stay away from the water.

The Peters family was not directly affected by the flood and Elizabeth used this miracle to help others. She opened her home to the public, called meetings with local women to share news of what was happening around town and invited workmen to come in and receive fresh clothing and warm drinks. She even arranged for coffee to be sent out to the men working on the flood waters, and made sure that everyone knew her home was a safe place to come. 'She has relieved a great number of people in the last few days,' said the *Fort Wayne Journal Gazette*, 'and given a beautiful example, which as many of her friends as possible have tried to follow.'

Eventually the waters subsided and the town got back to some semblance of normality. Normal for the Peters family was seeing Fred head off on a four-week business trip to California, with Elizabeth and the children moving into Alice's house while theirs was remodelled. On Fred's return, the family went up to their Rome City cottage and then moved into the home of friends while the Rockhill premises continued to be revamped.

From the outside, things seemed perfectly normal for the family and Fred continued entering – and winning – golf tournaments. He also spent a great deal of time campaigning with neighbours to receive compensation after some of their properties had been bought up in order to widen the road. They won, and received various amounts of money on 11 August 1913.

Elizabeth, meanwhile, helped her mother prepare for a trip to Europe and took part in tennis tournaments with other family members. On 6 October 1913, Jane was given a party to celebrate her 5th birthday.

Decorations were strewn all over the house in various shades of pink and white, friends came round to play and Elizabeth did everything she could to ensure the day was one to remember.

However, away from the hive of activity cracks were beginning to appear in the marriage. Fred's injuries from his old accident still gave him cause for concern; the largest of which was the continuing violent headaches that almost paralysed him. By several accounts, these headaches caused his temper to flare, scaring Elizabeth and the children in the process. Jane very rarely mentioned her parents' marriage during her lifetime, but did give a small insight when interviewed by Sonia Lee in 1934, 'Contrary to the general notion, I haven't had an easy time. I had a horrible childhood because my mother and father were dreadfully unhappy in their marriage. It left scars on my mind and on my heart.'

In newspapers published at the time there is no mention of the state of Fred's health and he does seem to have kept up with his business trips, holidays to the cottage and golfing activities. However, telltale signs of trouble are demonstrated by the family spending more and more time apart. Sons Frederic and Stuart went to stay with friends in Michigan for some of their 1914 summer holiday, Elizabeth joined some of Fred's siblings in a trip to Ann Arbor in October, and then Fred was seen with his brother instead of his wife at a dance club in December.

While he continued playing golf up to 1914, no mention of any games or tournaments can be found for Fred during 1915. Elizabeth's calendar, however, could not have been busier. Incensed that there were no women on the school board, she and various other women trekked to the railroad crossings in Fort Wayne and collected some 800 signatures in support of their campaign to get some elected. She also found time to travel to Chicago and then entertain not only her children but their friends too. In late May she gathered up Jane, Frederic, Stuart and other little ones, and took them all to the Jefferson Theater for an afternoon of entertainment, then on to a café called Aurentz's for refreshments.

Among her childhood activities, Jane had her first crush. 'Let no-one say that a child cannot be in love,' she told journalist Gladys Hall:

I mean, in love. No-one could tell me differently, because I was in love when I was eight years old. The very impossible; he was eleven, and he was named Ralph Pop. You may gauge the extent of my passion by the fact that at an age when the names Percival and Ronald and Curtis and so on were romantic names to me, I was able to idealize the name of Pop.

Despite writing letters, fighting off other suiters and stalking the young lad, Jane's love was unrequited:

I tell you, I was in love with Ralph Pop, and even now, after all these years, I can't really laugh at it, or about it. I felt all the pain, all the actual intense emotion, all the hurt pride and baffled hope of a woman for a man. Don't ever laugh at a child in love. Really, don't. It hurts.

Jane's recollection of the romance is slightly cloudy. Records show that a Ralph Pop resided in Fort Wayne with his family, but he was the same age as Jane, not three years older, as she believed. Her love must have happened before she was 8, since shortly before her 7th birthday her mother put together plans that would see her, the children and her sister-in-law, Helen, leave Fort Wayne in early October 1915.

# HEADING WEST

The trip West was described in the local press as an extended holiday to California, and this certainly seemed to have been Elizabeth's initial plan since she told her friends at the First Presbyterian Church that she would serve on the doll and infant booth at their Christmas sale in December. On 4 October 1915, the *Fort Wayne Sentinel* announced, 'Mrs. Fred C. Peters and three children and Miss Helen Peters left Monday morning for Los Angeles, California, to remain for several months'. The next day the *Fort Wayne Journal Gazette* told readers that the Peters' home would now be occupied by eight builders who were temporarily located in the city. Fred, meanwhile, moved in with his parents, John and Mary.

Carole herself spoke about the move in 1932, during an interview with the *New England News*, 'Mother wanted to rest and there was no spot like California. We planned to stay for six months, but luckily the climate lived up to even more than mother anticipated and now we're permanent fixtures.'

The family found themselves first in San Francisco but then very quickly headed south to Los Angeles, moving into an apartment on South Alvarado. No sooner had Elizabeth and the children settled in, however, than word came from England that her brother, Willard, had passed away. Elizabeth's mother, Alice, did not know about the death until reporters came knocking at her door, and she was absolutely devastated. While family flocked to Fort Wayne to comfort her and organise the body to be returned to the United States, Elizabeth stayed firmly in Los Angeles.

By mid-March 1916, word came that her sister-in-law, Helen Peters, would be returning to Fort Wayne within the week, but Elizabeth and the children decided they would be staying until later in the spring. With her children starting school in Los Angeles, it soon became clear that the woman actually had very little intention of ever returning to Indiana. While she felt the climate was better for the health of her and her family, Elizabeth's reason for staying permanently could have been Fred's health rather than her own. There are several indications that he was suffering during this period. First of all, on his return to the country club's tournament circuit, the once most formidable golf player lost his stride and was defeated in the Spring Championship. Then shortly afterwards he announced that he intended to quit golf for the next year, declaring that the rest would do him a lot of good. After that, instead of playing on the weekend as he normally did, he was seen watching his old pals from the sidelines. His attention then went into politics and he donated a whopping $500 to local Republican candidate Bob Hanna and became part of the advisory board for the campaign.

Settling into California did not mean that Elizabeth had any intention of getting a job. Instead, she relied on money sent from Fred for the care of his children and, at times, care packages from her mother, Alice. In April 1917, Fred travelled to California to see his family. If the purpose of the trip was to try and persuade them to return home, his pleas did not work. He was back in Fort Wayne by early May.

Shortly afterwards, his mind was on other affairs when the Horton Company premises went up in smoke after a machine caught fire. Two buildings were totally destroyed as a result. Fred's father, John Peters, told reporters that he normally made an inspection of the plant after lunch, but on that particular day he had taken his wife out instead.

'Of course it had to burn then,' he said. 'The plant was filled with new machines, machinery and materials and we were running night and day to keep up with our orders. The loss will reach about $150,000, with one fourth of it covered by insurance.'

Meanwhile in California, Elizabeth, Jane and her brothers continued to carve out a new life for themselves. Part of this was organising furniture from the Fort Wayne house to be shipped out to their new California home. When she wasn't in school, Jane spent a lot of time with her siblings and continued to grow up as a tomboy. 'Girls weren't rough enough for me,' she said. Although she was never particularly interested in playing house, in the rare moments when she did play with dolls the boys would laugh at her. Jane put them aside in favour of their toys instead. She would promise not to whine, cry or tell tales, and in return the brothers allowed her to join in with their favourite sports of baseball, tennis and golf. If she did begin to cry, however, the boys would leave her at home to stew; a punishment for being a 'whiney little girl'.

Jane would often tear her dresses while climbing over fences or scrambling up trees. She would get into trouble for such misdemeanours but, more than anything, Elizabeth looked on in wonder at her little tomboy and never pushed her to become more ladylike. At school Jane joined various teams such as baseball, basketball and track, and always on the sidelines was Elizabeth, cheering the young girl on and supporting her when the inevitable injuries happened. She had a unique style of mothering, which *Screenland* magazine described as:

> … just about 100 years ahead of her time. She does not believe in that sacred thing called parental rights. She is satisfied with the sincere friendship and love that her children offer her, and refuses to block with advice, tears or commands any course they care to follow.

As she did in Fort Wayne, Elizabeth busied herself with social events and parties and also became fascinated with numerology and the Baha'i faith; both introduced to her by a new friend.

The Peters family celebrated special days at the beach with their friends, and Jane also helped raise money for charity. On 13 July 1918, the 9-year-old served on Miss Morgan's chocolate booth during a fundraising fete to help fatherless children in France. At another benefit the young girl met legendary actor Douglas Fairbanks. Jane was so in awe of the great man that she later described not being able to take her eyes off him. It did not take him long to spot that she was a big fan, and leant down to give her a small peck on the lips. 'My determination to be an actress came just one second after Douglas Fairbanks kissed me,' she said.

In Fort Wayne, Fred reached the realisation that his marriage had ended. Any efforts he made to convince his wife to come home stopped, but he still kept in touch with his mother-in-law, Alice, and even attended a party at her home in June 1919. Aside from that, he tried to carve out a normal life in Fort Wayne, attending social events at the country club, playing golf, working at Horton and even attending gymnastic classes.

In California, the family moved around quite a lot. In the 1918 *Los Angeles Directory* they are listed as living at No. 626 South Catalina, but by 1920 they had moved to No. 605 South Harvard Boulevard. It was likely, while at this house, that the youngster got her first movie role, opposite actor Monte Blue in *A Perfect Crime*. According to Carole, a neighbour saw the 12-year-old in the garden and actually recommended her for the part. 'My mother rejoiced with me,' she said, 'and I had a glorious time for a few weeks.'

Her role in *A Perfect Crime* was brief; she was only on screen for a few scenes and no other roles came of the exposure. Carole was disappointed, but returned to school having been given a taste of what life could be like if she ever became a professional actress. The youngster continued her academic studies into high school, making friends with girls such as Sally Eilers, and renewing an earlier friendship with a young woman called Dixie Pantages. The family had also moved again. The *Los Angeles Street Directory* places them on El Centro Avenue at this time, but the 1923 edition has them at No. 154 South Manhattan Place.

Jane was growing up fast and she fell in love with a local boy. She recalled the experience in an interview with Gladys Hall in 1933:

> When I was in my teens, I was so crazy about a boy called Clive that I could think of nothing but making opportunities to be alone with him.

I didn't care about anything but being alone with him, because all I wanted from him were his kisses, his love-making. I didn't want to talk to him. I had nothing to say to him and he had nothing to say to me, nothing I was interested in hearing. We hadn't one taste in common. We didn't think alike. I didn't want to do things with him, go places, or play games, or read books or anything like that. The whole point was that I loved him, but I did not like him. If the quality of emotion had been subtracted from the little affair, there would have been nothing left.

The girl was becoming more feminine in her approach to life; brought on, it would seem, through a fascination with the actress Gloria Swanson. Jane loved her films and looks so much that she went to extreme measures to try and look like her idol:

I so much admired her turned-up nose that I spent hours pushing my own inconsequential nose up, trying to make it look cute like Gloria's. I thought her smile was so charming that I made myself look like a gargoyle going around showing my teeth as Gloria does.

Finally, the young girl caught a glimpse of what she looked like during her imitation. She stopped the game immediately. 'Instead of making myself look like Gloria, I was completely spoiling what little beauty I did possess,' she said in 1934.

At school, Jane took an interest in acting and was featured in several amateur productions. During one show she played the part of an old woman with a daughter. The girl who played her child was actually older than Jane, but that didn't seem to bother the organisers. Another time she played a villain with a large moustache. The student thought the stick-on facial hair was so massive that if someone had stuck a brake to her shoulder she could have made a very lifelike bicycle. Another part was as the May Queen, complete with royal regalia. Her siblings thought the whole thing was a gigantic hoot. 'My brothers kidded me to death,' she said, 'but I didn't mind too much. They let me wear a grand taffeta period gown and a tiara, and that was compensation for the razzing.'

Having got a taste for films, Jane began to take acting classes and went on auditions, one of which brought her face to face with Charlie Chaplin. He was impressed enough to give her two tests for a new film he was preparing called *Gold Rush*. She did not get the part but enjoyed the experience. Another time, it looked as though she might be signed by the Vitagraph Company, but that also came to nothing. Then Jane met famed director Cecil B. DeMille. The man was impressed by her photogenic qualities and interested in the tales her mother told him about already having theatrical training. Still, DeMille thought she looked a little young to be brought to screen on a full-time basis. 'My dear child,' he said, 'go back to school and see me in five or six years.'

In spite of any advice, Jane left high school as soon as she was able. Her education was not over, however, and she delved into acting classes, studying as much as she could. The young woman continued to go on auditions and was seen frequently on the Los Angeles club scene and particularly at the Cocoanut Grove, located in the Ambassador Hotel. Opened on 1 January 1921, the hotel was a mecca not only for tourists but the glamorous and seemingly sophisticated Hollywood crowd, too. Set in 27 acres of gardens, it had everything a visitor could want and a lot more besides.

It was not the pool or beautiful rooms that Jane wanted to see, however. Instead she would head straight for the in-house nightclub, where she would dance the night away with her friends. She was just 16 years old and yet, with her sophisticated look and fearless exterior, Jane seemed at least ten years older. Often dressed in black satin, the girl would wow the other Cocoanut Grove patrons by dancing up a storm and winning trophies in the regular competitions. Jane was proud to have won, but on many occasions she'd head back to the hotel the next day, trophies in hand, and sweet-talk the management into taking the prizes back and replacing them with cash. She did not care about parting with the trophies; she knew she'd win them back during the next competition.

In 1935 she said:

I went through the jazz-mad age with a vengeance, and spent almost every night dancing at the Cocoanut Grove. Dancing was all I thought of, and to be a superb dancer was the tops in my estimation. I'd have laughed at the idea of becoming a mere dramatic actress! It took me years to live down my reputation of being 'the Charleston Kid'.

In later years she looked back on her time as a teenager with no affection at all:

I never want to be sixteen again. I think that eighteen is the dullest age in the world. If ever I was unhappy, it was when I was in my teens. That's because you don't understand anything when you're that young. You're puzzled and so you're hurt. For only the things you don't understand have the power to hurt you, like the power of darkness. With age there comes a richness that's divine.

In spite of any unhappiness she may have felt inside, on the outside she was fearless. Because of this, it did not take long for Jane to be spotted at the Cocoanut Grove by various people who were anxious to further her career. Sometime during 1924 she was seen by members of a local dance troupe, the Denishawn Dancers, who had been booked to perform in the Cocoanut Grove. A touring company, they were due to leave for an eighteen month-long trip to India, Japan and China in 1925 and they were so fascinated by Jane that they actually asked her to accompany them. The adventurous young woman was excited to go, but her mother was not so keen and put a stop to the idea before it had chance to start.

# UP, UP AND AWAY

While Jane was disappointed that she would be unable to dance her way across the Orient, she didn't mope for long. She was soon to be discovered – though the way in which it happened is unclear. One of the official stories is that Jane was spotted at the Cocoanut Grove by a Fox talent scout, who invited her into the studio for a chat. This snippet of gossip was picked up by many columnists, including Edwin and Elza Schallert in their 'Hollywood Highlights' column for *Picture-Play* magazine. In the article the pair described how Jane was discovered by a film scout while on the dance floor at 'fashionable and exclusive social gatherings'.

A different story was shared by the actress during an interview in 1932, when she described being at a dinner party and sitting next to a studio executive. He was impressed by her company and asked if she would like to be in the movies. She said yes immediately and a test was arranged. 'I was dreadful,' she remembered. 'Even I knew that.'

Whatever her thoughts on the matter, the executives were impressed enough to sign the 16-year-old to Fox in early 1925. Jane was beside herself with excitement, but her mother was wary and wondered what was to become of her daughter's future. It had been clear for a long time, however, that Jane was never going to be anxious to settle down, no matter what her age or profession. Elizabeth understood this and, given the circumstances of her own relationship with Fred, would never think of forcing her into a marriage she did not want.

Carole said:

Too many women have just one ambition during their twenties. They want marriage. Then they settle down and become housewives and let their own characters go. Marriage is important, naturally, but it shouldn't submerge any woman's personality. It should not wholly consume her life. I tried to keep the canvas broad. To forget the temporary problems of love and a career, and see the panorama of my whole life stretching out before me.

Jane's name didn't thrill the executives. They decided it needed to be changed immediately, and Elizabeth and a friend who studied numerology suggested the name Carole. Jane had tried this stage name before and was somewhat lukewarm about it. However, she did like it a lot more than her real name, which she described as 'girly' and she never believed that it suited her. 'I was a tomboy of tomboys,' she said.

Lombard was suggested as a surname (after a family friend) and the two names went together well. Her new name would be Carole Lombard, though for years studios, reporters and magazine writers would never know if it was supposed to be spelled Carol without an 'e' or Carole with. This resulted in the actress being credited both ways for some years, though to avoid any confusion it will be spelled Carole in this book.

Carole's first real media mention came on 4 February 1925, when the *Los Angeles Times* featured a short piece entitled 'Society Girl Goes into Silent Drama'. The article described how the 'little miss' had recently been signed to Fox after a successful screen test, and would soon be appearing in actor Edmund Lowe's new movie. On 25 March her photograph appeared in the *Los Angeles Times* once more, this time in an article entitled 'How do you like these Newcomers?'

Carole was happy to finally have a foot in the studio door. However, she was also acutely aware of the fact that making movies was vastly different to winning trophies at the Cocoanut Grove. Later, she admitted to reporter George Madden in an interview for *Movie Mirror* that she managed to get through the first few years:

> Without knowing a thing about acting. I merely stood there in front of the camera and did what the director told me, and tried to keep my mind blank so I wouldn't interfere with his thought transmission. Something seemed to give forth on the screen, but I never knew how it happened. It was all an accident.

Lombard would lament to reporter George Madden that she was taken out of at least three movies around this time, purely because she didn't know what to do with her hands. 'I was always hanging on to something. If there wasn't a handy chair, or a railing, I'd drape both hands over one hip and wait for the director to have hysterics,' she said. But in spite of her lack of confidence, Carole was a fast learner and while she was merely used as decoration in her first few roles, she made the most of what she had and soaked up any piece of information like a sponge. In her spare time she would also study make-up, gestures, clothes and everything else required to be a good actress.

Carole soon realised that, in order to succeed, she would need mannerisms and she hooked on to this idea with great abandon:

> I learned that lifting my head and tilting it back like a pouty peacock, or lifting one eyebrow, or wearing a certain type of gown was Lombardesque. I was so pleased with these developments I ran them through every performance. Characterization and madames were as far apart as the poles at this stage of the game. Shop girl or society dame, I played them both alike. Of course it was all wrong, but I was developing something I badly needed, confidence in my little bag of tricks.

As mentioned in the earlier newspaper reports, Carole's first opportunity to do something besides look pretty came when she was cast alongside Edmund Lowe in the somewhat forgettable silent movie, *Marriage in Transit*.

Carole played Celia Hathaway, a woman who marries a secret service agent 'to save her from a rascal'.

While she was excited to be included in the film, from the very beginning Carole knew that it wasn't going to be her ticket to fame and she found it hard to sympathise with the character's plight. In a short interview with the *Galveston Daily News*, she told the reporter that in real life she would never be tempted to wed a virtual stranger as character Celia Hathaway had done. However, she was prepared to let her character do so because 'I had to. The man with the megaphone told me to.'

'I was pretty terrible in the picture,' she told Malcolm H. Oettinger, 'I rather expected I would be, having had no experience in pictures and no stage training. Besides I was pleasingly plump and that was no advantage, either.' During another interview, the actress gave a small snippet of what it had been like to work on the set of *Marriage in Transit*:

> If I was supposed to cry, I howled. If I threw something, I heaved it! Put me in a fight scene with an actor, and I tore him to pieces. Poor Eddie Lowe! They told me to tear him to shreds! To this day Eddie can't see me without ducking. For a while I overdid realism too, but at least it was a step in the right direction away from posing.

Carole may have thought she had overacted with Edmund Lowe at the time, but later she discovered that the actor had stolen quite a few scenes himself. While she was busy hamming it up, he was even more concerned with turning her back to the camera at every opportunity, leaving him with the scene to himself. The show stealing worked and she did not notice what he'd done until the film was well and truly in the can.

While *Marriage in Transit* was hardly the film of the year, some theatres went all-out to create publicity for it. One manager in Tampa, Florida, teamed up with Citizens Bank & Trust and together they installed a large poster outside the bank:

> What did the bride say to the groom while being married in transit? Code message – the first 25 people to cipher this message correctly will receive two tickets each to see Edmund Lowe and Carole Lombard in

*Marriage in Transit* at the Franklin theatre, Wednesday and Thursday, April 29th–30th. Mail answers to Franklin theatre.

The poster (complete with keys to the puzzle) drew crowds all day long and over 200 entries were received which revealed the answer, 'Open our joint account at the Citizens Bank – The big bank at the big building'. The bank and the theatre received great publicity for their companies, and positive reviews in the press. Unfortunately the same cannot be said for *Marriage in Transit*.

'Gossip reports there is nothing new under the sun. This picture rambles through five reels to prove it,' said *Photoplay*:

Again the weary secret service plot is taken off the shelf to provide a heroic role for Edmund Lowe, a wealthy youth yearning for adventure. He finds it in posing as an international criminal, getting what he goes after, marrying the heroine to save her from the crook, and finding Pollyanna's country in the confectionary finish.

The *Exhibitors Trade Review* gave the movie a much bigger review and while they did manage to mention Carole, their view of the film as a whole was not exactly positive:

This feature goes off to a ripping start and looks as though it is going to tear into the melodramatic homestretch a sure winner. But it doesn't maintain interest after the third reel begins, when the plot peters out lamentably, the mixed identity angles become sadly twisted and confusing and events are jumbled into a semi-burlesque mix-up … Carole Lombard is an attractive heroine and the support is satisfactory. Edmund Lowe is your best bet in exploiting this one; other members of the cast mean nothing to the box-office.

Although reviews were disappointing, any worries they caused were small in comparison to what Carole sometimes had to endure on the set of her early films. Some actresses, such as Thelma Todd and Marilyn Monroe, would often talk about the 'wolves of Hollywood', and Todd had walked out of an executive's office party when it became clear that she was expected to provide 'entertainment' to the guests. She was swiftly threatened with blacklisting, but even that didn't stop her from talking about it to several magazines, including *Photoplay*. Some years later, Marilyn Monroe would go through a similar experience when a would-be executive wanted her to act out a variety of questionable poses for him in his office. She too walked away and relayed that story and various others to a fan magazine.

While Carole was more discreet, the experiences she had early in her career were often the same. She hinted about the kinds of things she had to go through when she spoke to Gladys Hall in 1931, describing how men had tried their luck from the moment she first walked on to a film set. During the interview, Carole said that one man (who remained nameless but had apparently gone on to become a big star) had been so fresh that a studio electrician had to intervene in an effort to stop him from going further.

From that moment on, the still teenage Carole Lombard put up a barrier between herself and her male co-stars, and turned herself into a clown and told funny stories to try and distract them. If that didn't work, she would become unfriendly and aloof, often swearing and acting like 'one of the boys' to put the wolves off. As the years went by, her superstar status ensured that the actress would never have to go through anything untoward again, and her barriers came down. For now though, they remained firmly up.

In June 1925, Carole's next film, *Hearts and Spurs*, was released to somewhat mixed reviews. A melodrama western starring actor Buck Jones, the film gave Carole the opportunity to play Sybil Estabrook, Jones's leading lady. She also travelled with cast and crew for location shooting in San Bernardino County. Newspapers reported that, while there, Carole and fellow actress Jean Lamott were both initiated into the company with a variety of wild stunts and dares, including sitting on an electric chair and riding a wild bronco. As can be expected, daredevil Carole reportedly found the wild riding to be particularly good fun and mentioned the making of the film as one of the highlights of her early career.

Still, the actual part she played left Carole somewhat frustrated and confused. She told reporter Clark Rodenbach that westerns in those days just weren't vigorous enough. She complained that while the male actors were allowed to rush around on screen, riding horses and shooting each other, she was expected to stand prettily in the background. She would be allowed the occasional scream but, in spite of that, 'In those days the girl in a western was just a sprig of parsley,' she said.

Since she played a fairly substantial role in *Hearts and Spurs*, some reviewers gave the actress attention in their articles, both good and bad. *Variety* described her as 'attractive looking, particularly in the fashionable eastern clothes she is permitted to wear', but did not enjoy her performance. The reviewer – echoing Carole's thoughts on the subject – announced that 'she might as well have been labelled "for decorative purposes only"'.

*Motion Picture News* did not mention Carole's performance. Instead they concentrated on the action itself. 'There should be no question about this newest Buck Jones western satisfying the action lovers,' they said. 'They needn't look for anything original. In fact it covers old ground in its plot and the characters run true to type.' They did like particular parts of the movie, although they were quick to state that the drawing power would be for theatres catering to westerns, where Jones was popular. Meanwhile the *Titusville Herald* declared that Carole had a remarkable gift for drama and was an excellent co-star for Jones. This would have meant more had it not been for the fact that this particular 'review' cropped up several times during promotion for the movie and had actually been pre-written by the studio.

While the reception for *Hearts and Spurs* was mixed, Carole was teamed up with Jones again for another picture, this time entitled *Durand of the Bad Lands*. However, her part as Ellen Boyd was so tiny that she came last on the cast list and the only magazine that seemed to mention her even in passing was *Photoplay*.

Her next movie was no more successful. While historians cite Fox's *The Road to Glory* as Carole's next film, by the time it was released in February 1926 she did not appear anywhere in the reviews or magazine cast lists. This is most likely because, around the time she was making the film, Carole's world came crashing down and as a result she was unable to finish all of her scenes.

# CATASTROPHE

Carole thoroughly enjoyed the company of friends and, despite her fledgling film career, could still be seen on the Los Angeles club scene. During one particular evening in 1926, she was a passenger in a car being driven by her 16-year-old friend, Harry Cooper. Details of what happened next remain somewhat sketchy, but there are three possible scenarios.

The first story is that the car was stopped on a hill behind a truck. The truck driver suddenly lost control of the brakes and came hurtling backwards towards Cooper's car, crashing into the front and shattering the windscreen in the process. The second scenario has the car waiting at a stop sign and being hit by another from behind, knocking the passenger into the windscreen and shattering it on impact. Yet another story has Cooper bringing the car to a stop suddenly, causing a faulty catch on the passenger seat to become unhinged. The seat slid forward into the windshield, which caused it to break. The stories may be different but the outcome was definitely the same: as the windscreen shattered, a piece of glass sliced into Carole's face, leaving terrible gashes near her eye and on her left cheek.

The damage was not life threatening but the young woman was taken to hospital and ushered into surgery quickly. The process of stitching up her wounds was lengthy, but she was not given any anaesthetic as the doctor feared it would cause her facial muscles to relax and cause further damage to the area. Carole was in a huge amount of pain but lay deathly still during the procedure. She was later released from hospital with instructions to do nothing but recuperate. Doctors predicted that without the proper period of rest the shock to her nervous system could be extreme and would set her progress back considerably.

It has been said that news of the crash was quickly relayed to the executives at Fox, who decided they were better off hiring another actress for the parts they had planned. Then, when it became clear she would not be returning to work any time soon, they unceremoniously dropped Carole from her contract. The actress told a slightly different story to Dorothy Wooldridge some years later:

> I was terrible [as an actress for Fox] – worse than that, if possible. At the end of a year they threw me out. They should have done it long before. No girl should start picture work in a leading role. It's unfair to her and punishment to an audience. Right after Fox let me out, an automobile discharged me too. I came out through the windshield. They took twenty-five stitches in my face and to this day I carry the scars, but they're barely visible.

Another comment was made to reporter Mark Dowling:

> I had a lot of knocks, naturally. They were good for me. I was thrown out of one studio and I made plenty of bad pictures. But it's better to have your grief and hardships at that age, when you can learn by them, than to have too much early success.

At home, instead of wallowing in her downfall the actress spent the next few months obeying orders and making sure she was properly rested.

In time, Carole's mind turned to acting again and she immersed herself in self-study. She read plays (including Shakespeare), acted out small parts in the privacy of her bedroom and used every spare moment to better her craft. She was also visited by friends who would perch on the side of her bed and tell jokes, or sometimes cry at the unfairness of the crash cutting her career so short.

Carole told them that they mustn't worry, it was all okay. Underneath the bravado, however, the young woman was concerned that if the large scar on her cheek did not heal, her career would be over. Her prediction was almost proved correct, as by the time she had recovered enough to go back to work, many of the studios had forgotten all about her fledgling career and had no interest in reigniting it.

This lack of concern was upsetting but, in true Lombard fashion, she refused to let it get her down. Instead she vowed to do everything in her power to put the past behind her and move on with the future. Hollywood masseuse Sylvia Ulback recalled, 'Did she cry and moan about [the scar]? She did not. She didn't pay any attention to it, but went right on. And because of her attitude I tell you that scar is actually attractive; girls can learn a lot from Carole.' Still, the knowledge that she would have a scar for the rest of her life was well and truly on Carole's mind, and the subject would be brought up in articles and interviews many times over the years. During an interview with reporter Elisabeth Goldbeck, the woman told Carole that her face seemed to have changed. She asked if this could be a result of the crash. The actress was quick to defend her looks and jumped into a full explanation:

I have pictures taken before and after the accident, which prove that had absolutely nothing to do with it. They were almost identical. The accident happened six years ago, and it's only in the last three or four years that my face has changed. But it HAS changed completely. I think it changed as I changed mentally. Age changes you, and experience. It hollows your face and alters the mould. Your face can't help reflecting all that goes on in your mind. All the emotions you feel, all the troubles and heartaches and grief you experience, leave their mark if you're an actress.

Carole went through a great deal as she recovered during 1926. 'My upper lip was so stiff from this accident, that for several months I could hardly move it,' she told reporter Muriel Babcock. 'Massage did the trick. It is all right now.' By autumn she was well enough to rejoin her friends at the Cocoanut Grove in order to take part in another dance competition. Under her real name of Jane Peters she went all the way to the finals, where she competed against several dozen other youngsters, including actresses Joan Crawford and Billie Dove.

As 1927 dawned, 18-year-old Carole became even more confident about her new appearance, and on 12 March she attended a Junior Cameraman's Club dance at the Masonic Temple. There she spent time with artists such as Sammy Cohen, Nick Stuart and Barbara Luddy. However, while publicity appearances, dancing competitions and trips to the Ambassador were an excellent way to rejoin the outside world again, Carole ached for another chance in Hollywood. 'If I have the goods and get the breaks, I'll make good in the movies,' she said. Shortly after, she got the chance to do just that.

Hollywood mogul Mack Sennett had run a successful studio for many years. His organisation was a starting point for many huge stars of the era, such as Mabel Normand, Roscoe 'Fatty' Arbuckle and Charlie Chaplin. The company made literally hundreds of short movies per year and visitors to the set could often be witness to trained cats and lions taking part in a scene, or red-faced tramps throwing custard pies at a smartly suited man. Nothing seemed to be off limits where Mack Sennett was concerned.

In 1915 the producer decided to expand his enterprise by creating a stable of pretty girls, called the 'Sennett Bathing Beauties', which he used for his films as well as publicity. Together, the women would appear around Hollywood and beach areas such as Venice and Santa Monica, posing for photographs and making quite a scene wherever they went. The girls chosen as Bathing Beauties on the Sennett lot came from a variety of walks of life but, in some cases, they were young married women who were just looking to make a little pocket money to boost their husbands' wages. Some had ambitions to move into dramatic and romantic roles ('start with Sennett, get rich somewhere else' was a frequent quote heard around Hollywood), but for the most part these dreams did not come true. If you were a Sennett beauty, it was assumed that you would be happy to stay that way, and finding a way into drama was just luck, not normality.

By the time Carole walked into the studio in 1927 it had been running for some fifteen years and was starting to look rather rough around the edges. Certainly it had seen better days and the huge stars were long gone. Still, in spite of that, Carole was incredibly grateful for the opportunity to get back to work after her accident, especially since Sennett couldn't care less about the scar on her face; he much preferred that she had a good body for a bathing suit.

Reporter Marian Rhea saw Carole at the studio on the very day she was hired:

> She had just been given a job at Sennett's and she was walking on air. 'So you made the grade,' another girl said to her wistfully. 'Me – they told me there was nothing doing.'
>
> Carole reassured her. 'Oh well, you're sure to get a break some time.' And then she added, casually, 'Come on. I'll buy you lunch to celebrate my break.'
>
> No, it wasn't so much – to buy a lunch. Only the other girl's eyes filled with tears and the rest of us there realized then what Carole had seen right away – that there hadn't been too many lunches recently, for the girl who followed her out the door.

When it was time to begin filming, Carole was ecstatic to find herself in the old dressing room of Gloria Swanson, with Sally Eilers, who she had known at school. Carole enjoyed a good friendship with her, as she did with another Sennett actress, Madalynne Fields, or 'Fieldsie' as she was nicknamed. The two had known each other around town for some time, occupying the same social scene. While working for Sennett, however, the two young women became so close that they drove to the studio in Fieldsie's car and shared the cost of petrol. Eventually her new friend would become a constant companion and assistant for Carole.

Work took up a major part of her time, but Carole was still no stranger to dancing the night away. She and Fieldsie were frequently seen out on the town together, and joined various social clubs such as the Hollyhawk Club, where columnist J. Eugene Chrisman observed the young actress. 'I remember her as a girl with a husky voice,' he said. 'A loud and frequent laugh and a figure a few pounds overweight. Just one of a couple score of girls who were seeking movie fame.'

Carole thought herself very lucky to be given a chance for success as a Sennett Bathing Beauty, and soaked up all the comedic knowledge and timing to be found there. 'My best tutor was Mack Sennett,' she told reporter, Dorothy Wooldridge:

> [He is] the old maestro of comedies. Sally Eilers and I were the last of his featured bathing beauties to get somewhere. Mack Sennett is a wonderful teacher. His knowledge of comedy, of timing, use of pantomime, of sudden changes from comedy to tragedy, from laughter to tears – well he has grasped the psychology of the human mind.

When asked for information for her official Sennett biography, the actress told the publicity department that her drama experience came from the Potboilers, a theatre group in Los Angeles. Her height was listed as 5ft 5½in, eyes blue, hair blonde. Her hobbies included dancing and her skills were riding, athletics and, of course, acting. She preferred modern authors over classics, and her ambition was 'to be a star in pictures'. Nobody could deny the girl had ambition.

During her time at the studio, Carole played in a variety of comedies, with some more substantial than others. The *Film Daily* was one of the first to announce the actress's association, 'Mack Sennett will feature twelve girls in a new series of "Bathing Beauties" type, which Eddie Cline will direct. Sennett already has chosen Carole Lombard, Anita Barnes, Katherine Stanley, Leota Winter and Marie Tergain for the series.'

One of the first small parts was in *Smith's Pony*, a two-reeler that received favourable mention in reviews and kept audiences laughing. In *The Beach Club*, Carole was an extra, billed as 'girl in sports clothes'. Her scenes involved a small appearance in a hotel lobby and a beach club scene, which was filmed in Santa Monica. For her efforts, the actress was paid on average $15 per day and her part wrapped on 7 June 1927.

*The Bicycle Flirt* saw Carole (or Carrol/Carroll, as she was listed in production records) heading all over town during the summer of 1927. In her role as a young flapper, she filmed scenes in East Lake Park, Lincoln Park, Culver City and various streets around Los Angeles. Studio publicity described her character 'as full of love as an Elinor Glyn novel', while *Film Daily* said the finished movie was 'well gagged and moves at a snappy pace'.

*Run, Girl, Run* gave Carole a bigger chance at success playing Norma Nurmi, a star athlete. The character was described in the movie as having 'run a mile in almost nothing … and was nearly expelled for it'. Filming began on 16 September 1927 with outdoor scenes at Griffith Park and Paddock Field, and then a solo scene for Carole was completed on 21 September. Her wardrobe was comprehensive considering the relatively small role, and consisted of a one-piece dress, a hat, a fancy nightgown, slippers and a negligee. She was also filmed wearing black trunks and a jersey for her sports scenes.

Of the effort, *Motion Picture News* said:

While Daphne Pollard heads the cast in this comedy, the Sennett bathing girls garner most of the limelight. There are some sequences that present them in colour in a series of tabloids and they are not at all hard to gaze upon. As a matter of fact it would be a better picture if there were more of these colour sequences and the comedy effort were cut down a trifle.

Of Carole, reviewer Chester J. Smith had this to add, 'Miss Lombard is a beauteous and shapely blonde who wins the final dash for the college championship'. The *Exhibitors Herald and Moving Picture World* declared the movie to be a 'very high class and laughable comedy [with] some beautiful colour scenes'.

Carole had settled into her work with Mack Sennett and enjoyed the slapstick approach very much. She told reporter Cedric Belfrage about her time at the studio:

There won't ever be another Sennett's for laughs. Daphne Pollard and I were just in hysterics the whole time. We used to pull the worst gags on Matty Kemp and some of the boys over there. You should have seen that lot when the boys ran riot with water hoses – the mess we made off the set was often much worse than the one we did for the benefit of the cameras.

We had a great bunch over there, too. The so-called bathing girls, who did pretty much everything except bathe, were made up of all sorts. Some of 'em were as innocent as lambs and they went all the way down the scale to the super-sophisticates. Daphne Pollard, who was a real bathing girl because in every picture they made they turned the hose on her, was the best sport of the whole gang.

On 1 October 1927 the young actress began work on *The Swim Princess*. Location shooting took the cast and crew to all manner of places, including the Santa Fe Depot for a coach scene, Loyola College and Brookside Park. The latter, visited on 28 October, involved some drama when co-star Daphne Pollard almost drowned in the pool but was thankfully saved just in time.

While work kept her busy, the scar on Carole's cheek still bothered her, so she decided to sue for compensation. On 13 October 1927, shortly after her 19th birthday, the *Los Angeles Times* reported that the actress was claiming $35,000 not only from driver Harry Cooper, but his parents too. *Variety* repeated the story just days later on 19 October, telling readers, '[The actress is] charging her beauty was marred in an auto accident while riding with young Cooper in his parents' car'.

Judge Fleming of the Superior Court was in charge of the case, but before he was able to assess the damage caused by the crash, the suit was suddenly settled out of court. Carole attempted to keep the payment a secret from reporters, but it was quickly rumoured that she had accepted $3,000 from the family in return for a promise that she would not pursue the claim further.

As it turned out, the actress need not have worried about the scar ruining her looks on camera, as cinematographer Harry Stradling, (who worked with Carole later in her career) told *Modern Screen*:

I was worried that the scar would detract from her performance in close-ups. The object was to get the lights to hit her face so that they would fill in the scar and blend it with her cheek. But Carole knew even more. She said to me, 'Put a diffusing glass on your lens and I'll look okay'.

Stradling told reporters that he did as she asked, and the results were absolutely beautiful.

*The Campus Carmen* was filmed during the first two weeks of November 1927, and swiftly followed by *The Campus Vamp*, a story centred around a love triangle. Daphne Pollard and Johnny Burke headed the cast, while Sally Eilers, Matty Kemp and Carole were in supporting roles. Location shooting saw the cast and crew going from a sorority house not far from Carole's residence at No. 138 North Wilton Place, through to beach scenes and finally the Deauville Club in Santa Monica. Filming wrapped shortly before Christmas and the film was released the following year.

The rather successful cast was not enough to persuade *Motion Picture News* that *The Campus Vamp* was any good, however:

Some time back the appearance of a crew of Sennett bathing girls disporting themselves at the beach would have been sufficient to make any film a success, but on this occasion they register just so much atmosphere. Several Technicolor sequences that have been worked into this subject and featuring the girls are quite dressy, but lend very little to the entertainment value of the picture. It is the writer's opinion that producers of comedy should avoid sacrificing continuity and gags for an attempt at the artistic.

Unfortunately for many of the Sennett Bathing Beauties, the demand for their acting services was beginning to slow down and their films were not as popular as they once were. However, this did not seem to bother Carole, who was eager to start something new. During 1928 she obtained several temporary releases from her contract and went to act for other studios. One of those was Rayart, a lower-end production company that cast the actress in *The Divine Sinner*. The film disappeared without trace and Carole said that she had never even seen it herself. Next was *Power* at Pathé, then *Me, Gangster* for Fox – neither raised her profile.

Her time at Sennett was coming to an end and the last short Carole made for them was *Matchmaking Mamas*, playing Phyllis, a young woman whose mother is trying to set her up with a nice young man. Of course, as with all slapstick comedies, nothing goes to plan and the man she gets in the end is not quite who her mother had planned for her. By the time it was released, critics had simply had enough of the tried and tested slapstick of Sennett's comedies. *Motion Picture News* went so far as to declare *Matchmaking Mamas* 'good, although at times it looks (if one is to judge by the photography) a trifle old'.

'Mack Sennett's was the school of hard knocks,' Carole told Malcolm H. Oettinger:

> There I started working up from the bottom. It was the most delightful madhouse imaginable and life was one fall after another. There was a lusty, rowdy spirit of freedom there that I've never encountered anywhere else. I recommend it. It exposed the sham of pretension, it exploded the petty hypocrisies of people in high places, it flung pies at false dignity. What's more, Sennett's develops the sense of humour, toughens the constitution, nurtures ambition and teaches you the game as it should be played. Two years there gave me a thorough grounding. I left fully prepared to face the world.

Because of the downfall in the interest in Sennett movies, both the studio and the distributor – Pathé – were falling on hard times. 'I spent years wrecking one company after another,' Carole told *Picture-Play* magazine. 'I swear that I was no sooner signed up and at work than the company's finances would fall apart. I was a jinx. It's a wonder no one found out and blacklisted me.'

In a bid to rekindle their flagging assets, Pathé set about trying to discover new faces for their movies. They had already worked with her in *Power*, and now the studio wanted Carole full time. While it was intended that she would first work in silent film, in autumn 1928 the actress was given a test to see if her voice would be good enough for Pathé's talking pictures too. Sound executive Benjamin Glazer conducted the experiment, assisted by several other members of the studio. 'Glazer directed Carole Lombard, Junior Coghlan and

Robert St. Angelo in a 100 per cent talking test scene from a juvenile play, and they are reported to have registered perfectly,' wrote *Motion Picture News*. Louise Williams of *Picture-Play* told readers of Carole's supposed comments as she exited the test. 'We dumb artists don't know what will register on the microphone, but we're in good company. None of those experts in there do either,' she said.

On 2 October *Exhibitors Daily Review* announced that all Pathé features would use dialogue from now on, then shortly after *Exhibitors Herald and Moving Picture World* repeated the story and told how executive vice president, Colvin W. Brown, had been particularly impressed with what he saw during the tests. 'Brown is reported as having been much pleased with the sound tests … The results were so satisfactory that work was at once begun in putting dialogue into pictures now in production.'

Although there were several people at the studio who wondered if she would be able to make the transition from funny bathing beauty to real actress, 20-year-old Carole had no problems at all. 'I had a hard time convincing people I could do straight parts,' she said, 'But once they saw me do them, they believed me when I said I could. Sceptical, you know?'

# LOOKING FORWARD

A new journey had begun. While she had already taken and passed the talkies test, Carole and other young Pathé players were sent along to a special training class. There, they rehearsed plays and learned many different tricks for acting with sound under the watchful eye of Frank Reicher, a director who had much experience of stage and cinema acting. The classes were a new way of tackling the transition from silent movies to talkies, and Pathé was very proud of the results. While other studios were keen to hire New York stage actors to become stars, Pathé believed that the classes would enable them to develop previously silent talent instead. Other studios watched with great interest.

'Pathé's experiment of a training school for talkers, using young players exclusively, is bringing good results to the studio,' claimed *Hollywood Filmograph*. 'The work of Carole Lombard, who is highly regarded as a find by studio officials, after playing in two Pathé talkers, is cited as an example of the school's value. Miss Lombard, who had had no speaking experience professionally, had played mostly in Sennett comedies.'

Carole gave her opinion of acting with sound to Edward Stodel of the *Los Angeles Evening Herald*. According to her, having stage actors on set actually created more problems than it solved. 'The well-known stagey manner of delivering lines is taboo,' she said, before explaining that one stage actor she knew had a nasty habit of slapping fellow actors on the back during shooting. 'It nearly drove the sound expert crazy keeping him in control,' she added.

Rather bizarrely, during the late 1920s the actress was labelled as 'Carole of the Curves' and some reporters even went so far as to call her a 'plump, jolly girl'. This was a label that had haunted the actress since her Fox days, even though by today's standards she was certainly never what you'd call overweight. Nevertheless, it was decided that in order to go further in her career, particularly in the world of mainstream dramatic movies, the young woman should change her image and tone her body.

Sylvia Ulback was called in to see if she could help Carole get into shape. A legendary figure in Hollywood, Ulback's most famous story was that she had been inspired to take up exercise and diet when she caught her husband flirting with his skinny stenographer. Friends noticed her transformation and called on her to help with their own bodies too. She was so successful that eventually Sylvia decided to turn her part-time talent into a full-time business, with her first client being actress Marie Dressler in the mid-1920s.

When Sylvia first saw Carole, she was wearing a short, white sports dress, tennis shoes and carrying a beret. She was shouting hello to all the men she knew on set, and Sylvia described her voice as 'hearty and hale like, just as her figure looked'. The two were introduced, and the exercise guru vowed to change Carole's body in the space of four weeks. 'You'll be amazed,' she assured studio executives.

'I liked Carole right away,' she wrote in *Photoplay* magazine. 'You couldn't be around her and not like her. She was breezy and clever and so regular and oh, how badly she wanted to get thin! She knew how fat she was.' Carole threw herself into the task of losing weight and toning up with the same energy and gumption for which she approached all tasks, and within three weeks the happy actress was reported to have shrunk by two dress sizes. Sylvia revelled in the power she had over Carole and other actresses.

'A great deal of my success in Hollywood lay in making stars obey me,' she bragged. 'And they obeyed me because they knew that they had to. Unless their figures were nice their contracts weren't renewed.'

This no-nonsense approach was enough to convince Carole to do absolutely everything that Sylvia told her to do, which included two hours of massage and, rather strangely, lying on a bed while the trainer pulled hard on her leg. 'The stretching will actually pull fat away,' she said. 'It goes deeper into the fat cells than the hand can reach. It's marvellous.' This torturous technique of slapping, squeezing and stretching would cause the actress to scream so much that actors in the next dressing room would often shout over to see if she was okay.

Carole was placed on a strict diet. Breakfast consisted of a small glass of orange juice, a small glass of water, a slice of toast, black coffee and, if she was due at the studio that day, a soft-boiled egg. Lunch was a green salad with French dressing, followed by a small dish of gelatine, though she would occasionally be allowed a glass of iced tea and a small piece of angel food cake. Sylvia proudly told reporters that she allowed Carole this treat because she was 'such a good sport and never whined'.

The reforming of Carole's body and new outlook on her health had a very positive effect and Sylvia wrote that, after their treatments, she would have the energy of a child, bounding and dancing around the room without a care in the world. However, it would seem that Carole did not take everything she'd been taught to heart, and told several reporters that all diets were fads, and exercise and a well-balanced diet was the key to good health and a toned figure.

When she wasn't exercising and working, the actress spent her free time learning about fashion and tailoring. In 1933 Carole spoke about this period of time to reporter Rosalind Shaffer:

A small budget is hardly an excuse for a frumpy wardrobe. One of the smartest girls I know is a clerk in a small shop, who outshines many a picture star on her exceedingly small salary. The first thing to learn is how to handle a needle, for therein lies the open sesame to glamorous clothes. Don't moan and cry that you can't sew. Just persevere and try your hand at it until you DO capture the knack. I am talking from experience. Not so very long ago, I didn't know where the next hadly-needed frock was coming from. I had a friend who spent hours nightly, showing me something about the art of sewing. I bought inexpensive materials and patterns and soon, for ridiculously small amounts, I was acquiring adorable frocks. My mother did the fitting and I pedalled the sewing machine. Some of those dresses were just as clever as those I now wear from famous gown shops. It's the effect we girls want, not necessarily the label.

In addition to clothes, Carole also enjoyed collecting scents:

I really love perfumes. I don't buy the stuff for the bottles to be used as decorations on my dressing table. I open every bottle the moment I get it home and use it until I tire of it. I change perfumes on an average of once a week, returning to old favourites or new possibilities, and the stimulating effect of this variety in aromas is quite pleasant.

Carole looked at her time at Pathé as a refreshing chance to get into serious drama after her years of slapstick with Sennett. 'I just want to be happy,' she told reporter Louise Williams:

Just now I am crazy about the studio. I can't stay away from it. If they call me for four in the afternoon, I can hardly stay away at nine in the morning. I like to come over and see everybody, and feel that I am a part of what's going on. I've always wanted to act. I went to dramatic school for three years after I finished high school, and they couldn't hold classes too late for me. Then for a while I was crazy about dancing and swimming and yachting and riding horseback. Now I can't imagine wanting to do anything but making pictures. Later on, maybe it will be something else. Whatever it is, I'll do it. I always have a lot of fun.

Carole loved the way everyone at Pathé was allowed an opinion on their work:

We used to turn our hands to everything. We'd all get together on a story conference. If I had an idea I'd pop out with it and whether it was accepted or not, I was learning. I had a 'story' mind and found it helpful. In the easy camaraderie of a small studio we all had a finger in the pie.

Two films – *Show Folks* and *Ned McCobb's Daughter* – were released towards the end of 1928. The first was a yarn about show business which did not impress Norbert Lusk from *Picture-Play*, 'Tolerably interesting, because it is lively without being exciting – that's *Show Folks*, another picture of backstage life. The trouble is that these yarns of vaudeville performers are all more of less the same, except for the names of the characters.' He remained unimpressed with actress Lina Basquette's performance, and complained about the sound problems that caused actor Eddie Quillan's voice to jump towards the end of the film. However, he did note, 'Carole Lombard, a very pretty blonde, is worth watching'.

The actress also caught the attention of Welford Beaton, editor of the *Film Spectator*, 'There is a young woman in *Show Folks* whom I never saw before, and never even heard of. She is Carole Lombard and she is going to do very nicely on the screen.' He also gave the actress favourable mention for *Ned McCobb's Daughter*. The junior editor, Donald Beaton, mentioned Carole in his 'As They Appeal to a Youth' column, 'Carole Lombard plays a real heavy in *Show Folks*. She was in *Ned McCobb's Daughter*, and I must apologise for not saying how grand her work was in that as well as the former picture.'

On 4 December 1928 newspapers ran the story that Cecil B. DeMille – the director who had told Carole to come back when she was older – had borrowed her for a prominent role in the MGM feature, *Dynamite*. The young actress was due to play alongside Conrad Nagel and the project gave Carole a great deal of press attention and publicity, while also enhancing her profile socially. Reporter Grace Kingsley met the actress at a party given by Mitchell Lyson, Cecil B. DeMille's art director. She wasn't there merely as a guest, however, she was standing in for Lyson's wife, who was unable to make it. Kingsley noted that Carole took coats from guests, showed them around and then gleefully told the columnist that she had been at a party on Lyson's yacht. She had attempted surfing, she said, but had fallen in many times before learning how to stay on.

The DeMille film was to be a big break for Carole, and she told reporter Cedric Belfrage all about it:

> I'm the principal menace in C.B.'s next picture, *Dynamite*. As we wait for production to start, I'm getting accustomed to C.B. I'll say we get along just fine now, but at first I was awed by him. I used to go in his office to talk over something and he'd say, 'run along now, little girl; I'm busy.' It took a little time to get acclimated. But I've succeeded in getting the other side of C.B.'s majestic front, and I'm beginning to realize what a pleasant guy he really is. He's going to be great to work for.

Unfortunately, the whole affair did not work out. The official story was that while Carole was prepared to put in many hours of hard work, the film was delayed by an abundance of rewrites and story conferences. Sitting around for six weeks was no fun, particularly for Pathé, who were concerned that if the actress didn't make a movie soon she would be all but forgotten in the public's eye. They had big plans to turn Carole into a star – to put her into at least three films in a year – so, as time ticked on, they grew impatient. Urgent meetings were called and by 2 February 1929 various sections of the media reported that Carole's part in the project was cancelled and she had been recalled to Pathé. Back at the studio she was greeted with flowers and a note from Cecil B. DeMille, who had become very fond of the actress while on set. 'Miss Lombard is as wise as she is witty,' he told an interviewer in the late 1930s. He went on to say how much he admired the shrewd management of her career, along with her ability to play all kind of characters on screen.

While the recall story is the most championed version of events, there is another that seems equally as easy to believe. Apparently, as much as Carole wanted to, she did not work out in *Dynamite* due to the fact that she found it extremely hard to remember the lines and get into character. She put in a few days' work, and then assistant director Mitchell Leisen broke the news that she was no longer needed. DeMille then confirmed the dismissal with the roses he sent to Carole, along with a note telling her that he intended to give her part to actress, Julia Faye.

Whatever the true story, Carole was disappointed that once again her career had stalled. However, no sooner was she off *Dynamite* than she was cast in the talking movie *High Voltage* with William Boyd and Owen Moore. The intriguing story revolved around a busload of passengers who are stranded in a snowstorm. The small group find their way to an abandoned church, but it is discovered that a strange drifter is also in the building and does not take kindly to the invasion. Carole played Billie Davis, a young woman on the wrong side of the law, while William Boyd played the drifter.

While the film had potential, the shoot proved somewhat stressful, particularly when the troupe went on location to freezing Lake Tahoe. The actors were instructed to march through the snow over and over again, and by the time the director yelled 'cut!', they were wet through, freezing and thoroughly fed up. Carole remembered it as being the coldest film she had ever made and recalled how she had to wade through the deep snow in heeled shoes. To add insult to injury, the snow fell so heavily that the bus, which was needed for specific scenes, got stuck and filming had to be halted. Carole and actress Diane Ellis made sure they had fun while waiting by organising sledging and snowshoeing competitions.

Even on set in Los Angeles, away from snow and freezing temperatures, there were still problems. A flock of meadow larks invaded the Hollywood set and guns were used to scare them away. The shots coming out of the studio grounds were so loud that worried locals phoned the police.

Though the movie was shot with sound, there was a silent print available too. This led to a great deal of frustration from critics when the film was ultimately released. 'Producers are going to have a tough time in the silent theatres if they are going to re-cut silent versions from talkers and expect audiences to accept them,' complained *Motion Picture News*. '*High Voltage* was produced by Pathé as an all-talker. The silent print, put out for unwired houses, is a complete flop; using a subtitle every few feet to denote what the characters are saying.'

The story did not impress them either. 'The plot is maudlin and thin; in fact so much so that the audience knows what is going to happen miles in advance.' The only drawing power, according to the critic, was actor William Boyd as the drifter. 'Boyd will probably attract his following to this one,' they said, 'but they will surely be disappointed.'

While the reviews were lukewarm, it is possible that Carole gave them little attention, since she was now involved in one of her first big love affairs. The actress never disclosed who the gentleman was, but rumours over the years have pointed a finger firmly in the direction of filmmaker and entrepreneur, Howard Hughes. Hughes was putting the finishing touches to his epic movie *Hell's Angels* at the time, and was well known for his playboy dalliances. If he was the person she had her brief but intense affair with, Carole had plenty to say about him during an interview in 1935:

> About five or six years ago I fell in love with a young man who didn't know what he wanted from life. Everything, really, had been handed him on a silver platter; wealth, charm, position. Yet he was afraid of getting into the human struggle for success. He sat back and waited for things to come his way, refusing to thrust himself into the game. He couldn't make up his mind to what he wanted, what was worth going after. That is a popular pose among some rich men, but I have no sympathy with it. We were both very young – I was going into my twenties – but I was the more fortunate for I was less of a fatalist. I firmly believed that you must know what you want and try to get it.

In the years to come, the young man was still desperate for her attention:

> Not long ago, this young man called me up and said he wanted to talk to me. It had been several years since I had seen him. He asked me, in a sort of blind desperation, what he should do with his life. 'You must give me some sort of philosophy to carry me through,' he said. I told him that I still believed one must make up his mind to what he wanted and go after it. 'But be sure that what you want is worthwhile,' I said.

During 1929 Carole's media presence grew to epic proportions. Many publicity portraits were released to the press and dozens appeared in movie magazines around the United States. Not only that, editors began to realise just how well clothes clung to Carole's lithe body and used her in many fashion features. *Picture-Play* magazine featured her on many occasions: in April 1929 she was photographed wearing sports clothes, in October it was pyjamas and overalls and by November she could be seen wearing a motif sweater.

There were also films to make, including *Big News* with Robert Armstrong. Released in September 1929, the story revolved around a newspaper reporter (Armstrong) and his frustrated wife, who walks out on him because he is unreliable. He is soon fired from his job, only to discover a murder mystery the moment he walks out of the door. Of course he eventually ends up solving the mystery, writing a brilliant story and winning back his wife, too. *Variety* told readers that *Big News* was 'good stuff', though they did have a criticism for Carole, '[She] was a little too restrained, with both mic and camera; mayhap being a newspaper woman herself she had trained down emotionally to avoid the blue pencil'.

*Screenland* described the movie as:

> ... good entertainment – not brain-taxing, not spectacular, but melodramatic, amusing and never dull ... My only quarrel with *Big News* is that they have fallen for the fallacy that most newspaper women wear funny clothes and flat-heeled shoes and go about slapping everybody on the back. I worked on a newspaper once and I was always catching my high French heel in the headlines. It isn't fair. Carole Lombard, being a Mack Sennett School graduate, needs no advice as to how to look beautiful; but I do think she has something to learn about dramatic art. Gesture Six is a good gesture; why stick to Gesture One?

Carole had enjoyed making the movie. While on set she had water fights with the crew between scenes, and was visited by Edward Stodel from the *Los Angeles Evening Herald*. He found her holding court with a group of reporters, laughing and cracking risqué jokes. As she walked away, she turned to one of them, 'And me, what's a lady,' she said. 'That's my patented comeback around the studio,' she told Stodel.

It wasn't all film work that occupied Carole's time. Pathé also used her services while auditioning new young actors. Many years later, Bette Davis would tell interviewer Dick Cavett that she once did the same job, only in her case she had to lie on a couch and fake love with a long line of men. She described it as a ghastly experience, but luckily for Carole her time as a test girl was far easier, as she explained to Louise Williams:

> They wanted to make tests of stage actors, and thought it would be easier if they had someone opposite them. I made a test with a chap who had been playing in Candida. One night they handed me a copy of the play and the next day I did a scene with him. It was all so new to me and such an old story with him, I almost burst out laughing. I thought the test was terrible, but the studio liked it, so it's all right with me.

Even when she wasn't working, Carole would turn up at the studio to say hello, or see if there were any parts she could play at the last minute. Every night she would make a point of walking past the executives' offices to shout cheerio to each of them. Her mission? To make sure that no one could forget who she was, or her availability to play every role that came along. The tactic worked. The studio seemed to love her easy-going personality and put her into more and more pictures.

Made during the summer of 1929 and released in November, *The Racketeer* saw Carole take on the role of Rhoda Philbrooke, a broke society girl who is trying to raise money to nurse an alcoholic violinist back to health. In the meantime she ends up embroiled with a gangster played by Robert Armstrong. Describing the movie, Carole said, 'I don't play a sob sister. That's a distinction for me. I'm one of the few girls who hasn't played a sob sister this year.'

When it was released, Pathé posted announcements in various magazines, describing *The Racketeer* as 'Armstrong's latest and greatest characterization' and a 'box office headliner'. Some critics failed to agree, however. 'This is a rehash of several racketeer stories that have preceded it,' complained *Film Daily*. 'It has nothing noteworthy to pull it out of the rut. The action is rather thin and it is overloaded with dialogue.' Thankfully, their opinion of the movie did not reflect the way the magazine felt about Carole, '[She] proves a real surprise and does her best work to date. In fact this is the first opportunity she has had to prove that she has the stuff to go over. With looks, and a good trouping sense, she also has the personality.'

At the same time, *Picture-Play* magazine was lukewarm on the film. However, 'it holds one's attention by reason of Mr. Armstrong's quiet authority and the excellent acting of Carole Lombard'. *Motion Picture News* praised her too, calling her performance 'striking'.

# BREAKTHROUGH

While the actress hoped very much that she would have a permanent home at Pathé, when it was time for Carole's contract to be renewed the studio decided against it. *Variety* explained their decision, 'Pathé will make fewer but more elaborate productions for 1930–31. Studio has taken off the elastic on production, and henceforth will have no rigid production budget in advance. Company will also hereafter sell pictures individually and not in block.'

Carole's time with the organisation was terminated and rumours circulated that, in her particular case, it was because she looked too much like actress Constance Bennett. However, as always, she put on a brave face, shrugged her shoulders and just moved on. Stoically, the actress told friends that losing her contract was probably the best thing that had ever happened to her, and she was positive she would do much better at another studio.

Carole would joke to reporter George Madden that 'for ten years I've been the only person in Hollywood who believed in me, except perhaps

Pushface Lombard, who is a Pekinese'. Carole could always laugh and make many a witty comment about any potential trouble that came her way. However, away from the laughs, those early years in Hollywood were extremely hard and there was a time when she privately wondered if she was just too 'inadequate' to make it in the movies:

> All the time I was making seventeen flops in a row, I was scared to death they were going to call my bluff before I had a chance to really learn something about this business. There is no-one else on the screen who has had more consistently bad pictures than I. I doubt if anyone will ever know what I went through those first five years.

Someone who did believe in her, however, was Alfred Santell, the director of *The Arizona Kid*, which was being made at Carole's old studio, Fox. He remembered the 21-year-old and decided to sign her up for the role of Virginia Holt, a bad girl who fakes love for the main character, played by Warner Baxter.

The film required the cast and crew to go on location to a ghost town in Utah, which had been revived especially for filming. Accompanying them for at least part of the shoot was journalist Sydney Valentine. The author found the cast and crew in a series of makeshift homes which they had affectionately named after Hollywood landmarks. True to form, Carole's tent was labelled 'The Ambassador', while all around were false street signs pointing to imaginary Hollywood and Beverly boulevards. There was also a studio bulletin board giving instructions such as 'get to the refreshments tent on time' and 'no-one is to ride horses unless a special permit is secured. And there will be no special permits, so that's that.'

While the unit may have been surrounded by Hollywood memories such as the tent names, the imaginary streets and a few postcards scattered around, there was no actual glamour on set at all. The only luxury was a stove to ward off the freezing temperatures, and once the outdoor lights went off at 10.30 p.m. the resulting darkness meant that everyone had to be in bed, whether they liked it or not. By 6.30 a.m. the cast and crew were in the refreshments tent, the arrival of breakfast announced by a musical triangle.

The scenes were shot around an old church, a saloon and various other western themed buildings and facades. 'Unlike previous Western talkies,' said Valentine, '*The Arizona Kid* is having all its interiors filmed right on the spot, instead of at the studio weeks later.' Locals were used as extras in the production and would often storm the set even when not needed. Some enjoyed telling the actors about the old days when their families were pioneers, building towns and fighting off Indians as they did so.

Carole shared a few words about the making of the movie with interviewer Malcolm H. Oettinger. 'We went bye-bye for eight weeks,' she said. 'In the desert for two months, living in tents … Dandy. Then we saw the picture! It could have been made in a week in somebody's backyard, but it's making money and that's the answer.'

Work was completed by April 1930 and studio publicists began marketing the film. In adverts placed in movie magazines around the country, the studio declared the film to be a companion piece to *In Old Arizona*, a 1928 movie which also starred Warner Baxter. Unfortunately, at least one critic did not agree. The reviewer at *Screenland* magazine told readers that, while they may go in expecting another *In Old Arizona*, they would not get it. 'Like most sequels, this fails to arouse the enthusiasm of the first edition.' He did give a somewhat appreciative nod in Carole's direction, however:

> The feminine appeal is divided between Mona Maris and Carole Lombard, two of the prettiest girls on the screen. The blonde Miss Lombard is not quite at home in these outdoor surroundings; but La Maris is vivid and always interesting as the real romance in Chico's [Baxter] colourful career.

*Film Daily* did not mention Carole, but their reviewer felt that *The Arizona Kid* got off to a slow start and only began to pick up in the last moments. 'Here a strong finish and some tense suspense succeed fairly well in overcoming the slowness of the earlier reels. It is not as gripping as its predecessor, but the Baxter fans will like it just the same.'

The next release was Paramount's *Safety in Numbers*, though it had actually been made before *The Arizona Kid*. The film starred Charles 'Buddy' Rogers playing the role of aspiring songwriter Butler Reynolds, a man about to inherit millions of dollars. Carole played the role of Pauline, a young chorus girl hired by Reynolds's uncle (along with her two flatmates) to accompany him around New York. They all end up falling for the man, but it is one of her companions who he eventually falls in love with.

On its release in June 1930, the *New York Times* declared it to be ridiculous and gave favourable mention only to the musical interludes. The fan magazines were more positive, however. 'Young and refreshing,' was how *Screenland* described it, while *The New Movie Magazine* said it was the best Buddy Rogers film for a long time. *Educational Screen*, meanwhile, gave a special nod to Carole, stating that she and actor Roscoe Karns 'furnish the greatest amount of amusement'.

'Just when I was about ready to give up, I was offered a role in *Safety in Numbers*,' Carole told the *Screen Mirror*. 'It was a great break, but I didn't know it then ... I thought it would probably be followed by more months of idleness.' She was wrong. Encouraged by her talents in *Safety*, Paramount sent the actress to New York in June 1930. Her mission was to act in *Fast and Loose*, the movie version of a play called *The Best People*. The studio saw such potential in Carole that they decided to sign her to a featured player contract too. She was elated. 'I've known what it means to work for a living,' she told the *Screen Mirror*. 'I've known what it means to go without dessert for luncheon when it gets along toward the end of the month and that there is a landlord to be considered.'

On the way to New York, Carole returned to Fort Wayne for several days – a place she had not been to for many years. Her mother was already there, sorting out the estate of her mother, Alice, who had passed away in February 1930. The lady had been in the habit of spending her winters in California, and had been visiting one of her daughters when she suddenly became ill and did not recover. *Variety* covered the death by telling readers that Carole had been left a bequest of $5,000, which was a considerable inheritance at the time.

The actress refused to officially confirm how much money she was to receive. 'Because everyone would be wanting to borrow from me,' she joked. More seriously, she told reporters that the inheritance would not affect her screen career in any way, and she would continue to work as long as producers wanted her to.

By the time Carole arrived in Fort Wayne, Elizabeth was not only involved in estate procedures but also in organising a large family get-together. The actress enjoyed the company of her Fort Wayne kin and then went to her old childhood home, No. 704 Rockhill Street. There she stood quietly on the top step, looking out over the street and telling companions about the fun and games she once had there.

During the three-day trip, Carole also went around town looking at the new buildings and lamenting how much the place had changed since she left all those years ago. She also made a rare visit to see her father, which she had not done in some years. It was a private matter, though some glimpse into how his life (and that of relatives) had been affected by Carole's growing fame can be gleaned from an article in *The New Movie Magazine*:

> Her father is retired and remains in the city most of the time. He generally attends the private previews of his daughter's pictures when they come to the Paramount Theatre. And then her numerous aunts and uncles on both sides of the family keep in touch with the actress by following the chatter columns.

Before long it was time for Carole to leave for New York. The actress was excited about the journey ahead:

> We have a troupe composed of New York actors. Frank Morgan and Miriam Hopkins, and Dave Hutchison, from *Sons o' Guns*, and it's all quite dignified. Correct, you know? No horseplay and a far cry from the water fights we staged at Sennett's during any old picture. In the middle of a scene you could expect a bag of water on your head. It was real sport. Then you'd fill a bag and dash after the enemy. In Manhattan it's all different. It seems we're artistes here.

During the 1930 trip to New York Carole gave an interview to reporter Herbert Cruikshank for *Motion Picture*. By this time Lombard felt she'd spent enough time in New York. She was homesick and desperate to get back to Hollywood. Sitting down in the lounge of the Algonquin Hotel, the actress sipped on tomato juice, treated the reporter to her imitation of Greta Garbo, told him that she chose her name thanks to an interest in numerology and provided funny stories about her fellow actors back in Hollywood.

At the next table, an excited (but mistaken) diner could be heard telling his companions, 'Look, there's Constance Bennett!' while Carole herself seemed not to notice. Much of the interview was run-of-the-mill stuff, but an interesting aspect is the strength of character displayed by Lombard even though she was still in her very early twenties. For instance, Carole told the reporter that while she had been cast as an ingénue in several past films, what she wanted to do more than anything else was act in comedies. However, she would also be thrilled to play the dramatic role of Sadie Thompson in Somerset Maugham's *Rain*. This was a part she coveted, though never won, and it eventually went to dance rival Joan Crawford in 1932.

During the interview, Carole disclosed that her idols in the acting business were Gloria Swanson and Ann Harding, while her male obsessions were Fredric March, Bob Armstrong, Robert Montgomery and Charles Kaley (with whom she was also rumoured to be having a love affair). Cruikshank told his readers that they must not be surprised if she ended up married to Kaley one of these days. 'A girl must marry some time,' he wrote excitedly, though his comments were widely off the mark.

While rumours swirled about Carole's love life, she remained tight-lipped on the subject. However, it would seem that during this time the young actress had become involved with publisher Horace Liveright. He was twice Carole's age and had recently been employed by Paramount as a story researcher. It was during this time that the two met and became close, though not on a physical level. During an interview with Gladys Hall, Carole talked about something she termed as 'companionship love'; a relationship based on friendship rather than emotion. From what she described, it seems likely that she was talking about Liveright during the piece:

I had Companionship Love. He was a slightly older man. They usually are when they play this role. I admired him enormously. I liked everything about him. I liked his mannerisms and his manners,

I liked his style. I liked his tastes, his hobbies, his friends, the things he did and the way he did them. He taught me things, lots of them. He opened doors to me. He brought out 'the best' in me. And I would have been positively ill if he had ever kissed me. The thrilling ingredient that sets friendship on fire simply was not there.

# MR AND MRS POWELL

Carole's next movie was *It Pays to Advertise*, a quickie she made between 18 December 1930 and 3 January 1931. Just days after wrapping, the 22-year-old began to work with an actor who would change her life and career forever. Born in 1892, William Powell was a successful actor and well respected by his peers. However, he was a good sixteen years older than Carole and not known for his patience towards young or inexperienced actors. So when she was cast opposite him in *Man of the World* many people wondered how they would get along; especially since Carole was becoming extremely well known for her feisty and forthright manner, and salty language.

To try and ward off any uncomfortable moments on set, the two were introduced in Powell's dressing room a while before filming began. Powell recalled the first meeting to reporter Walter Ramsey:

The day I met Carole I had the same feeling as a sixteen-year-old boy on his first date. I was embarrassed and fidgety. I worried over whether or not I was making a good impression on her. It just so happened that immediately after our introduction, which took place at the studio, we were left alone to talk over the picture we were about to do together. But we didn't talk about the picture. We talked about men and women and things that happened to them and ourselves. Suddenly, in the midst of this talk with the most beautiful girl I had ever known, a thought came to me: Someday I am going to ask this girl to marry me!

While this was all very romantic, if Powell thought that Carole was going to be a pushover for his sophisticated charm, he was wrong. During an early date, the subject of marriage was brought up in conversation and the actress wasted no time in telling the actor that whatever her future held, it was not marriage. A short time after meeting Powell, Carole gave her thoughts about marriage to journalist Ruth Biery:

I think marriage is dangerous. It spoils beautiful friendships that might have lasted for years. The idea of two people trying to possess each other is wrong, and I don't think the flare of love lasts. Your mind rather than your emotions must answer for the success of matrimony. It must be a friendship; a calm companionship which can last through the years.

The media questioned whether or not the two actors would become a serious item. *Picture-Play* described them as being 'torridly fascinated by each other' and cited the fact that while Powell's last wife was a brunette, Carole, as a blonde, was in complete contrast. The reporter also wondered if any marriage plans would interfere with the actor's reputation for preferring the company of his buddies (Ronald Colman and Richard Barthelmess) over women. Reporter Marie House asked him about this, shortly after meeting Carole:

It's true, I like the companionship of men. With men you can be yourself. Let down. Be comfortable. They talk the same language, have the same viewpoint. With women you must be more formal. And besides, we like to keep our private lives to ourselves.

Because we do not choose to parade our amours, if any, to the show gaze of the public, we are labelled 'women haters'. That is such a farce ... I think the ideal relationship is between a man and a woman. The one woman, who could be everything to you. It is deeper, more elemented than any friendship could be. I won't say more lasting – but it satisfies the soul hunger, the heart hunger.

Carole greatly enjoyed Powell's company. 'Bill knows about words,' she told Helen Louise Walker:

He has a passion for them. He pours over dictionaries and he has given me a respect for language that I never dreamed of before ... It is so grand to have somebody with whom you can talk, with whom you can exchange ideas ... You find out what you think about things, yourself. Your opinions take shape!

Despite that, Carole remained firmly ensconced in the home she shared with her immediate family:

You simply couldn't go wrong with a mother like mine. I think the 'life of the Lombards' is the real reason for my shying from the matrimonial leap. Our house is usually ringing with laughter. My brothers are wits in their own right and they do a good deal of practising about the house. Freddie and Tutti [Stuart] always bring home a few friends apiece for dinner, and those added to a few of mine makes the Lombard mansion a little like a madhouse. But I love it. I am afraid that when I leave home for one of my own I'll be gnawed with homesickness and loneliness.

On 28 March 1931 the Powell/Lombard movie, *Man of the World*, was released. It told the story of Michael Wagstag (Powell) who enjoys blackmailing wealthy Americans, along with his accomplice, Irene (Wynne Gibson). Potential victims are found in Mary (Lombard) and her Uncle Harold (Guy Kibee), although Wagstag does not expect to fall in love with the woman. His background means that the story can never end happily and he ends up losing Mary and – after a spot of blackmailing – he is forced to remain with Irene.

Of the film, *Screenland* magazine said, 'This isn't one of Bill's best, but he is well worth seeing. Powell appeals – and Wynne Gibson, as his faithful accomplice, and Carole Lombard as the blonde, are delightful.' *Variety* was more concerned with the Parisian inspired costumes, saying that in this area Carole had received 'swell treatment from the costume department'.

Now that work on the film was finished, the romance could have fizzled out like so many other on-set dalliances. However, it carried on regardless, though even from this very early stage the romance wasn't as straightforward as it could have been. The summer before the couple met, Powell had travelled around Europe with buddies Ronald Colman and Ernest Torrence. 'We had no set itinerary,' he told reporter Marie House. 'Decided one day to go someplace and were off. Vagabonding.' The trip was interesting, but at times frustrating. 'I was absolutely surrounded by play-boys and play-girls of the play world,' he told reporter Walter Ramsey. 'Everyone around me seemed to be having a most glorious time … yet I was, if possible, even more lonely than I had been at home.' Still, Powell loved the freedom of travelling and this appeared to be the way he wanted his life to go in the future. His biggest dream was to fish, camp, make one or two movies a year and travel with his partner. He was not ready for retirement, but certainly all signs pointed towards slowing his career a little and enjoying the simpler way of life.

Carole was on a totally different path. While rumours of marriage between the two continued to heat up during 1931, reporter Ruth Biery hoped that she would be able to share some happy news with her readers. She was disappointed, however, as Carole confirmed there was little hope of a marriage any time soon:

Bill wants to travel. He wants an interesting, friendly person to travel with, but I'm not ready to travel. I have to concentrate on my career. When I can't go – and he wants to go certain places – he can't seem to understand – now. And if we were married …

Carole's voice trailed off and the interview was brought to a close, but not before Ruth Biery decided the romance between Lombard and Powell was 'a sad little story' and the timing was all wrong. The outcome of the relationship would be 'in the lap of the gods', she said. Perhaps this was a little too dramatic, but certainly both Carole and Powell gave many comments that made the idea of a lasting relationship seem unlikely. When asked by Marquis Busby if the two would marry any time soon, Powell shook his head, 'I don't know. We're always too busy making pictures. Carole has made four this year at Paramount and has four more to make before fall. This doesn't leave much time for extracurricular activities. Anyway, it will be a long time.'

When asked the same question, Carole was just as unsure. 'I don't know that we will ever marry,' she said. 'If we don't, we will always be good friends. If we do marry, here's wishing luck to both of us. Bill is a grand person to know and be with.'

Personality wise, the couple seemed poles apart. Bill described Carole as the frankest girl he had ever met, while his orderly life seemed to grate on her nerves. 'We'll never get on,' Carole said:

> Bill will strangle me – or, at least, he'll want to. He likes order and dignity and an organized sort of life. I can't live that way. I always do whatever occurs to me at the moment. Bill won't be able to stand me. He wants to marry and settle down. I couldn't settle down. It would kill me!

In the meantime, reports surfaced that Powell had told his girlfriend he was not interested in exploring Hollywood's nightlife on a regular basis. Instead, he preferred to dine quietly with friends. For now, Carole gave up her frequent trips to the Cocoanut Grove and Roosevelt Hotel and pretended to enjoy the quiet life. She confirmed this to *Silver Screen* magazine, saying that while she used to go out dancing, she now spent her time indoors with Powell and his cronies.

Their taste in sports did not match either. A keen tennis player, Carole loved running around the court on a regular basis. Not Powell. While he would escort her occasionally to games at his friends' houses, during their courtship the sport did not seem to excite him at all.

'It isn't conversational enough,' he said. 'You just don't discuss a certain serve, or a particularly good play in tennis.' Instead, Powell preferred to play golf, just as Carole's father had in Fort Wayne. 'You have time to enjoy the scenery, and the nineteenth hole is always a cheerful prospect. You get together with a few friends and review the entire morning's play. Bridge is about the only other game in which you can indulge in such fascinating post-mortems.'

Carole took on a game of tennis in exactly the same way she took on her career – with determination. 'Carole has natural good form,' her tennis coach, Eleanor Tennant, said. 'And I've never known anyone who wasn't up in tournament play, who didn't have tennis in their blood, who got tennis-drunk the way she does. "Now I have it!" she'll yell when we're having a lesson. "Keep shooting them at me!"'

Two more movies were made in the months ahead: the first, *Ladies' Man* and the second, *Up Pops the Devil*. The former saw Paramount take advantage of the romance between Carole and Powell. It was the story of a man (Powell) who lives off the gifts and good graces of women, but the character did not exactly endear him to audiences. By the time it was released, the actor had become lukewarm on the project and described his appearance as an error of judgement. He told reporter Marquis Busby:

> Americans can never forgive such a character. In Europe the gigolo is more or less accepted, but not in this country. You can find some redeeming traits in a man who steals, takes dope, drinks too much, beats children, or murders his wife, but there are none for the type of character I played in *Ladies' Man*. He's something you find when you turn over rotten logs.

Despite their conflicting personalities and the fact that the two actually hadn't known each other very long, Powell still stuck to his initial idea that it would be good for them to be married. During 1931 their lives adopted something of a routine. The actor would ask Carole to marry him, she would say no and give a list of reasons why, then the relationship would go on as before. A few weeks would pass and the matter would come up again. Carole would turn him down, he'd sulk for a while and then move on. He joked to reporter Walter Ramsey:

I think I asked Carole to marry me on average of every half hour. At first she was a bit dubious ... so many professional marriages fail to work out ... I had experienced one failure in matrimony previously, [and] Carole was just starting out on a career that was tremendously important to her.

Carole told Ruth Biery that her partner wished her to give up her career and live exactly as he chose to. She stood firm and told him in no uncertain terms that this would never happen. In the months ahead, Powell admitted to friends that he was now seeing things differently; he intended to be supportive of the actress's career and lifestyle from now on. This sudden shift was unexpected but appreciated by Carole, and after yet another marriage proposal she surprisingly agreed to marry Powell after all.

The pair set about organising what they hoped to be a quiet, intimate wedding with only a few friends and family in attendance. In June 1931, just a few days before the big day, Powell spoke to reporter Joan Standish about their future plans. 'Carole and I spent our lunch hour today, figuring out where we wanted to live when we get back from our honeymoon in Hawaii,' he said. 'Frankly I have a leaning toward a house. Somehow, marriage always seems more "settled" in a home of your own.'

'Will you hate to give up your freedom?' asked Standish.

'Good Lord no,' replied Powell:

Freedom is one of the great disillusions of the world. We think we want it above all things, and when we get it, what in the world can we do with it? What's the fun of going places and seeing things if there isn't someone important to share the thrill of travelling? What's the fun of accomplishing things if there isn't someone who means a lot to applaud and tell you what a remarkable fellow you are? I've had a great many years of the 'coveted freedom'. I've found that I can be the loneliest in the most crowded places when all I have to celebrate with is – freedom.

I think I'm getting the most wonderful girl in the world. Freedom? I'd trade every bit of it just for a few hours with Carole. We've opened secret doors in one another's personalities. We've found that we are new people – to each other.

The couple were married on 26 June 1931 at No. 619 Rexford Avenue, the home of Carole's mother, Elizabeth. The 22-year-old bride wore a simple blue gown with large flower corsage which she had received from her fiancé with a note, 'Dear Miss Lombard, will you kindly see that these reach the future Mrs. Powell and that she wears them?' Her father was not in attendance. Instead, the bride was walked up the aisle by her future father-in-law, Horatio Powell. Reverend W. L. Barth presided over the ceremony, while the best man was Carole's brother, Frederic.

There was a small hiccup involving the nervous groom having trouble finding the right finger for the ring, but otherwise the ceremony went according to plan. Everything, that is, except for the presence of several newspaper reporters and photographers at the windows, trying to get a glimpse of the famous couple. Carole joked that between the laughs with the ring and the noise of the press, she wasn't sure if the minister had actually reached the end of his wedding speech, but 'I hope for the best!'

The next day, Carole's film, *I Take this Woman*, was released, at the same time as the newlyweds sailed to Honolulu for their honeymoon. While Carole was happy to get away from Hollywood, the vacation as a whole could have been much better. The actress became extremely unwell while in Honolulu, suffering from a severe case of the flu. By the time the couple arrived back in Los Angeles on 7 August she had taken a turn for the worse and her condition deteriorated throughout the month.

Studio executives had not been keen on Carole taking time off for the wedding and were anxious to get her back to work. They gave her a part in *The Greeks had a Word for It*, which revolved around three women trying to snare rich husbands by pretending to be millionaires themselves. This film provided the inspiration for Marilyn Monroe's 1953 film, *How to Marry a Millionaire*, which incidentally co-starred William Powell.

It could have been incredible, especially as executives hoped it would team Carole Lombard with bombshell Jean Harlow, but it was not to be. In the end Jean could not get permission to take the role, and Carole's health took a turn for the worse and doctors diagnosed her with pleurisy. The start date of 26 August came and went, and new stars were immediately sought. Rumours abounded that Loretta Young or Thelma Todd would take on the roles, but in the end the parts went to Joan Blondell, Madge Evans and Ina Claire.

As time went on, worries over Carole's health subsided a little. The Powells tried to settle down to a peaceful life together quietly dining with friends and attending the Southwest Tennis Championships. This reflected how Powell had envisaged his marriage to be. 'After our honeymoon,' he explained before the wedding:

> We're going to settle down in the old-fashioned idea of a calm and very unexciting life – as exciting lives are judged in Hollywood. We have a few close friends who mean much to us. We're going to play tennis, and quietly attend theatres other than opening nights, and take drives to the beaches and get our own meals on the cook's day out, and go places and do things – always together. I've found a pal, a sweetheart, a friend, a wife.

Lombard tried to become a partner whom Powell could be proud of. In this regard, she set about honing her cooking skills and bought flowers every week to brighten up their home. She spent time playing with Bill's son by his previous marriage, shopping for curtains and pictures and carefully choosing items of furniture that she thought her new husband would like. She had an acute eye for detail and told reporter Gladys Hall that Powell was so excited to have a real home of his own that he spent ages walking slowly around the rooms, patting the furniture and telling her how 'cute' he thought particular items were.

Carole jokingly called him 'pathetic', but shared her admiration for her new husband with Hall. 'I'm divinely happy,' she said. 'I didn't know there could be such happiness as I am having now. I'll never forget it, not one instant of it, so long as I live on this earth.' In a complete turnaround from comments made before the marriage, the actress also told Hall that Bill was not in the least bit jealous and said that while her husband often made comments about men she worked with, it was all done in fun.

'The whole explanation of our marriage and our happiness is that we understand one another,' Carole said:

We took time to do it – eight months of going together every available moment. And where there is understanding, there is no possibility of misunderstanding. How can there be? I can't see the sense in these so-called modern-marriage pacts, talking things over, planning what one will do in this or that emergency, making charts of emotions. After all, emotional matters cannot be charted. If there is perfect understanding between two people, what is there to plan about? Bill and I do, and intend to do, what we feel like doing, where and with whom. But – we both know what the other feels like doing and why. That's all there is to it.

Carole embarked on a new film – *No One Man* – on 12 November 1931, and then after it wrapped on 5 December, she and Powell set about organising Christmas. They sent out a joint card which showed a cartoon couple with the inscription, 'Merry Christmas and a Happy New Year – Mr. and Mrs. William Powell'. *Silver Screen* told readers that while the 'Mr and Mrs' inscription seemed rather formal, their message never went out of style. 'Incidentally, this is the first greeting of any sort bearing their married name in a formal style,' the reporter said.

As 1932 dawned, the marriage looked to be perfect and the couple went to great lengths to show the world just how much they adored each other, even posing together by the fireplace and out in their sunlit garden. But while the photos were designed to show great love, Powell found them somewhat laughable. 'It makes you feel a little self-conscious posing for them – when you realize that half the time in cases like that the divorce papers are filed before the magazine even gets on the stands. It's almost a challenge.'

Friends told reporters they had never seen Carole happier; that she had become more sensitive and her sarcastic wit was gentler. But in spite of all the outward shows of affection, cracks – however small – started to appear in their otherwise perfect existence. One of the main problems was Carole's health. She had not recovered fully from the honeymoon illness and had frequent relapses throughout the first year of marriage. Bill was so concerned about his wife's health that he encouraged her to take time off from her career, or give it up altogether. This was not something Carole was prepared to do.

The age gap also presented a problem, though Powell was quick to toss aside any questions related to it:

A great deal has been written and said about the difference in our ages. It's a lot of nonsense! We are in love with each other … what then, does a few years difference make so long as Carole likes to do the same things I do, and I enjoy doing the same things Carole loves to do. Companionship and congeniality – not age – are the important things in any marriage.

In spite of Powell's feelings, it was quite an adjustment for Carole to live such a quiet life with her husband; she was only 23 years old after all. A telltale sign of her frustration came when *Screenland* printed a story about trying to impress men. They asked Carole for her opinion. 'Don't try affectations, baby talk, mystery poses or pseudo-sophistication,' she said. 'You can't keep it up unless it's natural, and nothing is worse than a life-long attempt to be something you distinctly are not.'

On 30 January 1932, *No One Man* was released. Carole played the role of divorcee Penelope Newbold, a woman who cannot decide what she wants from marriage or who she desires to share her life with. Alongside her were Ricardo Cortez and Paul Lukas, playing the love interests. The film received fairly positive reviews. *Film Daily* said, 'Excellent work by a good cast of troupers, plus capable direction, make this a satisfying dish for those who like domestic tangles with class background and more dialogue than action.'

*Silver Screen* described Carole as 'alluring', while the *Motion Picture Herald* dedicated most of its time to giving away the plotline. However, they did add, 'The audience at the New York Paramount gave every evidence of having been well entertained by the adaptation and quite satisfied with the work of Miss Lombard, blonde and attractive.' As well as reviews, the film also inspired some beautiful publicity photographs of Carole, and a fashion spread in *Photoplay* magazine. 'Much of the action of *No One Man* takes place in Florida,' it said, 'so Carole's clothes make an excellent forecast of what you will be wearing this summer.' *Variety* also picked up on the costumes in a small article in their 26 January 1932 issue. In it they described the outfits and noted that it seemed as though Paramount was grooming the actress for fashion stardom.

In complete contrast, a review printed in the very same issue described the film as 'Unimportant screen material, which will probably get by lightly at best because it's from the same cloth as many preceding money pictures'. As if that wasn't negative enough, the reviewer then insulted Carole directly by saying she suffered:

> … a two-way handicap to overcome for sympathy. One is the character she plays and the other is the camera. The lens has been none too kind to her here. Gorgeous in 'stills' the reproduction on the screen for her is such as to cause audible unfavourable comment from women in the audience.

They ended the review by saying that *No One Man* was sure to end up as 'just a picture'.

Carole began making *Sinners in the Sun* on 8 February 1932, but she wasn't in the best of health. The long waits between scenes were just too much for her nerves, and the actress tried to fill the time as best she could. On one occasion she spent a few hours between scenes being interviewed by reporter Wood Soanes. Watching the actress sitting on a divan in her dressing room, what struck and disturbed Soanes most was the way she continued to knock the back of her head against the wall as she spoke. To the reporter, it seemed as though she was totally unaware of the action.

Filming ended on 11 March 1932, but the rumours about her marriage coupled with her film career were all just too much and she suffered a nervous breakdown shortly after. For two weeks the actress lay in bed, first crippled by the breakdown and then by a severe case of grippe.

As if that wasn't bad enough, Powell then became ill with a very bad cold and the two were incapacitated. On 27 April 1932, the *Washington Post* reported that Carole was past the crisis but would still need another week or so to fully recover. The breakdown, it said, was brought on by severe overwork.

Eventually she regained her strength, and as she did so Carole tried to reclaim a portion of her former self. She told Powell that they really should go out more; it was their duty to spend money and therefore create custom for those people working in cinemas or waiting tables in restaurants. Subsequently, the couple were seen occasionally at restaurants and the cinema, and Carole opened her mind to Powell's love for travelling:

> Sometimes we suddenly decide, at two or three in the morning that we want more than anything to go to Mexico – or Santa Barbara, or Arrowhead, or Palm Springs. So we simply put on coats, stick toothbrushes in the pockets, get in the car and go. Drive all night and arrive exhausted in the morning with just enough time to grab a bit of sleep before we have to turn around and race back in time to get to the studio next day. There's not much sense to it, but it's swell fun, and we've done exactly as we wanted to do. That's the way I like to live.

# REBELLION

I n May 1932 *Sinners in the Sun* was released, though by this time Carole had become more and more disenchanted with Paramount. She was particularly frustrated with the amount of money she was being paid and wasted no time in complaining:

In the business world when a man or a woman reaches the high salary class, his or her earning power is just beginning. Each dollar that is earned is building up a return for years to come. That isn't true in Hollywood. Only here, is the life of a high salaried person limited in part of years. A screen star must get what he or she can for services within five years. Look at the number of box office names who burn out within a year.

Shuttled from one mediocre picture to another, she wondered if she would ever be cast in anything worthwhile. 'She gives excellent performances in pictures that create no stir,' said reporter Laura

Ellsworth Fitch in the summer of 1932. Carole shared her own opinion with the same writer:

> I love movies. I must, otherwise I'd have got myself a saner job long ago. I hang on stubbornly, hoping that someday I'll have a crack at a really intelligent, fine picture. I laugh about the stupidities afterward, but at the time it is heart-breaking and nerve-racking. The stories, little confections that have been stirred up by half a dozen hands into a tasty morsel that would drive any adult to acute nausea! The whole system is so cockeyed. The talent is there, but it is so badly used – the wrong people doing the wrong things, world without end, amen! Casual anecdotes of ordinary studio routine are more harrowing than the darkest Russian tales you can name. It's such a pity – directors and writers forced into niches where they don't belong. And of course the actors are eventual victims too.

By late summer 1932 Carole signed another contract with Paramount, but just a month later it was reported that she remained discontented with the parts being chosen for her. 'I don't want anything more than is my due,' she told reporter Grace Kingsley, adding that she knew she would not be on screen forever. 'I think it is only right that an actress should be willing to step down and give the new girls a chance.' Unknown to Kingsley, just a day before the column was printed Carole had been suspended from Paramount and taken off their payroll.

The studio had once again loaned her out. This time to Warners, where she was expected to make a movie with James Cagney. Paramount executives approved the script, but Carole hated it and refused to report for work. Both studios were livid and she was suspended, though it took several days for the news to hit the press. On 17 October 1932, while the suspension was all over the trade magazines, newsmen rushed to Carole's door to see what her side of the story was. They were left disappointed. The drapes remained drawn and nobody came to the door.

Executives at Warners and Paramount were at a loss as to what to do next. The suspension had not changed Carole's mind as they hoped it would, and instead she dug her heels in even more. Consequently, by

18 October it was announced that actress Mary Brian would take the role. Paramount was furious and issued a statement announcing that it 'would not embarrass Warners by tolerating players' indifference and refusal to function as they thought best'.

In an interview with *Picture-Play*, Carole put her side of the story across:

I have an instinct for business. I know every word of my contract, know what my rights are and demand that they be respected. My creed is 'Look well to this day.' I am not temperamental. When I was accused of walking out on Warner Brothers it was not because they meant to lend me out. I didn't mind being leant. But a role Warners wanted me to play was not suitable for me. It was a typical Mary Brian role. In time the studio was convinced I was right. It wasn't true, either, that I got riled up because my then husband, William Powell, did not get a role assigned to Jimmy Cagney.

While all this was going on, *Virtue* was released. The film was the result of Carole being loaned out to Columbia, and was the rather dark story of Mae, an ex-prostitute who is trying to change her ways and get out of the business. She falls in love and marries Jimmy (played by Pat O'Brien), only for him to find out shortly after the wedding that his wife has a shady past. As if that isn't enough, she is then accused of a crime she did not commit, which complicates the already rocky relationship.

Reviews were favourable, although while *Film Daily* praised the performances of all cast members, they did find the film on the whole a tad melodramatic. *The National Board of Review* magazine gave *Virtue* the thumbs up for a mature audience and said that it was 'another story of a girl's troubles in living down her past, with a murder to help straighten things out, but it is lively and interesting, with human portrayals by the actors and brisk, engaging direction'.

*Motion Picture Herald* addressed a serious issue in their review:

Possessed of a certain dramatic effectiveness and succeeding in becoming reasonably entertaining, this picture nevertheless presents the exhibitor with something in the nature of a problem in selling. The reason is that the theme is concerned primarily with the attempted and finally successful return to respectability of a girl of extremely easy virtue.

Carole's suspension was over by 30 October 1932 and the *Los Angeles Times* announced that she had been loaned to Charles R. Rogers for a part in *Billion Dollar Scandal*. However, by early November she was off that picture and instead cast in Paramount's, *No Man of Her Own*, replacing Miriam Hopkins who was originally signed to the role.

The film saw 24-year-old Carole work with actor Clark Gable for the one and only time of her career. Gable – the 'King of Hollywood', as he would become known – was seven years older than Carole and had most certainly made his mark on the industry. He had paid his dues, developing from a young theatre actor to a fully-fledged movie star, and had recently acted with a young Jean Harlow, an actress who would become his regular co-star in the years to come.

*No Man of Her Own* was a fairly simple film and Carole played Connie Randall, a small-town librarian. She meets gambler Jerry Stewart (Gable), who is currently hiding out in the town, and they decide to get married on a toss of a coin. While she is madly in love, Stewart could not really care less about her until he eventually falls in love just in time to go to prison for three months on a gambling charge.

Throughout production, Carole and Gable thought nothing particularly significant about each other; for them it was purely just another job. Things went relatively smoothly, although filming was held up for a short time when both actors came down with a bout of flu. While the actor may have been gathering quite a following of young admirers, Carole was not charmed by him at this point. By the end of filming she made her feelings known in the form of a gag – a big cut of ham with Gable's face firmly pasted on the wrapper. Pictures of the gift-giving were published all over fan magazines and the actor thankfully saw the funny side of it.

On 25 November 1932, *No More Orchids* – another Columbia movie – was released. Then, a short time later, *No Man of Her Own* premiered. Reviews for the latter were fairly positive. *Film Daily* said:

Just a nice little piece of entertainment, in which Clark Gable again is transformed by love from a tough guy into a tame one … Gable is in his element and Miss Lombard gives a natural impersonation of the smart country girl. Lots of laughs are produced by Director Wesley Ruggles' handling of situations.

Next Carole made *From Hell to Heaven*, though the media were still far more concerned with the state of her marriage. *Modern Screen* printed a story about the actress's marked change of personality:

> Since her marriage, Carole hasn't been the same girl. Gone is that one-time Lombard buoyancy. She has been seen rarely at social functions, with or without Bill. She looked and seemed unhappy. And only natural that Hollywood should conjecture these symptoms as trouble in the Powell family.

This quick conclusion infuriated Carole:

> As a matter of fact, I've been quite ill. And one can't appear hilarious under those circumstances, even if she does love her husband. I can't predict the future of my or anyone else's marriage, but right now everything is smooth sailing between Bill and myself.

Journalist Elisabeth Goldbeck felt compelled to give her opinion on the effect of Carole's frequent illnesses on her marriage:

> It seems to be the consensus of Hollywood opinion that an enthusiastic bridegroom might get pretty tired of this. What fun can it be to have an invalid around all the time, instead of the lively, luscious girl you married? That's the impertinent question Hollywood asks.

When given the opportunity to ask Powell what he thought, his answer seemed to reveal an actual enjoyment of his wife's ill-health:

> Carole's illness has done more to cement the affection between us, than anything else could have, and given us a companionship that few picture couples are ever allowed to have. For months Carole was unable to work. Ordinarily, she would have been at the studio most of

the time since our marriage. But her illness gave us a chance to know each other intimately.

The fact that I make a limited number of pictures a year and have a great deal of time off made it even better. We were able to live almost like normal people. If Carole had been well, marriage and I would have been just sandwiched in between pictures. This way it was her whole life. And I think her illness saved us from the pitfall of conflicting careers, which is a very difficult adjustment to make in the first years of marriage. Professional jealousy – not only jealousy of the other person's success, but jealousy because his work seems more important to him than you are – is apt to rear its ugly head in any marriage of an actor to an actress. We were spared all that, and I think we understand each other well enough, after this year of being together, to weather anything of that kind that may come in the future.

When Goldbeck asked Powell about the couple's plans for the future, he gave a rather provocative answer:

How can you make a statement about anything as un-volitional as love? I don't know how it will be. I wouldn't want to swear that Carole and I will feel the same way a year from now … Marriage itself is dangerous. It professes to be able to control love. It says, 'Now that you've said these words, you've got to go on loving this man or this woman.' You chafe under it, naturally. And the Hollywood idea of making long speeches about love and expecting them to hold good a month or two later, when the interview comes out, is absurd.

While the interviews given by the couple during 1932 and 1933 were meant to assure the public that everything was okay, the somewhat negative answers did the very opposite. However, the world had bigger problems than the success of a Hollywood marriage. By this time it was gripped by the Depression – a period when people quite literally found themselves standing in a line, waiting for handouts of stale bread. While everybody seemed to be hoarding any spare cash they had, Carole went out of her way to try and encourage those who were better off to spend money. This, she felt, would help to kick-start the economy once again.

May 1933 saw the release of two movies, *Supernatural* and *The Eagle and the Hawk*. Then the actress gave an interview about the current economic climate to Faith Service from *Movie Classic* magazine:

We haven't any right to stay away from the theatres and cafes and shops and clubs. These aren't just pleasure places. They are places where people are earning livings – and helping other people to earn livings. We haven't any right to 'do without' clothes and furs and parties and cars. Because if we don't spend and give other people work, they're going to be out of jobs before long. And where will they get other jobs? How will they live? And if we refuse to spend and other people lose work because of it, their ability to spend will be cut off. And that will, in turn, hurt you and me. It all works in a circle. We can't hope to reap good times again, unless everybody helps to sow them. And EVERYBODY means both you and me.

The Depression has been used as an 'out,' an excuse for not buying and giving by too many people, who have been scared by the old bugaboo of fear. I am not talking of course, of those who cannot do it because they simply haven't GOT it to do with. They are the victims, at least partially, of those of us who can, but are afraid to, be extravagant … The only difference Bill and I have made in our shopping this past year has been to buy practical things for the majority of people, not only for Christmas, but for birthdays and anniversaries and for all the occasions when giving was at all possible. Things they needed – because the majority of people have not only avoided extravagance; they have also gone without the necessities.

# DIVORCEE

Carole traded a lack of excitement in her marriage for an obsession with buying material items such as gowns and shoes. She also upped her magazine subscriptions and trips to local book shops, but still she was bored. The love between the couple seemed to be turning into a brother/ sister relationship rather than something between lovers. As time wore on, Bill complained to friends that perhaps his wife wasn't as interested in the marriage as he had hoped she was. It rumbled on, but tellingly Carole's free-spirited nature and health were beginning to return. It was clear to her, at least, that she couldn't stay cooped up for much longer.

Finally, in early July 1933 after a long period with very little communication, the couple sat down for a serious talk. They had both come to the sad but inevitable decision that the marriage must end and, after agreeing to remain friends, the two went their separate ways. 'For Carole and me, there simply was no married life,' Powell told reporters.

Carole shared her own thoughts in *Movie Mirror* magazine:

Because I am so constituted that I refuse to stand still, it was inevitable that my marriage with Bill must fail. We couldn't make each other happy because there was never complete contact between our minds and our natures. Marriage should result in the flowering of two personalities – of increasing their perceptions and their capacity for achievement. And even though we were devoted to each other and still are, our marriage was doomed to failure. For it contributed nothing to our individual growth as entities and personalities. Nothing is good – nothing is worthwhile – if it roots our feet to one spot; if it slows the mind with indifference. If it harnesses our instincts and our ambitions.

It wasn't long before news of the separation reached the press and public, with stories surfacing that William Powell had left Los Angeles in order to seek out some peace. Meanwhile Carole took what she hoped would be a quiet and secret trip to Reno, in order to file for divorce. The story soon hit the press, however, which infuriated the actress; especially when quotes from 'friends' appeared in the papers. Since reporters could not receive statements from either Powell or Lombard, it was left to Carole's mother, Elizabeth, to make the official announcement. On 7 July 1933 she gave a short statement. 'They just decided all of the sudden that they could not agree,' she said, before going on to confirm that a settlement had already been decided between the former couple.

In Reno, Carole employed the services of divorce attorney George B. Thatcher, and then moved into a house in Lake Tahoe, where future actor Robert Stack and his family were residing for the summer. There she spent time with the Stack family, and the teenager taught her to shoot clay targets. The actress also found time to entertain her mother, brothers and several friends, including columnist Louella Parsons. In her 16 July column, the writer told readers that if it weren't for the rumours and gossip surrounding the state of the Powell marriage, she doubted they would have ever split up.

Meanwhile, Carole made a public appearance at a dedication ceremony for the Tahoe Rim-of-the-Lake Highway, and then divorce proceedings took place on 18 August 1933. During the six-minute exchange, the judge asked the actress why she was seeking a divorce and Carole appeared uncharacteristically downcast. 'Mr. Powell is a very emotional man, and is cruel and cross in manner of language,' she said. She added that in the two years they'd been married, her husband had shown his temper almost repeatedly from the day of their wedding. William Powell decided not to contest the suit; by this time he was resigned to the fact that his marriage to Carole was over.

As soon as the hearing was done, the actress flew back to Los Angeles. After the stifling situation she had found herself in, Carole's first priority was to make sure she was living as independently as she possibly could. Never was this more apparent than when her mother insisted she move back in with her family. Although she loved her mother dearly, describing her as 'a peach of a sport' and thanking her for helping to maintain a balanced life, the very idea of living with Elizabeth again horrified Carole:

> Since my divorce I have learned to live my own life. To have the courage to say to people – even to my mother whom I adore, 'This I will not do because it is bad for Carole the person and Carole the actress.' I refused to move back in with her because I knew that only when a woman is definitely on her own; when she has no-one to lean upon; when there is no-one around to absorb her weaknesses and minimize her strengths – does she have a chance to grow.

On the set of *White Woman* at Paramount Studios, Carole spoke to reporter Alanson Edwards about her divorce. While she did not divulge much about her own personal circumstances, she did speak frankly about Hollywood marriages in general:

> There are just as many happy marriages among the stars as there are among other people. It's easy to understand how such an impression grows. Every time a movie star gets a divorce, it's an item for the newspapers. Often, as has just happened, a number of film divorces occur in quick succession, so Hollywood gets a reputation.

Could a difference of personality be the reason marriages fail, Edwards wondered? To which Carole replied, 'The causes of divorce in Hollywood are the same as they are anywhere else. I don't believe temperament is an overshadowing cause. Certainly it was not in my own case.' This was an interesting statement considering that Powell's temper was exactly the reason she had given in the divorce court. Still, Edwards did not mention the slip and instead wondered if she would ever consider getting married again. Carole was forthright in her reply. 'Nobody can read the future, of course,' she said. 'How can I tell if I'll ever marry anybody else? All I know is that I haven't met the man yet.'

The divorce came just in time for the friendship with Powell to remain relatively unscarred. The two saw each other socially and were spotted together at the Brown Derby, the Grove and the Clover Club. They also accepted invitations to parties held by mutual friends and attended at least one film premiere together. However, any rumours of reconciliation were quickly quashed when actor Gary Cooper was seen popping into Carole's dressing room on several occasions. The actor had long been fond of Lombard and described her as lots of fun with a good sense of humour.

The actress remained quiet about the romance stories, so reporters asked Bill Powell instead. He seemed appalled and told them they were all crazy to think such a thing. Other romance rumours involved George Raft and Gene Raymond, though Carole was quick to assure reporters that she would not be marrying any of them. 'I do not believe that screen stars should marry,' she said.

In private, the constant fascination with her love life drove Carole to distraction. She told reporter Dorothy Manners that the stories were actually destroying her social life:

There have been nights when I have actually wanted to go to the Cocoanut Grove, or one of the other dancing spots with some casual friend. And yet I have hesitated to do so because I knew we would be met by a battery of news cameramen all set up to shoot the 'evidence' of our flaming love affair!

While the world waited to see who she would date next, Carole was quite happy to go it alone for a while. There were even times when she actively sought out quiet evenings on her own, and was known to sit in the dark pretending she was out when would-be admirers came to call. The reason was simple. First of all she had no wish to become gossip fodder for the newspapers, but also she actually felt as though the divorce had led to a turning point for her. Carole was enjoying just being herself, as she told reporter Sonia Lee:

In the past year I have found release from everything – from all those minute and irritating demands which have definitely hindered me as a person and as an actress. For the first time in my life I am free – mentally and spiritually. I have reconstructed my ideas about living and about acting. I am no longer afraid of myself or of the future.

By autumn 1933, two more movies had been released: *Brief Moment* for Columbia, and then *White Woman* for Paramount. The latter saw her acting with Charles Laughton, whom she described as a genius. 'He works hard but he admits a God-given instinct. I acted with him in [*White Woman*] and he taught me a great deal.' The film received mixed reviews. *Photoplay* described it as a 'strong enough horror for anyone … a masterpiece of thrills and chills. Not for children.' *Film Daily* said:

With Charles Laughton and Charles Bickford for characterisations, plus Carole Lombard as eye interest, any picture is bound to hold more or less fascination, and that's the chief reason for whatever enjoyment this affair contains. Basically, it's another of those tropical yarns about a couple of men fighting over a woman.

The first months of 1934 saw the 25-year-old actress release two more movies: *Bolero* and *We're Not Dressing*. Then she embarked on *Twentieth Century* with acting heavyweight, John Barrymore. The thought of working with the legendary actor made Carole uncharacteristically nervous:

I'll never forget my first day on the set. There was an air about the studio that reminded me of our school when the teacher promised us a nice visit from the crabby old principal. For years ever since I was a tiny kid, I had heard of the exploits of 'Wild Jack' Barrymore and of what he had done to people who had blown their lines or muffed their cues. Then I met Barrymore. I can see him now, standing there with his legs apart, his head bent forward so that he looked out at me sort of through his eyebrows. 'You look like a good kid,' he growled. 'I hope things go well.' He didn't say them, but I felt that the words 'for your sake' belonged in that sentence.

Luckily for everyone, the shoot was not as stressful as Carole thought it might be. 'Don't let anyone ever tell you that John Barrymore isn't the greatest actor of his day,' she told reporter, George Madden:

Perhaps he isn't now the great star he once was. But star or not, he knows more about acting than most of us will ever learn. He taught me more in the six short weeks it took to make the picture than I had learned in five years previous. It would take a book to cover all the things he did to help. But perhaps the greatest was the subtle way he built my self-confidence and flattered me into believing I was good. In place of wandering away after he had completed his own scenes, he'd stay on the set and watch me go through my paces. The picture was a comedy, and I'll never forget how swell I'd feel to hear that booming laugh of his. It was the most subtle flattery in the world. I worked like a dog to earn those laughs of John Barrymore's.

Barrymore gave her advice all the way through the shoot. She must always value her instincts, he told her, and not forget to abandon herself fully to the role. This advice was something Carole took forward into her future career. Afterwards the actor presented her with his portrait, with the inscription, 'To the finest actress I have worked with, bar none'. She was absolutely thrilled. 'I knew that all those hard years of striving had brought me to my goal, and that I had at last been accepted by the inner circle; that at last I could call myself an actress.'

*Twentieth Century* was released on 11 May 1934, then from 18–20 May Carole and stars such as Bing Crosby, James Cagney, Claudette Colbert, Charley Chase and Edmund Lowe took part in The Film Stars' Frolic at Gilmore Stadium. The Screen Actors Guild festival comprised many different entertainments, including circus themes and gypsy choruses.

The Dominos Club, an acting organisation with actresses such as Thelma Todd and ZaSu Pitts as members, put on a play called *Ladies of the Masque*, while others recited nursery rhymes and Shakespeare sonnets. The local media declared the event a success but, according to the guild, it was actually a financial catastrophe which wiped out their treasury. Several actors, including James Cagney and Eddie Cantor, had to step in and privately loan the guild money in order to restore funds.

Carole made another film; *Now and Forever*, for Paramount, but while work remained important her social life was gathering steam. After the divorce she was seen partying at the various nightclubs around Hollywood and dancing became a way of channelling her excess energies. It was through this renewed interest in her social life that she struck up a friendship with Russ Columbo, a crooner she had met as a young flapper in the 1920s.

Born on 14 January 1908, Columbo was famous to millions of moviegoers and radio listeners as the beautiful voice of songs such as *You Call it Madness, but I Call it Love* and *Too Beautiful for Words*. He was also a composer, violinist and actor, with his film career bringing him into contact with the likes of Gary Cooper and Lupe Velez.

Good looking and charming, Russ was romantically linked to various actresses over the years, including Sally Blane, who accompanied him to many Hollywood events. However, it was his romance with Carole Lombard that caught the media's attention. As they danced their way round Hollywood during the early part of 1934, people began to wonder if the velvet-voiced singer was about to settle down with Hollywood's most famous divorcee.

Carole enjoyed Columbo's company, but the relationship went much further than that. She took a great interest not just in his personal life, but his career too. The pair would often discuss movie roles, and Carole gave the shy singer tips for becoming more outgoing when it came to handling executives and other people in Hollywood. In addition, she accompanied him to the studio, not only to show her support for his career but also to learn the mechanics of life at a radio station.

While Carole was outgoing and Russ quieter in nature, they quickly became inseparable and were seen all over Hollywood, playing tennis, dancing in nightclubs and spending time with friends. Their friends looked on in wonder at how happy and settled Carole had become. In Russ she found someone to share all of her interests, which was in complete contrast to the somewhat boring marriage she had shared with Bill Powell. 'I simply must laugh and clown through life,' Carole once told reporter Ruth Biery; a motto she lived up to for most of her days.

Russ was a very intense individual and his relationship and love for Carole seemed to be the most important thing in his life. He began asking her in earnest to marry him. She balked at the idea, content to go about their relationship in the way she always had – without any legal attachment. Carole spoke to reporter Sonia Lee about the reasons for her hesitation:

> I really believe [Russ's love for me] was paramount in his thoughts. It even dwarfed his desire for fame and recognition. He was completely content to sit of an evening and just watch me – without saying a word, without moving. He had no life apart from me. He was lost if we were not together.

It was that very adoration that made her delay letting their relationship become more serious, but as with Powell before him, this did not stop Russ continually asking the question. Always Carole would give the same answer – pretty soon:

> I was not afraid that marriage would in any way define or modify or intensify my love for him, I was afraid that marriage might stultify him with contentment. And I wanted him to accomplish great things, to take his place on the screen as an important actor.

While Russ's romantic love could not be denied, Carole seemed to care for him in quite a different way:

> [I loved Russ] not only as a man, but as a mother would love her child. He was a very rare, a very unusual person. I knew it – and I loved him for it. But no woman dares to be the one goal in a man's life. If she loves him, she must seek to be only a part of his entire life, a part of his ambitions, a part of his fulfilments.

Interestingly, Carole also spoke about this kind of 'maternal love' to reporter Gladys Hall, a short while before she became romantically involved with Russ:

> In every love, I think, there is some element of the maternal, or there should be if the woman is a thoroughly normal woman. But that is not what I mean now. I mean the love that is all maternal, that takes a man and makes a little boy of him, spoiled, dependent, indulged, forgiven of all things. The love that assumes all of the responsibility for everything, takes all the burdens, makes all the decisions. This is the love that usually comes to strong and dominant women for rather weakling men. They become mothers of these men. That is what they want to be. They are never attracted to men who are stronger and more dominant than they.

This sort of love had, according to Carole, happened to her long before the relationship with Russ, but it had been something of a disaster:

> I fell in love with this boy. I tried to make him over. I wanted to replace his habits with other habits. I tried to find jobs for him, and when he had a job I kept it for him, or thought I did. I tried to protect him from criticism and from unkindness on the part of other people. I finally discovered that he was as yellow as the yolk of an egg and that nothing I could ever do would improve him one iota.

# SUDDEN HEARTBREAK

Throughout 1934, Carole revelled in making her house into a home. She employed interior designer William Haines and the resulting makeover was featured in a Hollywood fan magazine. There she was photographed standing in front of the beautiful fireplaces in her drawing room and bedroom. Other photos showed Carole reclining on her huge chaise longue-style bed and standing in the front garden.

The drawing room, decorated in six different shades of blue, became a popular location for friends and family and she hosted several parties there. During one such event, all guests were asked to dress up in their most elegant gowns only to find that the room had been transformed into a log cabin with several camp fires scattered around. The table was low and long, covered with a red tablecloth, and required guests to eat steaks from tin plates and drink wine from tin cups while wearing their best finery.

Carole's love for outlandish parties stemmed from having more than her fair share of boredom while attending other people's events.

'Did you ever come home from a party and wonder what on earth possessed your hostess to give it?' she asked one reporter. 'Sure you have. Everybody has. Well, that's what I try my best to avoid.' Carole hated the pompous way most Hollywood parties were handled, including stiff-backed chairs, dinner jackets and brand new dresses. Instead she always endeavoured to give her guests a good time, and if they had to sit on a bale of hay or a giant beanbag to do it, then so be it.

Still, Carole was adamant that she didn't give as many parties as everyone imagined she did:

Because I've given one or two unusual parties, the word has gone round that I'm a caution and a scream and that the parties I give are hysterical and sensational. I really entertain very little, as Hollywood knows, but people think I greet the dawn every day in my evening clothes.

If she didn't entertain very often, the results when she did were often hilarious and talked about for months and years on end. One party was a hospital themed event, where she greeted guests dressed in a nurse's uniform. Her friends were then issued with hospital robes to put over their expensive outfits and then led to the drawing room. If anyone doubted Carole could actually make her home look anything like a clinic, they were wrong. The actress moved all of the furniture and turned the living room into a ward, furnished with only beds and medical equipment. The guests had their own beds to sit on, while a butler dressed as an intern served refreshments in medical beakers, tubes and dishes. She told *Photoplay*:

I wouldn't think of giving a dinner, even a small one for six people, without at least a week of planning. This gives everyone in my household time to organize details. It gives me time to plan a menu, my cook time to carry it out, and the stores time to order any special or out-of-season foods. And then it gives me time to arrange my own engagements so that I won't be all tired out for it.

For those interested in Carole's advice for a successful party, here are some suggestions from the lady herself:

> Don't serve hors d'oeuvres unless they are superb. There is nothing more dismal to the palate than a mediocre bit of fish and egg heaped on a piece of too soggy or too brittle toast. Unless you can attain hors d'oeuvres that cause oohs and aahs, serve your cocktails unaccompanied … Music, if it is good and also impromptu, is a hostess' most benign ally. When an evening at my home finishes up with all the guests crowded around the piano singing at the top of their voices, I know the party can be checked off as a success.

In August 1934, Carole and Russ attended the funeral of her baby nephew together. It was a sad affair, and led the singer to think poetically about his own life and place in the world. On the way home Russ mournfully told Carole that if anything should happen to him, she should see to it that his funeral became his 'final performance'. The actress tried to shake the idea off at first, but for the next few weeks a feeling of sadness seemed to engulf the pair. 'Russ and I felt something cataclysmic hanging over us,' she explained. 'He and I sensed a presence near us, felt a peculiar apprehension. We were depressed without knowing why.'

This gloom was also mentioned by author William French, who spent time with the singer a few months before his death. Columbo was concerned that the house he was leasing at the present time might be a bit too close to the road for his mother's tastes. He was determined to find something quieter and took French along with him for the ride. When the writer asked why he needed to find something right away instead of after he had finished working on his latest film, Russ replied:

> Maybe I'm funny about it, but I want to grab some of the nicest things for mother right now. You know how it is. The old fellow with the scythe is always around the corner. I am planning to build [a home] but I don't want to wait because you never know what might happen.

For example, suppose one of Hollywood's famous damn fool drivers happened to be coming down here just now, wide open. I'd have a great chance to build a house after that wouldn't I?

Russ had suffered great loss in his life, including the tragic death of his brother in an automobile accident. That, coupled with the knowledge that Carole had once been badly injured herself, made him obsessed with the idea that something terrible was going to happen to her. The actress had been working on *Lady by Choice* for Columbia and was exhausted. Now with every day that passed, Russ was convinced that it would all lead to disaster. 'I was frightfully tired [and] I tried to say that that was the only cause of our depression,' Carole said. Her assurances did nothing to prevent Russ's worry, however, and he travelled to the studio almost every day, just so he could make sure she was alright. 'He watched me every moment and I felt more at ease when he was with me or near me.'

While she may have tried to convince Russ that she was fine, deep down the actress was becoming worried about the amount of exhaustion she was suffering from. Eventually she visited her doctor to gain his advice. After an examination, he recommended that as soon as her latest film wrapped, Carole should head out of town for a week in order to regain her strength and recover from the flow of work.

When she told her boyfriend what she intended to do, he suggested that instead of travelling alone, he should come too. However, before any plans could be put into place, Russ's mother was rushed to hospital with a heart ailment and the singer was sent into a panic. For weeks Russ and Carole had predicted something terrible was to befall them, and it seemed this was to be it. The singer dashed to his mother's bedside where he discovered she was in a serious but stable condition.

Any plans Russ may have had to accompany Carole out of town were no longer an option. However, instead of cancelling the trip altogether, the actress told her partner that she would go to Big Bear for a day or two, then drive back to Hollywood to visit him and his mother. She told Russ that he could then come with her when she returned to Big Bear. 'He consented to that because he was devoted to his mother and, of course, wanted to remain near her,' Carole said.

The day after his mother's emergency trip to hospital, the couple attended the preview of Columbo's film, *Wake Up and Dream*, which coincidentally coincided with the release of Carole's film, *Now and Forever*. During the evening he gave an interview to William French from *Modern Screen* magazine, and he seemed upbeat:

> Life really began today. Just write 'Friday, the 31st' in red because it starts Chapter Three in the story of Columbo. And put it down that today Old Man Hard Luck lost my address. Everything good happened today. I made the first of my new broadcasts, I saw my first starring picture and I made four recordings on my new phonograph contract. What a lucky day this was!

After the glitzy preview, the couple headed to the Cocoanut Grove where Russ played in the orchestra. His good mood of earlier, however, seemed to have evaporated somewhat and he became despondent. Russ's best friend, Lansing Brown, had been in the audience of *Wake Up and Dream* but had slipped off early as he had a photographic assignment the next day. The fact that Lansing had been unable to tell Russ what he really thought of the film was troubling. 'Russ depended on Lansing's judgement,' Carole told Sonia Lee, 'and considered his criticism extremely valuable.'

Russ spoke about this himself in a conversation with reporter Rilla Page Palmborg:

> Lansing Brown is my best friend, the best friend a man could have. He has been my confidant, my adviser for ten years. I never make a move without first consulting Lansing. He has always thought of me, not of himself. We start out in a car for a party and he gets to planning my future! We forget everything until hours later we find ourselves down at the beach or out in the country – too late for the party.

The day after the premiere, the thought that he had been unable to speak to his friend was still fresh in Russ's mind. He told Carole that if Lansing didn't get in touch with him, he would take a trip to his house the next day. She agreed and then left on her scheduled trip to Big Bear with her secretary. As she drove out of Hollywood, she felt a sense of doom cascading over her. 'I was strangely uneasy,' she recalled. 'I'm not a hysterical person, I'm logical and I think, pretty well balanced, but on the drive from Hollywood I almost turned back twice. It seemed as if something were calling me, telling me not to go up there.'

Despite her misgivings, she continued to drive into the night, and at 10.15 p.m., arrived at Big Bear. Once in the accommodation, the actress was dismayed to find that the telephone exchange had closed for the evening. This meant that she was unable to contact Russ to make sure everything was okay and this led to an incredibly restless sleep. 'I was in a frenzy of nerves,' she explained. Several times her secretary woke up to the sounds of Carole's cries and knocked on the door to see if everything was okay. Assuring her that all was fine, the actress told the woman she was just exhausted, before adding rather poetically; 'I wish I had been able to call Russ. I've got a horrible feeling that something is wrong.'

The next morning, Sunday, 2 September 1934, Carole thought for a while about returning home to Hollywood, but then, in a decision she later described as 'utterly stupid', she decided to stay put. She tried to call Russ but there was no answer; the singer had already left to visit his friend Lansing V. Brown. Sitting in the library, they spoke at length about Russ's new film while looking at Brown's collection of vintage firearms. Before long, the subject turned to the old duelling pistol Lansing kept in his desk drawer, which was then brought out for them to both admire. As they talked, Brown began to absentmindedly fool around with it.

'We were talking about his next picture and his plans for the future,' Brown said. He then went on to explain that he'd been holding the pistol in his hand and snapping the trigger without paying much attention to what he was actually doing. 'All I know is that there was the explosion,' he said. This came as a tremendous shock, since he was unaware of the existence of powder or bullets in any of his vintage firearms. 'I had never made an examination to see whether they were loaded; they were so old.'

He told reporter Rilla Page Palmborg:

When I bought them seven years ago, the antique dealer assured me that they weren't loaded. We had all looked down the barrels of them dozens of times. We had even run a pencil down to dig out cobwebs. But the expert who examined them [on] Monday said they had been loaded not less than seventy-five years.

Carole confirmed this. 'We had toyed with those two old duelling pistols a hundred times,' she said. 'We poked our fingers into the barrels and held them up to our eyes to squint up into them. Yet nothing had ever happened. We never dreamed they were loaded.'

Unfortunately the duelling pistol was indeed loaded and went off without warning; the bullet ricocheting off a mahogany table and going straight through Columbo's left eye. 'There was an explosion,' recalled Brown, and after he had composed himself from the shock of the noise, he looked over at his friend, finding him motionless, slumped in the chair:

It was all mighty fast. I thought he was clowning ... Russ and I used to do a pantomime when we heard an automobile backfire. We'd clutch our chests and exclaim, 'Ach! They got me!' I looked at Russ, expecting him to say it. Then I saw blood gushing from his eye.

As soon as Brown realised that his friend was not messing around, he tried frantically to revive him while shouting hysterically for his mother. By the time his shocked parents arrived they were horrified at the sight that greeted them. 'When we entered the room my son was bent over his friend, pleading with him to speak,' said Brown's father, Lansing Snr, during the inquest. An ambulance was called and the singer rushed to the Hollywood Receiving Hospital in a bid to save his life. There was nothing that could be done there, however, so he was transferred to the Good Samaritan Hospital where special surgeons hoped they'd have more luck.

Once at the facility, brain specialist Dr George W. Patterson tried in vain to halt the blood that flowed from Columbo's head, but found the wound too delicate to operate on. Knowing it was a losing battle, it wasn't very long before his family were called. Actress Sally Blane – a recent love of Columbo's – arrived and although their relationship was over she stood in the corridor with his distraught family, none of whom were allowed to see the singer. Finally a doctor left his room and informed those waiting that there was only the slightest chance of survival.

Carole was still at Big Bear when a call came from the doctor, breaking the bad news to her. 'I was told that he had been accidentally shot,' she told reporter Radie Harris, 'and that there was no need for me to hurry to the hospital.' She went into further details with Sonia Lee:

> I knew instantly that Russ was dying. I questioned the doctor closely. Was there a chance? Would he regain consciousness? I wanted the truth and I got it. Russ was dying. Russ would never regain consciousness. There was no use, he said, in my taking a plane to get to his bedside.

On the evening of 2 September 1934, Russ Columbo was declared dead. 'I'm very surprised he lived so long in view of his condition,' stated Dr Patterson. An X-ray revealed that the bullet had entered the brain through his eye and lodged itself in the back of the skull, causing a fracture as it did so.

Carole's shocked mother telephoned her daughter, but she was already on her way back to Hollywood. At one point her dog began to whimper and nuzzle against her neck. She checked the time on her watch and later wasn't surprised when she heard when Russ had passed away. 'Russ had died in that very second,' she told Sonia Lee. The doctor told Carole to head to her own home, where the news was confirmed to her. Although she expected it, the actress said she was still 'shocked beyond words' and immediately rushed to the hospital.

She and Russ had planned to have dinner that evening at her mother's house, but instead she found herself viewing his body and grieving with his heartbroken family. As she left the facility, a reporter pounced from the shadows and abruptly asked how she felt. Through her tears 25-year-old Carole managed to give a brief comment. 'It is impossible to express in words how deeply shocked I am to learn of the tragedy,' she said, before getting into her car.

Later, once the news had sunk in a little, she managed to release a longer statement which was reported around the world:

His death is a terrible shock to me, as it must be to all his friends and admirers. It is particularly tragic at this time, for I know Russ was destined for the most successful year of his career. He had told me of several offers he had and he was to take up a new radio contract within a few days. Only last Friday night we saw together a preview of his latest picture.

Lansing V. Brown was questioned by police about the incident and an inquest was held. It was quickly decided that no one was to blame. It was a tragic accident; a misadventure that had resulted in the loss of an emerging star. Brown, meanwhile, was so choked by the incident that he was in a near state of collapse and ended up handing all his guns to the police with instructions that he never wanted to see them again. He told interviewer Rilla Page Palmborg:

Russ got everything he ever wanted. As he reached each goal he had set for himself, he immediately commenced to plan for another. He always had to have something to strive for. How could a person with so many plans be gone – at twenty-six? I want people to realize the awful loss I have and not think of how much I am going to suffer.

Columbo's family – though in pieces over the tragedy – were more than forgiving towards the young man. They released a statement declaring the whole thing 'an act of God … He is taking the whole thing much harder than any of us,' they said. In a bid to help the family, Carole took full control of the funeral. It took her mind off the tragedy, but on the day itself the grief hit hard. As she stood with fellow mourners, it was clear to everyone that she was absolutely distraught. As she leant on Russ's brother and her doctor for support, friends described her as being completely white, wretched and gaunt. As singer Bing

Crosby headed the team of pallbearers, Carole tried desperately to hold everything together.

Crosby himself was overcome at the loss of Russ Columbo. Radio stations had long since created an imaginary feud between the two singers, which their audiences seemed to lap up hungrily. Just a day before his death, a fabricated picture was posted in a newspaper, showing Bing Crosby shooting Russ Columbo. It was terrible timing and Crosby felt awful about it. 'I hope no one took that seriously,' he said:

> I tell you it gave me an awful shock. A creepy feeling. Everybody who knew either of us intimately knew there was nothing to that feud idea at all. It was started back east, by the radio people [but] after both of us settled in California we were together many times at my house and at Carole's. Few people felt Russ's loss more than I did – because, somehow, it seemed we should be sailing along together, as we had been the last three months of his life. I was proud when asked to officiate at his funeral as a pallbearer, and to play some small part in his last rites.

Shortly before Russ passed away, Carole gave an interview to Elisabeth Goldbeck, during which she spoke about how her life had been affected by various twists and turns:

> I've been able to take a peculiar advantage of everything that has happened to me. Though I might be wretched and heart-broken about something at the time, still I throw it off just as soon as I can, put it in its proper relation to my life, and use the experience as a stepping stone, to give me greater understanding of life and develop my character.

She then went on to describe her belief that time healed all wounds:

> If I were told that I would never again see someone I'm terribly fond of, I would suffer for a while, but not for long. I'd throw it off, because I know there's nobody you can't get on without. And it's ridiculous

to carry on about something you know is going to seem relatively unimportant tomorrow.

With the passing of her love, Carole's bravado softened. One of the last times she ever mentioned Russ in public was during an interview with Sonia Lee, which was published in the December 1934 issue of *Movie Classic* magazine. 'Russ and I loved one another,' she said:

> Eventually, I believe, we would have married. How soon, I don't know. His love for me was of the kind that comes very rarely to any woman. I never expected to have such worship, such idolatry, such sweetness from any man.
>
> The whole tragedy seems to have been a chain of circumstances leading to death. If I had turned back to Hollywood, Russ would have been with me. If Lansing had been able to telephone him on Saturday, Russ would not have gone to see Lansing on Sunday. Yes, I am certain that no matter what we might have done, Russ would have died that day. I am convinced that if he had not met his death through that ricocheting bullet, he would have met it some other way. His number was up. There isn't a question in my mind about that. I am desperately lonely for Russ. We were so very close – together so constantly. I'm just beginning to feel the loss. I feel as though I were suspended in air, only slowly coming alive.

In an unexpected twist in the story, his mother Julia (aka Julio) was still in hospital at the time of her son's passing. As she was incredibly weak, doctors and family members decided it best not to tell her of the tragedy, unsure as to how she would take it. At first everyone told the enquiring woman that her son was on location, with the intention of admitting the truth when the time was right. However, there would never be a good time to break the news and, unbelievably, for the next ten years the family devised a number of stories to keep Columbo 'alive' in his mother's eyes, including an elaborate series of excuses as to why he couldn't possibly come to visit her.

It was a mammoth task, but they succeeded by sending postcards from around the world and playing Russ's records in a bid to fake his radio show.

They even came up with a story that Carole and Russ had married in secret to avoid publicity and then sailed away to England. From there, cables were sent and 'signed' by the happy couple and news was reported back from the honeymooners. Carole was fully involved with the plan and wrote several letters to Mrs Columbo; keeping in touch until her death some years later.

# HANDS ACROSS THE TABLE

I n September 1934, just days after her boyfriend's death, Carole
headed to New York with her mother to take her mind off the
tragedy. It was an impossible task. Rumours began to surface that
the actress had a tremendous falling out with Russ just hours before
his death, and that she was secretly planning a reunion with ex-husband
William Powell. Some reporters went so far as to falsely claim that on
leaving Hollywood, it was Powell who had given her a tearful farewell.

The stories exasperated the actress to such a degree that when the
studio called to tell her she'd been cast in a new movie, she was relieved.
She told reporter Radie Harris that the call was probably the best thing
that could have happened:

> I have my work and I'm going to plunge into it with an all absorbing
> interest. This call from the studio, summoning me back to Hollywood
> to play the feminine lead in *Repeal* [later retitled *The Gay Bride*] is a
> far greater anodyne than the holiday I had planned.

On 18 September 1934, Carole went to MGM to make the film. Once there, it was discovered that the resident studio costume designer, Adrian, had not been assigned to her picture. Instead a costumier by the name of Dolly Tree was to make the outfits. Columnist Read Kendall got wind of this development and tried to make something of a scandal about it. Why would Adrian, designer for the likes of Jean Harlow and Joan Crawford, not be involved in a Carole Lombard film, he wanted to know. Had there been some kind of falling out between star and designer?

Adrian was quick to send the reporter on his way. 'I would like to have designed Miss Lombard's gowns,' he said, but then explained that the job had always belonged to Dolly Tree; he had never been considered. Read then asked Carole for her opinion on the matter, but instead of a slice of gossip, all he received was a compliment towards Ms Tree and a quip that she was delighted with every costume designed for her.

While she may have been pleased with Ms Tree's work, Carole's favourite designer was Travis Banton, who seemed totally in awe of his star client. Frequently he named her his 'best dressed actress' and always lavished praise on her. 'Carole is crazy about clothes,' he said. 'She is eager to experiment … She works for her laurels and deserves winning them.' He expanded on this while talking to reporter Virginia Lane:

> The more interesting a woman is, the more sides there are to her personality. When she understands the trick of selecting clothes to match each mood, and of varying her headdress and make-up as she varies her costumes, then she has glamour. That, really, is the secret of Carole Lombard's allure. [She is] twelve persons in one.

Read Kendall approached Banton to hear his version of why Adrian had not designed costumes for *The Gay Bride*. He was forthright in his answer, declaring that he would have loved to design the gowns himself, but was 'fully acquainted with the situation'. His decision not to become involved with any gossip surrounding Carole was probably a mixture of loyalty and fear of upsetting his client. Just weeks later it was announced that the actress had employed him as her primary designer, both off set and on. 'I consider it a great honour that Carole has asked me to pass on every article in her personal wardrobe from now on, and I am happy to be able to design things for her to wear in private life, as well as on the screen,' he told reporters.

Carole was equally as admiring of the designer:

Travis Banton, who is to my mind one of the best clothes creators in the business, uses discretion for us [actresses]. If he is dressing Ruth Chatterton, the browns set off her personality. If he is dressing me, the style will be entirely different, since I am not at all like Ruth.

Carole finished the movie and returned to Paramount in mid-October. Then in December 1934, *The Gay Bride* was released. Carole played Mary, a woman who marries a gangster for his money, only to see him murdered, therefore making her a widow in search of real love. She was accompanied by Chester Morris and ZaSu Pitts, with Nat Pendleton playing her heavy husband. Pendleton had been playing fairly dumb roles in the past, but was desperately trying to break away. 'I had to change,' he said:

Movie audiences are funny. They associate you with the character you play. If you kick or kill somebody, they think you're that kind of person in real life. It holds you back in your career. I haven't been playing unsympathetic parts in some time. Comedy, yes, but not mean heavies. I struck out in that direction in *The Gay Bride* in which I played Carole Lombard's husband.

The British magazine, *Film Pictorial* called it a 'cheery comedy':

The film has its moments. There are excellent performances from ZaSu Pitts and Nat Pendleton. It is well directed, and has bright dialogue, but we would like to see such first-rate artistes as Carole Lombard and Chester Morris in productions that give them more scope for their talents.

The storyline of the movie attracted a great deal of attention from theatres. The idea of Carole playing a 'gold-digging chiseller' inspired the Loew's State Theatre in New Orleans to give out special 'Chiseller's Club' membership cards to their patrons, with Carole listed as secretary. Nearby stores were also utilised and included movie-inspired flower displays in bridal shops and hair displays in a beauty parlour.

Away from work, Carole still enjoyed spending a great deal of time with her mother and her brother's wife, too. In early December 1934 the three attended an event at the Assistance League to listen to friend Frances Layng Spence talk about books. Carole joyfully told reporters that when the woman planned to travel to Washington later that month, she would do so with a luxurious suitcase, on loan from the actress herself.

As 1935 dawned, Carole decided she wanted a break from acting, and applied for a passport. Her intention, she told reporters, was to travel to New York and then on to Paris for a long awaited vacation. 'I really feel that I am entitled to a rest,' the actress told columnist Edwin Schallert. 'I want to go to Europe. It will be my first visit there, and I want to see a lot of places, especially Italy and Budapest.' She intended to travel with friend and assistant Fieldsie, but the actress was not positive about her chances of actually getting to her destination. She told the reporter that knowing her luck she would be called straight back to the studio, as she had been once before. 'If possible I'm going to put an ocean between myself and Hollywood,' she said.

Carole was correct in her prediction of problems, and the journey itself was an indication of just how unsuccessful the trip was going to be. On 7 January it was reported that the actress had left California and was due to arrive on the east coast by the 8th. However, her plane had an unexpected problem and was forced to land in Abilene, Kansas, instead. Carole revelled in telling friends and reporters about the adventures she and Fieldsie had during the trip, which involved a drunk pilot, an overheated cabin and a train that dropped the pair off in the middle of nowhere. Eventually – and much to their relief – they reached New York, arriving on 10 January and installing themselves in a suite at the Waldorf Astoria.

As the actress prepared for her trip to Paris, news came from Hollywood. The studio would need her back in Los Angeles within the next few weeks. There would be no time to fly to Europe, so instead Carole planned to travel to Miami, then on to Havana for a short rest. Before she could do any of that, however, she fell ill with a case of grippe, which she had recovered from by 24 January when she finally headed for Florida. After spending several days there, she went to Cuba before going back to California in early February 1935.

While waiting to see what the studio had in store for her, Carole's next movie was released. *Rumba* was the story of Joe Martin (George Raft), a cabaret dancer who meets holidaymaker Diana Harrison (Lombard) while dancing in Havana. The two do not hit it off, but their feelings change after Diana dances with Joe in order to thwart a gangster threat. The film had been made between 9 November 1934 and 27 December 1934, although it had been due to begin slightly earlier. The delay came because Carole and Raft were not sufficiently prepared for their dance numbers, though this seems to be more the fault of the latter, since production records show he only attended rehearsals once. Just days after the cast finally made it to set, hours were lost because Carole's costumes needed to be altered, then shortly before wrapping, they lost more time when her dress ripped and needed urgent repairs.

When it was released, the film received somewhat lukewarm reviews. *Variety* was keen on the dancing and rated it a 'good looking production'. *Film Daily*, however, labelled it:

> A rather punchless story. Plenty of production effort has gone into this picture in the way of attractive backgrounds and musical trimmings ... so that between this and the able cast there is about enough to hold interest for fans who are not too meticulous. As for the story, it is below par.

In February 1935, Carole received the tragic news that her father had passed away following an operation. The death garnered very few media mentions, and anyone who expected Carole to run home to Fort Wayne for the burial was disappointed. Instead the actress gave word that she would stay away for fear that her presence would only make the day into a spectacle. She stayed home in Hollywood, while her Indiana relatives took care of proceedings.

After being recalled from her proposed European vacation, 26-year-old Carole was frustrated to be offered several projects that she had no wish to be associated with. The studio was keen to change her mind but she refused to move, determined that she would not be browbeaten into parts she did not want. 'These days a girl has to be modern or else be a wallflower,' she told reporter William F. French:

> The year 1935 hasn't time to stop and pay its respects to the old-fashioned girl who is sitting quietly in the corner. Instead of waiting to be asked, a girl has to get out in front of the parade, where she'll be seen. The time is past when a girl can attract attention being a passive verb, so to speak. She must be active, and in time with the times. She must be modern.

In spite of any plans made by the studio, Carole stopped working for the first time in years. She went to the desert and up into the mountains, then once home continued her interest in interior design; something she had loved for a few years. She spent time with writer and love interest Robert Riskin, and indulged in a new hobby of learning to fly. A solo flight followed, and Carole enjoyed it so much that she became obsessed with the idea of qualifying as a licensed pilot. 'I'm taking up flying because I think it's part of a present-day education, and because I think we will all be flying before long,' she told reporter William F. French.

Bringing her down to earth, executives offered Carole a role in *The New Divorce*, which would see her teamed up with Gary Cooper. For a while it seemed as though it would come to fruition, and the project was officially announced in March 1935. However, the part eventually went to another actress and Carole was assigned to another movie, *Hands Across the Table*.

Before she began filming, Carole hosted the most famous party of her life when she hired the Venice Pier Amusement Park for the exclusive use of her friends. Everyone who was anyone was invited, including Ruth Chatterton, Zeppo Marx, Cary Grant and Carole's co-star from years before, Edmund Lowe. Studio grips, technicians and other crew members were also in attendance, and all were greeted at the door by Carole and Fieldsie.

Most of the guests threw themselves into the proceedings, gaining many bruises and scratches along the way. The action was so raucous that columnist Tip Poff predicted that the actress may even be sued for the damages sustained by the other celebrities. Some Hollywood stars, however, decided the affair was far too much for them. Press reports the next day showed that actor, Clifton Webb, director, Wesley Ruggles and producer, Jesse Lasky all preferred to stand on the sidelines and watch the others having fun. Rumours surfaced that Carole had invited the notoriously uptight group in the hope that they could finally let their hair down and have fun.

Errol Flynn's wife, Lili Damita, had a shock when she entered the building wearing a rather sensible skirt and jacket. Some enterprising soul decided to press the button for the air machine at the exact moment she passed by, sending her skirt skywards. She was not amused and spent a long time afterwards putting herself back together again. Louise Fazenda suffered a similar fate when her button front skirt flew up and the buttons ripped straight off. Meanwhile, actress Josephine Hutchinson had such a terrible time on one ride that security had to come and haul her off for her own safety.

Carole, Cary Grant, Claudette Colbert and Marlene Dietrich had no such trouble. Photographs of the three show them having fun on a variety of rides in the fun house. Treats included a spinning turntable and slide, a silhouette artist and caricaturist. At one point, Claudette Colbert went flying off the turntable and had to be rescued by Cesar Romero after tennis player Eleanor Tennant landed on her head. Marlene Dietrich suffered injuries when she was pushed down the slide in an old sack while wearing shorts. She didn't seem to mind, however, and was soon seen on several different rides.

Carole, Claudette Colbert and Marlene Dietrich were great friends, and it was actually because of this friendship that the party happened, because the actress wanted to thank mutual friend Will Stewart, who had entertained them all during a visit to New York. Carole would speak about a particular evening during the trip, where Marlene offered to make the group some scrambled eggs:

Most of the party – not knowing the girl as some of us do – were sceptical about her ability. But they went to Will's home, willing to take a chance on Marlene's cooking. Of course they weren't disappointed. Marlene not only prepared eggs, toast and coffee to the liking of everyone but – and here's the thing that amused us most – cleaned up the kitchen floor when she dropped a jar full of sausages.

While the Venice party made great press, her next episode wasn't quite so much fun. Carole had sent her maid on an errand in her car when she was involved in an accident. The driver of another vehicle hit the side of Carole's and failed to stop, sending the servant heading straight into a fire hydrant. She became hysterical and the actress was summoned to the police station to pick her up and calm her down.

Away from parties and road accidents, it was time to get back to work. It had been quite some time since she had gone anywhere near a soundstage, and executive A.M. Botsford was beyond frustrated. On 26 July 1935 he wrote that Carole had not been in a film since 8 November 1934 and despite signing a contract for eleven films some seven months ago, she was yet to make a single one. The actress was due to go to Universal to make a movie in November 1935, which meant that if she was to fulfil her promise to Paramount, Carole would have to work constantly from then until the end of her contract.

On 1 August 1935, she finally walked on to a Paramount soundstage for her role as Regi Allen in *Hands Across the Table*. Co-starring Fred MacMurray, the film tells the story of a young manicurist (Lombard) who plans to marry someone rich. MacMurray is a playboy who wants to do the same thing. The two meet and, despite their grand plans, end up falling in love and setting free their rich admirers.

Carole told reporters that the film would give her a great opportunity to cast off the glamorous gowns she was famous for and instead play a genuine woman with simple tastes in clothes:

I'm going to catch the fellow who started all this 'glamour girl' stuff about me some day, and cuff him to death with his own typewriter. If I look cold, sophisticated, aloof on the screen, that's not my fault. It's the way the camera picks me up. Heaven knows if that were so I wouldn't have any friends … [in *Hands Across the Table*] I'm going to be flesh and blood for a change.

For Fred MacMurray, the film was a learning experience as well as a job. Still a relatively shy young actor, he did not know how to take the wisecracking blonde and made a point of keeping out of her way. However, one day the actress roped him into a game of Monopoly. From then on the two became friendly and MacMurray learned a lot from her. 'More than anything else, Carole has proved to me that there is nothing so serious you can't have fun out of it,' he said. 'It isn't that she isn't sincere about her work, but she's discovered how valuable it is to know when to let down.'

This was felt by the director, Mitch Leisen, too:

She helped make Fred MacMurray what he is. He was stiff and scared in *Hands Across the Table*. She kept kidding him, and with Madalynne Fields, her best pal, she once sat on Fred and plucked his eyebrows until nothing could upset him anymore!

As production went on, MacMurray continued to gain confidence and slotted in nicely with the other members of cast and crew. During one scene, he even had the courage to tell director Mitch Leisen that he wasn't comfortable with a particular line and substituted it for one of his own. 'It's a good sign when an actor begins doing that,' said Leisen:

Of course they can go to extremes, but you see what it means in Fred's case, don't you? It means that at last he's reached the place where he can throw off his self-consciousness and really feel the character. In *Hands Across the Table* Fred was one of the most difficult actors to direct that I had ever handled. For one thing, he used to have a tendency to talk his lines too fast. It was because he was scared of them, of course, and wanted to get them over as quickly as possible. But not anymore. Working with him is a pleasure now.

The film was not only a sparkling comedy, but a heartfelt and beautiful story too. The entire cast gave stellar performances and this was demonstrated in the array of positive reviews. *Film Daily* gave a glowing report:

> This love yarn, best described as in the *It Happened One Night* class, is delightful fare that will meet with a merry reception anywhere. With Carole Lombard and Fred MacMurray making a dandy romantic team, helped by a script with lots of intriguing developments and cute lines, plus Mitchell Leisen's nicely handled direction, it can't miss. Miss Lombard, [is] looking like a million bucks and at her very best histrionically.

# THE KING AND QUEEN OF HOLLYWOOD

By the end of 1935, Carole's relationship with writer Robert Riskin had become serious enough to warrant a degree of column inches. They were photographed going to the Santa Anita racetrack and out to polo matches. As she had with Russ Columbo, Carole also wanted to help further his career. In that regard she called a meeting with her agent, Myron Selznick, and the two decided to approach producer (and Myron's brother) David O. Selznick to see if he would be interested in signing him. Riskin's screenwriting contract with Columbia was to expire shortly and this, in part, interested David a great deal.

On 5 December 1935 he wrote to colleague John Hay Whitney to tell him that Carole had been in touch, with what he was sure was a fantastic idea. Calling him the top writer in the film industry, David decided that if they were able to sign Riskin, even the highest amount of money he demanded would be more than worth it to have him on board.

Added to that, he was convinced that with Riskin's talents the company could utilise him as an associate producer on the screenplays he had written. This could amount to three or four a year, the executive hoped.

Helping Riskin wasn't the only thing on Carole's mind. During the meeting with David O. Selznick, she told him that she wanted to sign with his company after her current Paramount contract came to an end. He had recently seen *Hands Across the Table* and was of the opinion that it was her only important film to date. He was sure that the actress was on her way to becoming a new Joan Crawford and was eager to sign her up.

There was just one potential problem. He had once before approached Paramount executives about signing some stars who were about to finish contracts. The executives told Selznick that if he did not try to raid their stock they would perhaps be happy to loan him an actor or two in the future. At that time Selznick had agreed, but now that Carole wanted to come on board he changed his mind. Declaring that he'd made just a 'vague promise', the producer made clear that if there were any talented stars to be had he would certainly be in the running to get them.

The Mayfair Party, a grand event for Hollywood's elite, was held at the Victor Hugo Restaurant on 25 January 1936. Carole was chosen as hostess and took her duties extremely seriously, organising the ball with exactly the same enthusiasm as the parties she gave at home. The result was spectacular, and consisted of white decorations and furnishings all over the restaurant and the guests dressed in white – evening gowns for the ladies and ties and tails for the gents. Carole also insisted on six footmen, complete with full regalia, to announce each guest as they entered the room. Two bands – Cab Calloway's Orchestra and Eduardo Durante's Rhumba Band – entertained the crowds, and as a special touch Carole asked them specifically to play tunes related to the people in attendance. Before long, the likes of Bing Crosby were up and crooning along to the music.

The next day the papers were full of articles about the success of the party, but it took several months for fan magazines to pick up on a more interesting story. A reporter for *Screenland* discussed the matter in full:

> The party displayed signs of a new romance – Gable and Carole Lombard, who ran the show. Clark arrived with Louella Parsons and sat across from his former wife, who studiously looked the other way. Then he moved to Marion Davies' table, and when last seen, he was dancing with Carole, whose party he joined. Carole arrived with a contingent of young men; Robert Riskin being ill. She had Cesar Romero, Walter Lang and sundry other young men at her table, as well as Bing and Dixie Crosby ... Clark drifted very definitely to Carole ...

The former wife mentioned in the article was Rhea, a woman much older than Gable, who had wed the actor in 1931. Theirs was not a marriage based on love. If anything, it was as a result of a morality clause in Gable's MGM contract which had ultimately forced them to tie the knot. The actor met Rhea while he was still a young actor in New York. She had fallen madly in love and he – enjoying the attention – was happy to go along with the relationship. However, as his star began to rise, the young actor grew bored and was more than happy to let the romance come to a natural end. He began staying away from the house that he and Rhea shared. He had affairs and kept a separate bedroom. Despite her desire to get married, he gave clear signs that he wanted a clean break.

Rhea was incensed that Gable would want to leave and took her woes to executives at MGM. She told them her story and said that it would be extremely unfortunate if the newspapers got wind of the rising star living with a woman he was not married to. MGM had invested money in Gable and was not willing to let a scandal jeopardise it. Instead, executives told the actor that by living with Rhea he was in violation of the morality clause in his contract. Whatever he thought about the situation was unimportant; for now he was coerced into marrying a woman he did not love.

By 1935 the marriage was over and the Gables had formerly separated, though not divorced. That technicality was not enough to stop the actor having relationships with other women and his head was certainly turned by Carole Lombard. Though the two had worked together on *No Man of Her Own*, the Mayfair Ball was the first time any attraction between the pair became apparent. The two seemed inseparable, and as they danced together people began to gossip. Even when Gable left rather abruptly, onlookers wondered what magical things were going on between the pair.

Their next meeting, however, would be slightly more tempestuous. On 5 February 1936 Carole hosted a table at the Brown Derby for friends and various film executives, including David O. Selznick, Samuel Goldwyn, Darryl Zanuck and Irving Thalberg. Several days later, one of her guests, noted screenwriter Donald Ogden Stewart, invited her to a party he was giving for his wife. Dubbed 'The Nervous Breakdown Party' because Mrs Stewart was recovering from one, it was held at high noon so as to not to cause exhaustion for the guest of honour. Despite that, everyone was asked to come in full evening attire.

They all did as they were told, though Carole thought she would take the breakdown theme quite literally and arrived in an ambulance instead of a car. The party was in full swing, and everything stopped when Carole was carried into the room on a stretcher. As guests gathered round, the actress jumped off the gurney and burst into peals of laughter before joining in the festivities. Some people thought the prank was funny, but others stood agog, not knowing quite how to react. Gable was one of those who thought it in mighty poor taste and he spoke to Carole about it. The two exchanged heated words, though by the end of the night things had calmed down and they happily played a game of tennis together in their evening wear.

Carole's romance with Robert Riskin had cooled off somewhat, and she was seen on the arm of Cesar Romero and several other admirers on more than one occasion. There was something intriguing about Clark Gable, however, and just days later she made her feelings about the actor known when she decided to play a little Valentine's Day prank.

Gable was a big fan of cars, not only driving them but repairing them too. Over the years he was photographed frequently working on his automobiles; it was a perfect way to wind down after a long day at the studio. Knowing about his interest, Carole bought the actor a beat-up old Model T Ford from a local scrapyard. She had it painted with giant red hearts, filled it with ribbons and flowers and attached a note which read, 'You're driving me crazy'. She then had it installed in Gable's parking space. When the actor found it there, he thought it was hysterical. He immediately made a date with Carole and turned up at her front door in the old car. Despite wearing a beautiful evening gown, the actress played along and the two headed off to the Trocadero.

Several months later, Read Kendall of the *Los Angeles Times* reported on the story. He told readers that Gable had since had a new engine fitted in the jalopy and was hoping to race it around the Muroc Dry Lake. Offers flooded into MGM from people who wanted to buy the vehicle, but Gable refused to sell.

March 1936 saw the release of *Love Before Breakfast*, a yarn where two men (played by Preston Foster and Cesar Romero) are both attracted to Kay Colby (Lombard). Through underhand tactics, Foster's character manages to get Romero out of the way, therefore opening the door to win Kay's affection.

It was Carole who actually lobbied for Preston Foster to be offered the part of Scott Miller in the movie. She saw potential in the actor, as Foster explained to interviewer Paul Russell:

Cliff Reid, producing at RKO-Radio, recalled my work in a Fox picture, *The Man who Dared*. He was preparing *The Last Days of Pompeii*. Ernest Schoedsack, who was to direct it, was sold on me for the lead. Then they were delayed in starting. But Reid, bless him, put me under contract meanwhile; he cast me in *The Informer*, and then with Barbara Stanwyck in *Annie Oakley*. If it hadn't been for his giving me this latter role, which was fairly romantic, Carole Lombard wouldn't have chosen me for her hero. And I wouldn't be as happy as I am!

At the end of filming the director, Walter Lang, was due to set sail for China, and Carole decided to throw a party at the ship, just before sailing. Inviting friends Jean Harlow, Bill Powell and Gloria Swanson, she organised for Lang's luggage to be covered with a variety of 'Just Married' signs and paraphernalia. As he boarded the ship, she then pelted him with rice and old shoes. He said that for days on the ship he was met with congratulations about his marriage, even though his 'bride' was nowhere to be seen.

On the film's release, *Screenland* described *Love Before Breakfast* as 'A rollicking film that rolls along to the tune of your chuckles, giggles and some big laughs. Carole Lombard gives it lots of bubble and sparkle ... For a gay and frivolous evening, be sure to see this one!' The *Los Angeles Times* was just as eager in its praise, describing it as 'exceedingly funny', 'stressfully entertaining' and 'quite mad'.

Carole's next project was acting as a guest editor at *Screen Book* magazine. This consisted of posing for photographs and supplying a very interesting article about how budding actors could break into the business. She wrote:

> Since this, in all probability, is the only 'editorial' I'll ever have the chance to inflict on the public, I've given its subject matter considerable thought. And I've decided to devote this page to a heart-to-heart talk with those of you who are ambitious to become actors and actresses.

To youngsters desperate for fame, she asked a number of questions:

> Have you a vibrant, emotionally-expressive voice? Have you the trained intelligence necessary to learn dialogue or interpret a role? Can you act? Do you understand timing? Have you mastered the technical fundamentals? Unless you can answer every one of these questions in an unqualified affirmative, you are not ready for the Hollywood of 1936.

In her encouraging manner, Carole then went on to give concrete advice for anyone wishing to break into movies. Ironically, since she was not a stage actress herself, she spent most of the column encouraging would-be actors to train in the theatre. 'Hollywood hasn't time to train beginners,' she said. This was no doubt a nod in the direction of her own start, when she had felt totally out of her depth during her first screen appearances.

She was a long way from there now, yet some of her roles still left audiences cold. Released in May 1936, *The Princess Comes Across* was something of a disappointment, and filming had been quite tense. Carole was ill with throat troubles and had reported to the set against doctor's orders. As well as that, co-star Fred MacMurray was involved in a battle over his right to earn more money now that he was officially a star. Carole heard about his predicament and was very forthright in her advice. The actor must go on strike; there was no other option, she said.

He did as he was told and, on various days, would go out to visit friends instead of reporting to the studio. On his return home MacMurray would find messages from executives threatening him with termination. The actor was concerned about the demands but Carole advised him to stay firm as she was sure they were bluffing. She also reassured him that no matter what, she would not be prepared to work with anyone but him. These supportive comments from the actress gave MacMurray the strength to carry on his battle. He eventually returned to the studio with a new contract and would forever tell reporters that he owed it all to Carole.

It was hoped that the finished print of *The Princess Comes Across* would make up for any problems behind the scenes, but the reception was disappointing. *Screenland*'s review pretty much summed it up. Their view of Carole was favourable, but not so much for the film as a whole:

> If you want to see the best Dietrich-Garbo imitation you ever dreamed of, be sure to catch this new Carole Lombard picture. It starts off like a whirlwind with the lovely Carole combining an impersonation of Marlene and Greta with uncanny accuracy. If you want to know how one girl can imitate both Dietrich and Garbo, you'll have to go to see for yourself – it's worth your trouble. Go, watch the first two or three reels; then if you're bored don't blame me, but steal quietly away and go home and wait for the next Lombard-MacMurray romance, which had better be better than *The Princess Comes Across*.

Her romance with Clark Gable continued to hit the headlines. Around the time of the release of *The Princess Comes Across*, rumours abounded that Carole had attended a prestigious ball on the arm of Gable. The actress's secretary, Fieldsie, was assigned to squelching any stories that could ruin her employer's reputation. When asked by columnists about her presence at the ball, Fieldsie denied all knowledge and told everyone that Carole could not possibly have been there with Gable, as she was at home, face covered in cold cream and playing Double Solitaire with the secretary until 2 o'clock in the morning. Few people believed her.

Sometime later, Carole gave her own version of events:

Fieldsie and I were sitting at home playing cards. One of the big social shindigs was on. We had the radio turned on to a station that was broadcasting the doings. Very colourful. Very beautiful. Until the announcer said, 'And folks, there's Carole Lombard.' Well, Fieldsie and I forgot the score. That baby described what clothes I wore, who I was with, what a swell time I was having. It was really something. Sometimes I surprise myself at the way I get around.

13

# MY MAN GODFREY

Despite all best intentions, eventually it was pointless to keep denying the romance between Lombard and Gable. Stories appeared that they had been seen all over town, and *Photoplay* printed photos of the couple looking lovingly at each other while at a tennis match. These articles infuriated Rhea Gable. She had been used to Gable's affairs during their marriage but the Lombard romance was very different. For the main thing, his past dalliances had always been covered up by the studio in order to save his reputation as a married man. Now that he was separated it was a whole different story.

The studio turned a blind eye to the new couple, and fan magazines revelled in telling readers how they spent their evenings popping corn, and their weekends going to the races. 'And who do you think Clark Gable took to the circus?' asked *Silver Screen* magazine. 'None other than Carole Lombard. And it's a well-known fact that the boys always take their best girls to the circus.'

They were the new big thing, and the media enjoyed dissecting Gable's marriage to Rhea in order to make the new courtship even more of a fairy tale. 'Clark Gable's Romantic Plight' was the title of one *Photoplay* article. 'Bachelor or benedict, which is he? Never before have the problems of a Hollywood marriage aroused so much interesting speculation.' The article then went on to declare that the Gable marriage had never stood a chance, due to Rhea's 'grace and charm [that] belonged against the background of a smart drawing room'. In contrast, they decided, 'Clark, with his love for roughing it and his preference for open shirts rather than stiff-bosomed ones, just wasn't the man to fit into the picture'.

Another article – this time in *Movie Classic* – told readers that Gable had just met with his lawyer to discuss the situation with Rhea, while Carole had stormed out of an interview when asked about her relationship with the actor. 'Touchy is an inadequate word to describe the way Carole Lombard has suddenly gotten about her – uh – *friendship* with Clark Gable,' it said.

The unwanted attention was deeply embarrassing for Rhea. While they were merely separated, the woman could still go around town as Mrs Gable and enjoy all the perks the title gave her. Now, however, her celebrity status was quickly diminishing and it was more than apparent there was a new Mrs Gable waiting in the wings. Despite previously appearing to want a quick end to the marriage, Rhea now made a decision. If Gable no longer wanted her in favour of a much younger woman, she would not go quietly. If her husband wanted a divorce, he would have a very long time to wait.

The announcement that Carole's next film would also star ex-husband William Powell made gossip columnists gasp. Was this a reunion, they wanted to know? Had the actress fallen once again for Powell? Had she left Gable? The answer was a simple 'no'. While their marriage may have ended in a divorce court, Bill and Carole still actually had a lot in common and enjoyed a rather good friendship. Carole spoke about this with reporter Dorothy Wooldridge a couple of years before:

> I admire him as an actor and as a man. I know that we are vital to each other. We have a mental balance founded on respect. We meet on a

friendly basis, and when you speak of friendship after marriage, know that it is possible only when there has been no quarrelling. Respect dies with quarrelling and fighting … I think it is fine when two persons who have separated can meet as friends and go out together with no feeling of bitterness.

The story of *My Man Godfrey* revolved around two sisters, each trying to outdo one another on a scavenger hunt. Carole's character – Irene – manages to convince a homeless man called Godfrey (Powell) to become her prize, and she takes him home and wins the hunt. However, the 'forgotten man' then gives a speech so critical of what she has just done that Irene takes pity on him and employs him as the family butler. He then manages to turn the house – and its crazy inhabitants – around and many lessons are learned along the way.

'She told me that *My Man Godfrey* was her toughest picture,' said friend and director Mitch Leisen, 'because she had to be nutty, slap-happy, goofy and her lines lacked continuity, were unrelated and without thought. They were hard to grasp. Incidentally, to get into her screwball character she sat beside her director's secretary, who was just the type, for weeks studying her!'

Carole talked to reporter Gladys Hall about screwball versus dramatic roles:

They're not really so different. You know the old thing, comedy and tragedy are akin? Like lots of old things, it's the truth. Back of all comedy there is tragedy; back of every good belly-laugh there is a familiarity with things not funny at all. There must be. You laugh with tears in your eyes, don't you? Most of us do. And Irene in *Godfrey* was, I'd say, the most difficult part I ever played, because Irene was a complicated and, believe it or not, essentially a tragic person.

To research his role, Powell studied his own butler at home. He told reporter William F. French:

It's true I'm living the part of Godfrey off the screen as well as on, and that my butler has grown to be a new man to me since I've been studying him to learn butlerage. For although Godfrey in the picture was a gentleman, he could buttle as buttling should be buttled. He was a much smarter fellow than I, and didn't have to follow his butler around the house watching him, until the poor fellow felt that his employer was out to steal his job. Godfrey was an observing lad, and had unconsciously assimilated the needed knowledge. He knew his man better than his man knew himself. Although my butler has been serving me for years, I realize now that I never saw him clearly before; never noticed how he did things or his manner of service. But now I could qualify in the most exacting family.

When reporter Elizabeth Wilson visited the set she was surprised by what greeted her:

I may say that I have made some pretty crazy places in my life … and some of my best friends have been crackpots and lunatics … But never have I run into anything so insane, really so stark, staring mad, as the set of *My Man Godfrey*.

Wilson arrived just as the cast was shooting a scene where everyone reveals what they found on the scavenger hunt, and the set was full of all manner of things, including a monkey cuddling up to William Powell and a goat chewing on Lombard's Travis Banton-designed evening gown. When she saw what was going on, the actress apparently pulled the dress out of its mouth and told it to 'shoo!' 'I hate goats,' she said in the creature's direction. 'Now don't take it personal. I just don't like goats in general.'

After watching the making of the movie for a few hours, Wilson came to the conclusion that:

*My Man Godfrey* is going to be a knock-down, drag-out laugh riot that will have you reeling from the theatre in a complete hysterical collapse. It's a screwy story to begin with, and directed by Mad Gregory [La Cava], and with those gay cut-ups, Lombard, Powell, Brady and Pangborn giving of their insanity it just can't miss being the funniest picture of the year. I'm laughing already.

Carole, too, enjoyed working on *My Man Godfrey*. 'It's the maddest picture I ever worked in, and I love it,' she said. 'Everybody here is a specialist in his or her type of madness.'

There is little doubt that the cast had a ball and the jokes on set amused Carole no end. One popular choice involved tricking actress Alice Brady into saying the wrong lines. 'Every time she gets a difficult line to read, they whisper tongue-twisters at her,' explained Carole. 'She sells sea shells on the sea shore. They've made her say the wildest things. Heaven knows the lines are crazy enough anyhow, without those imps twisting them around.'

The way the movie was shot was quite different to how most of the cast were used to working. The director, Gregory La Cava, encouraged and endorsed creativity and each person frequently brought their ideas to him for approval. It was suggested that everyone watch the daily rushes, and if anyone had suggestions for things they could do better, they were told to say. Carole hadn't worked this way since the early days of Sennett and Pathé, so the making of *My Man Godfrey* proved to be light relief.

'You think *Godfrey* is a good picture?' Carole asked reporter George Madden:

Then credit seventy-five per cent of it to Gregory La Cava who directed it, wrote all the dialogue and literally gave birth to it. To me, La Cava is the great directorial genius of Hollywood. I'm not saying there aren't other ones, but when you see a La Cava production, you're seeing a one-man creation.

At the end of filming, Carole, William Powell and Gregory La Cava threw a huge party for cast, crew and friends (including Gable) on the soundstage where they had been working. A bar was installed and gifts were presented; Carole's being a large set of garden tools due to her enthusiasm for designing her home and garden. She entertained everyone with her wicked sense of humour and salty language.

All around Hollywood, Carole was known for throwing curse words into conversations; a habit that earned her the nickname, 'the profane angel'. Her friend and fellow actress Patsy Ruth Miller talked about the issue in her autobiography, *My Hollywood*. Patsy was married to John Lee Mahin, writer of the Jean Harlow and Clark Gable movie *Red Dust*, and became quite good friends with Carole during her relationship with Gable. Miller described the actress as being 'impossible not to like', but one thing she just could not get used to was Carole's constant swearing. Miller thought of herself as being very prim and proper and this piqued Lombard's interest. Instead of holding back her language purely to satisfy her friend, Carole would deliberately swear in front of her, just to get a reaction. The look on Miller's face never disappointed.

Carole explained that the reason she liked to swear so much on the set of movies was simply because things could become rather fraught with the long waits between scenes. Swearing was her way of letting off steam, so that any frustration she may be feeling off screen did not show up on it. In recent years, evidence of Carole's language has come to light with the release of outtakes from *My Man Godfrey*. The clips show the actress fluffing her lines, and accompanying her annoyance is a stream of 'shit', 'Jesus Christ' and 'Nuts! Son of a bitch!'

*My Man Godfrey* turned out to be one of the funniest and most successful films of Carole's career and a glittering premiere was held at Pantages in early September 1936. On its release, *Screenland* called it 'more fun than any picture of the month. For real amusement value, here's your best current movie "buy". It's perfectly mad, it's silly, it's sheer nonsense; but thank Heaven and Hollywood for such film fare, I say.'

The *Los Angeles Times* agreed that it was 'quite a bit mad', and gave it a stellar write-up, while *Photoplay* told readers:

> In as mad and gay a picture as we've seen for months, William Powell and Carole Lombard continue where they left off when their real life divorce so rudely interrupted their cinematic fling ... You may see bigger and more spectacular productions this season, but we wager you won't have any more fun and that you will enjoy it to the utmost. See this if it takes your last penny.

*Film Daily*, meanwhile, agreed with Carole's opinion of the director. 'This is one of the wildest farces that has come to the screen in a long time,' they said. 'It is loaded with laughs and much credit is due Gregory La Cava, who produced and directed.'

Because of the success of the movie, many fans and corners of the media still wondered if Carole and William Powell would get back together. This all stopped at the end of September 1936, however, when the actress petitioned to have her name legally changed from Jane Peters Powell to Carole Lombard. This, she said, would mean less confusion when dealing with business matters. 'I have used the name of Carole Lombard professionally for several years,' she told the court. 'And it has come to have a value to me which I want to safeguard.'

Carole would be nominated for an Academy Award for *My Man Godfrey* (though the award eventually went to Luise Reiner for her role in *The Great Ziegfeld*), and the acclaim of that, plus the fantastic reviews, boosted Carole's confidence. She found herself becoming more and more opinionated on what was best for herself and her career:

> I'm not vain about my career anymore, but I want to be able to be proud of it. I'd much rather make a good picture than a so-called important one. Harold Lloyd has had one of the longest careers in films making good pictures. Even when he branched out, calling his own shots on stories and producing his own films, he never dashed off into costume pictures just to prove what an important star he was.

Nowhere was her new confidence more apparent than when Paramount wanted Carole to appear in their new film, *Spawn of the North* with Cary Grant. While they took out large advertisements in trade magazines throughout summer 1936, the film was actually a sore subject with the actress. She had campaigned for Gable to be given the role but the studio declined, claiming it would cost too much money. This decision left her still assigned but desperately trying to find a way of getting out of it. Her escape came when the cast and crew were told they'd be heading up to Alaska for shooting. Carole visited her doctor, and was suddenly diagnosed with secondary anaemia. Of course, he 'strongly recommended' that she cancel the trip to Alaska, much to her relief. The project was put on hold, but when it was eventually made she was long off the cast list.

Carole was not only turning down parts she did not care for, but interviews too. Whereas her dressing room door had previously been open to almost every reporter, now certain members of the press found it firmly locked. She was still happy to talk to those she trusted, but more and more frequently members of the press – women mostly – geared their questions towards her relationship with Gable. Carole did not appreciate it. 'They come to me for what they call personality stories,' she said, 'and get my private life all mixed up in them. If they can't be honest, I'm not talking.' Her standard response to being asked about love life rumours was always, 'Aren't they silly?' and then she'd move the topic swiftly on.

When Carole did agree to talk, it was still with the honesty she was famous for. When asked if she preferred socialising in New York or Hollywood, she replied:

In social activity right now Broadway, compared to Hollywood, is like the old one-horse town. I haven't seen so many white ties and tails for at least six years in the film colony. Parties are larger and gayer. Everywhere there's an atmosphere of confidence – people are out for a good time again. I'd say that Hollywood at present is gayer than Broadway has been in years. Easterners who entertained the film celebrities in New York are having the compliment returned in a big way out on the West coast.

Carole's confidence as a person and a movie star carried over to the people around her. She was well known around the studio for her good deeds and promotion of people she thought deserved a leg-up, and as her star rose to its highest she helped out more and more. One day she discovered a young assistant at Paramount, who wanted desperately to make it as an actor. Carole decided to help him out and every day would send him to the executive's office and front desk on a variety of fake errands. That way, she hoped he would be brought to the attention of the powerful bosses and given a chance as an actor.

Another protégée came in the shape of a young woman who worked in the costume department. Carole took the girl under her wing, then encouraged and helped her to set up a dress shop. She also found several young women who could not afford to go to college without adequate funding. The actress not only paid their expenses, but clothes and Christmas presents too. 'You have to be careful what you say to her,' said friend Madalynne Fields, 'because if on May 10th you say, "Oh Carole! That quilt's divine!" you're likely to get a quilt like it on 25 December. Unless you have a birthday in the meantime!'

The list of her good deeds went on and on. One contract player found herself out of the studio because a producer did not think she had what it took to become a star. Carole personally convinced the man to take her back, and would accept no gratitude from the actress whatsoever. 'Skip it', was all she said when the girl tried to say thank you.

Perhaps the most famous of all her kind gestures was when Carole found out about Margaret Tallichet, a beauty contestant who had come to Hollywood looking to become an actress. She somehow found herself as a secretary in the publicity office instead. Margaret had accompanied a newspaper reporter to Carole's dressing room, and when the interview was done the two women got talking.

Margaret told Carole all about her dreams and hopes and, before she knew it, the actress had called an agent and film executive and demanded they come to meet the new face. Margaret remembered the gesture, 'And then she arranged for the studio dramatic coach to give me lessons, and she had Loretta Francell, her hairdresser, cut and dress my hair. And after that she asked for a portrait sitting for me.' As well as all that, Carole invited Margaret to parties, dinners and other social functions so that she could meet potential employers. The hard work paid off and the young woman eventually broke into movies.

Sometimes Carole's good deeds would be combined with a joke, too. One Christmas she asked her hairdresser – Loretta Francell – what she would like as a gift. The woman told her that she desperately needed a new toilet seat. It came with a note attached – 'When you use this, remember Carole loves you'. Another gift was slightly more glamorous: a Ford car for a special birthday present. She was generous to a fault and her determination to help all in need earned Carole a nickname from friend and assistant, Fieldsie. She affectionately called her 'little champion of the downtrodden'.

She was no stranger to helping people in more forthright ways, too. 'I do walk off sets,' she said:

> … but not for the reasons you might suppose. I'm not temperamental about myself. I can take care of myself, all right. But I do get temperamental when I hear some little would-be Napoleon of a director, some little killer-diller of a petty czar cursing out extras, grips, electricians. I've walked off sets when things like that happen. And I will again, if and when they happen again. I've said to the pettifogging Nappies, 'Why don't you bawl me out if that's the way you feel about it? You don't dare to bawl the stars out, do you? They could bark right back at you, couldn't they? So you have to light on the little fellows, the ones who can't talk back, don't you?' It's an obsession with me, the bullying of men who can't defend themselves by men who, not necessarily stronger, are in stronger positions. I've tweaked more than one nose, twisted more than one ear until it rassspppped for that sort of thing.

Along with her confidence on set came a view that being labelled a clothes horse was not something to be proud of. When asked about her title as the best dressed actress, she replied:

> I can't imagine a duller fate than being the best dressed woman in reality. When I want to do something I don't pause to contemplate whether I'm exquisitely gowned. I want to live, not pose! So far as clothes go, all I try to do is be well-groomed. I don't spent two thirds as much on my wardrobe as a number of the stars. I don't believe in being lavish that way. It'd be a career in itself and there are too many other things to enjoy. Besides, I couldn't afford it!

A more interesting occupation came in the care and upkeep of her home. By now she was living in a new house dubbed 'the Farm' and was revelling in the change. 'Suddenly the owner [of my last house] announced my rent was to be tripled. I thought that unreasonable, so I politely bid him goodbye.' The new house was described as somewhat small. 'There's no dining room simply because the building was too small for one!' she said.

But while the house may have been too small for a dining room, it certainly wasn't too little to house Carole's growing menagerie. When *Motion Picture* magazine came to visit, they found ducks wandering around the rooms, a rooster named Edmund and a good supply of dogs, cats and birds. 'That house is mad,' Fieldsie told reporter Harry Lang. 'There's all that and who knows what else there'll be tonight, because Lombard's out shopping right now.' She was right to worry. Not long after, Carole bought another dog, a spaniel called Smoky. 'I'll probably have more,' she said. 'I can't resist pets and I can't walk by a pet shop.'

The house brought out Carole's crazy sense of humour, demonstrated when she received a gag gift of a bee-bee gun. Her normal aim was a target on a bush, but occasionally Fieldsie would be on the receiving end. 'I don't dare go out in that yard when Carole's got the bee-bee gun, without wearing a red hat. With that gun, Lombard is just too bad!' But it wasn't all gags. Carole adored the garden and spent many hours working there, tending to her trees and flowers and just enjoying life with Clark Gable.

On 13 November 1936, 28-year-old Carole began work on Paramount's *Swing High, Swing Low* with Fred MacMurray and director Mitchell Leisen. Once again, Leisen loved working with her:

When she's in a picture, she never says 'I think I should cry in this scene,' but rather, 'I think the girl should cry in this scene.' She always refers to her role in third person, which shows projection. One day, Fred MacMurray came up to me and said, 'Mitch, this guy just wouldn't talk that way.' That was the day I knew he'd become an actor. Because at last, he was referring to his role in the third person.

The film called for Carole to sing, but by her own admission she wasn't the best person to carry a note. In fact, in two previous movies

– *White Woman* and *Brief Moment* – her singing voice had actually been dubbed over. The actress asked Leisen if he intended dubbing her voice this time and when he assured her he did not, she was mortified. The director would not be moved though, so instead Carole took classes with voice coach Al Siegel. In the end her voice did not improve much, though her somewhat awkward renditions were covered by strategic trumpet playing and just small snippets of the songs.

Carole insisted on a closed set with very few interviews for fear of being asked about Gable, but despite that, reporter Jeannette Meehan somehow managed to find her way onto the soundstage. Staying for most of the day, she witnessed the cast filming a scene in a makeshift Cuban café. There, she was surprised to see Carole giggling off set one minute and crying on set the next. When she had chance, Meehan asked the actress how she managed to do such a thing. She shrugged. 'The scene itself does it,' she said. 'That's all there is to it.'

While all this was going on, Carole signed a very flexible contract with Paramount that ensured she made two films a year for them, at $150,000 a time. While it gave her a lot of freedom to work with other studios, Carole remained characteristically blasé. She told Meehan that while the money enabled her to make her family's life comfortable, 'Other than that it simply means that it's possible for me to look forward to the day when I shall be able to retire on a comfortable income.' The reporter was shocked. Surely she couldn't be serious, and yet Carole assured her she was. 'I don't want to be any broken-hearted "has-been". As a matter of fact I doubt it if I ever make another picture after this contract is up.'

While working on *Swing High, Swing Low* Carole asked for an unexpected day off. The newspapers soon heard of the request and took the opportunity to make up a story. 'Six times in six months, the rumour goes out that I'm dying with pneumonia,' she told Edward Churchill:

People must think that I'm a walking, all-year round resort for germs. They can't resist me and I can't resist them. I was making [*Swing High, Swing Low*] and asked Mitchell Leisen, the director to give me a day off. Some fun! The word started bouncing around that I had a cold, the next day it was pneumonia. And this is the worst of it

... Mother was actually seriously ill. She worries when anything is wrong with me. The rumour grew and grew until I was supposed to be gasping my last. In some way she heard the wild story, and she became so upset her recovery was set back several days. It just goes to show you the damage that idle gossip can cause.

On 1 December 1936, David O. Selznick once again showed an interest in having Carole work for him at Selznick International Pictures. Writing to colleague John Hay Whitney, he confirmed that under her current Paramount contract the actress could make four outside pictures in the coming few years. The amount called for – $150,000 per movie – he believed to be quite steep, but he was excited at the thought of possibly teaming her with actor Charles Boyer. This he believed, sounded quite 'hot'.

His office agreed, and on 2 December it was noted that already Warner Brothers and Twentieth Century Fox were both eager to get Carole for one of her permissible outside movies. There then followed a variety of memos, telegrams and notes between the Selznick staff, discussing whether the deal should go ahead (yes, if they could get her immediately; no if they had to wait two or three years), how many movies they should make with her (preferably four), and what – if any – film they had in mind for her to act in.

Carole was very much in favour of doing a film with Selznick. Since she'd enjoyed success with the zany *My Man Godfrey* she now wanted to become known for straight roles too. 'I had to struggle for years to do comedy,' she told reporter Ben Maddox:

But I don't think I was at the top when I was merely an insipid ingénue and I don't agree that I'm so proficient in comedy as I can be in straight drama. It's my goal, professionally. Otherwise I want a sane private life. That's why I look at those so-called glamour yarns as more of a handicap than a help. Fun's fun, in its place. I don't laugh always, though.

While she was eager to make a drama with Selznick she came across the script for *Dark Victory*. The story revolved around a woman who has an incurable disease and her relationship with the doctor who is looking after her. Carole was desperate to play the lead and even more keen for it to be made at Selznick International. She told her friend and director Mitch Leisen about the project and he was so enthusiastic that he called writer Van Upp to write a treatment. On 25 January 1937 – the very day production closed on *Swing High, Swing Low* – Carole telephoned David O. Selznick to inform him about the *Dark Victory* project. She told him that if he agreed to make it, she was sure she could get actor Ronald Colman on board too. Selznick was not convinced. He owned the rights to the screenplay, but had come across so many stumbling blocks while trying to make it that he had frankly gone cold on the subject.

Nevertheless, he agreed to have a meeting with Carole and Leisen to discuss the venture. The pair shared their enthusiasm for the project but Selznick was still sceptical. He told colleague, Dan O'Shea, that he doubted anyone could persuade him to make the film but was willing to look into it. His decision to go along with Carole stemmed from the fact that she was more than willing to try and push everything herself. Selznick was perfectly content to sit back and see what she could come up with, though in the end, as he predicted, *Dark Victory* came to nothing. Selznick eventually sold his rights to the screenplay and it was made with Bette Davis in the starring role and George Brent as the doctor. Davis was later nominated for an Academy award for her stunning performance in the film.

When *Swing High, Swing Low* was released in March 1937 it was a big success. Carole played Maggie, an entertainer who marries struggling trumpet player, Skid Johnson (MacMurray). However, their happiness is short-lived when Skid goes to New York for a job and Maggie believes he is having an affair. When she sues for divorce, Skid no longer cares about his career and it quickly goes downhill. By the end of the story, however, both his dreams and his love are safely reinstalled.

*Modern Screen* called the film:

… more than agreeable entertainment, mainly because of the engaging presence of Carole Lombard and Fred MacMurray and the intelligent direction of Mitchell Leisen. Miss Lombard demonstrates a surprising ability for heavy dramatics. Her comedy sequences, of course, are handled with her usual flair. Another Lombard surprise is her singing of *I Hear a Call to Arms*, which she vocalises with excellent results.

*Film Daily* was equal in its praise, 'This is an ideal vehicle for Carole Lombard and Fred MacMurray and should score heavily at the box office. They both have sympathetic roles and troupe effectively.' They ended the review by saying that the direction was 'fine' and the photography 'first class'.

**14**

# NOTHING SACRED VERSUS TRUE CONFESSION

B ack at Selznick International, David was still looking for
suitable vehicles for Carole to star in. He bought the rights to a
book called *Of Great Riches* by Rose Franken, and sent it to the
actress for her perusal. She loved the story and phoned Selznick
to say not only was she 'crazy' about it but she was also convinced they
should make it together. While Selznick was pleased, he wasn't going to
hand it to Lombard outright. Instead, he wrote to director Frank Capra
in February 1937 and told him that, along with Carole, other actresses
he was considering were Claudette Colbert, Jean Arthur, Janet Gaynor
and Irene Dunne. The co-stars he had in mind included James Stewart
or Henry Fonda.

Unknown to Selznick, while he was pondering the actors Carole was
brooding about the film. While she had been praised for her role in
*Swing High, Swing Low*, the actress wasn't convinced that critics liked
the dramatic parts of the production. This cast doubt in her mind as to

whether or not she was suited to drama after all. She telephoned her agent, Myron Selznick (David's brother), to tell him her concerns, and he then relayed the information to David on 19 March.

The producer began to wonder if trying to get Lombard to sign was at all worth it. On 6 April 1937 he wrote to colleague Lowell V. Calvert, asking him for a lowdown on what kind of business *Swing High, Swing Low* had done, so that he could decide just how 'important' Carole was as an actress. He received a reply the next day, saying that the film had been a success but making clear that, in the Paramount theatres currently showing the film, managers seemed to credit Lombard and MacMurray as a team rather than Carole as an individual.

While digesting this news, Selznick came up with an idea that he believed could be the answer to everyone's problems. He decided to team Carole Lombard with actor Fredric March, in the Ben Hecht screenplay, *Nothing Sacred*, and shared the news with his colleagues. He was pleased they agreed with his plan, and in fact one colleague said it was the greatest news he'd heard in a long time and predicted a sure box office success. At the same time, Carole read the screenplay and gave her consent and good wishes.

The story of *Nothing Sacred* revolved around a woman called Hazel Flagg (Lombard) who has always dreamed of leaving her small town to head to New York. During a doctor's appointment, Hazel is shocked to discover she has been diagnosed with radium poisoning and is given only six months to live. Her heartbreaking story hits the desk of New York journalist Wally Cook (March) who immediately sees a human interest tale that will gain him favour with his boss. Cook wants Hazel to travel to New York, but there is a problem: she has found out that the diagnosis was false and she will not die after all. However, in order to live her dream of going to the big city, she persuades her doctor to keep the news to himself and the 'dying' woman heads off.

The story of poor Hazel goes down a storm with the readers of Cook's newspaper, and all kinds of events are arranged in her honour. She laps up the attention and quickly falls in love with Cook. However, when it is discovered that she isn't dying at all, Cook is furious and the two get into a huge fight. Eventually, they find a way of keeping the news of her false illness to themselves; Hazel fakes her own death and then she and Cook sail into the sunset together.

As soon as Selznick heard the positive reaction from his colleagues it was full steam ahead to get *Nothing Sacred* into production. He wrote a press release and predicted that production would begin towards the end of May or beginning of June. Since this was to be a colour movie, he booked Carole in for a test on 12 May 1937. As with all things related to the Selznick/Lombard deal, however, nothing was ever going to go smoothly.

Carole arrived at the studio as instructed, took the test and then sat down for a meeting with secretary, Fieldsie, and dress designer, Ernest Dryden. Ernest Dryden was a Viennese costumier who had worked as a poster designer in Berlin before the First World War and then moved on to designing menswear. He became a fashion magazine illustrator and finally a Hollywood costumier. In that regard, he had worked on the 1936 film *Garden of Allah* and, a year later, *Prisoner of Zenda*. However, he had never worked with Carole before and that created a problem.

As everyone was aware, Travis Banton was always her number one choice for designing not only film costumes, but daywear too. Before meeting Dryden, Carole spoke to friend Marlene Dietrich, who had worked with Dryden on *Garden of Allah*. 'He is terrible,' the actress told her, and Carole immediately became distrustful. She told Dan O'Shea that she was not sure if Dryden was the best way to go, but he persuaded her to meet him anyway and then told Selznick that if they were going to get Carole to even consider working with him, he must have all his best sketches with him or else design something specifically to show her.

When the two finally met, it was a cordial affair. Carole smiled and nodded in the right places, but her heart was not in it. Afterwards she asked Fieldsie to tell Selznick's colleagues that while she found Dryden's sketches very nice, she did not want to go ahead with him as the designer on *Nothing Sacred*. Instead, she came up with the somewhat bizarre idea that perhaps he could design some dresses (at the expense of David O. Selznick) and take the risk that she may actually reject them once finished. If she did like them, she explained, she 'might' agree to work with him on the film.

Predictably, O'Shea did not like this idea, but the next request was even more frustrating. Fieldsie told him that the designers Carole would rather work with, were (in order) Travis Banton, Bernie Newman and Irene. Dan O'Shea telephoned Fred Lahey at Paramount, and was told that Banton was slow, cost a considerable amount of money and was most certainly classed as a luxury item. Besides that, he was working on another movie for the next three weeks and while he'd be available after that, it would be on a part-time basis only.

O'Shea told Selznick about the meeting and conveyed his belief that no matter what the costumes looked like, Carole was never going to work with Dryden. He had heard rumours that she considered him untrustworthy and, besides that, he knew she had talked to Marlene Dietrich and listened to what she'd said about him. While all this was going on, Ernest Dryden was growing bored and decided to force their hand. 'If you don't put me on payroll,' he whinged, 'I am going to Honolulu on vacation.'

Selznick was furious. On 13 May he sent a message back to O'Shea, instructing him to tell Fieldsie that Dietrich had actually loved working with Dryden until the two had a falling out. Furthermore, he personally considered him to be one of the three best male designers, the others being Adrian and possibly Banton. Under no circumstances would he work with Bernie Newman, whom he considered to be 'ghastly', adding that he didn't even consider him to be a designer, more a supervisor. He agreed that Irene could be a good choice, but more than anything else he wanted Dryden.

O'Shea was sent to the designer with the news that Selznick was fighting hard for his services, but if everything fell apart he would consider it entirely Dryden's fault. He had never known such a brilliant and quick designer, he said, but if Dryden couldn't sell Lombard the idea it was because he was too lazy to sit down and draw enough beautiful designs to get her attention. Throughout it all, Carole stood her ground and refused to be swayed. In the end, Travis Banton was contracted to design her outfits, with additional help from Walter Plunkett. Dryden never got an opportunity to work with the actress; he died less than a year later, the victim of a massive heart attack.

Five days after Selznick conveyed his thoughts about the designer, a memo was sent from Dan O'Shea to tell him that Carole's colour tests looked fantastic, but she was now insisting on lightening her hair and changing her make-up. Further tests were made on 20 May 1937, during which time staff noted that she was exceptionally co-operative and had indeed bleached her hair. Carole made an appointment to look at the tests during Saturday 22 May but also told O'Shea that she wanted yet another series made, this time with her Paramount cameraman, Ted Tetzloff. O'Shea convinced her to at least wait until Selznick had watched the footage himself, though noted that in terms of keeping Tetzloff off set they could have a fight on their hands.

The contract negotiations were now in full swing and on 2 June 1937 Carole contacted Dan O'Shea to change three clauses. First, she wanted to ensure that the studio would not tie her name to any commercial product without her say so. Then she requested that her working hours would never go before 9.00 a.m. and after 6.00 p.m., unless doing a night shot. This seemed fine with Selznick, but the third query – to eliminate the morals clause – prompted a definite 'no'.

On 7 June 1937 the world stood still when Hollywood's beloved 'baby', Jean Harlow, passed away from kidney failure. The industry was in a state of shock and Carole felt the loss deeply. At the time of her death, Jean had been dating William Powell and the couple would often spend time with Gable and Carole. Furthermore, Jean was a regular co-star of Gable's, and a good friend and rumoured love interest during the early days. All this ensured that when it came to social and emotional interest, Jean was firmly in the life of Carole, and vice versa.

The funeral resembled a state affair, with fans and admirers lining the streets for miles around. Stars were photographed walking into the chapel, and on this occasion Carole and Gable could not have cared less about being seen together. The funeral was a major spectacle and prompted Carole to start thinking about her own mortality. She begged Gable that if anything should ever happen to her, he must ensure her own funeral was kept quiet and dignified. He promised he would.

While Carole comforted William Powell and mourned the loss of a friend, Clark took Jean's death very personally. He had been working with her on *Saratoga* when she fell ill and was one of the last people to see her alive, having visited her at home just before her death. Later, he spoke lovingly about his co-star to reporter Gladys Hall.

[Jean's death] just about did knock me flat. Jean and I sort of began together, you know. We started together, here at MGM, worked together in *The Secret Six* with Wally Beery and Lewis Stone as the stars and with us as very important minor players. We didn't even have our own dressing-rooms then. We wondered whether we would ever get another job after that picture was finished. We made more pictures together than we made with anyone else, I guess. I was awfully fond of Jean. She was always a big kid to me, a kid with a heart as big as all outdoors, generous and swell and real.

I felt her passing more than I've ever felt anything … so I needed a rest, a change a break. I didn't go far away. I wanted to go to China, I planned to stay there about three months. But before I got going the war got going and that was that.

'Wouldn't Carole mind you going so far away for three months?' Gladys asked.

'It would have been okay with Carole,' Gable answered. 'She was all for it. She was working, and she's not selfish. She knew that I wanted to go and so she wanted me to go. That's the way she is.'

On 14 June 1937 production officially began on *Nothing Sacred*. Just a day later, a change was proposed to the original Lombard/Selznick contract. This time it was suggested that they make three films together, instead of the previously discussed two. When Carole was told about the new idea, she suggested that if she were able to get Gable to work on a picture as her co-star, a percentage deal should be worked out, too. Selznick thought this was a fine idea, firstly because he did not believe she would ever be able to get Gable on board, but secondly because he very much enjoyed percentage deals. A meeting was held to discuss the contract on 21 June 1937, and the first draft sent out several days later.

While contract negotiations were taking place, Columbia Pictures held their annual sales convention and took the bizarre decision to announce that Carole would be playing in one of their new productions.

The story was reported in newspapers around the country on 1 July, one of which reached the desk of David O. Selznick. He was furious and immediately sent a memo to Dan O'Shea, asking if he knew what was going on, and whether or not they should write a clause in their contract limiting the number of films Carole could make in a year. O'Shea got on the phone to Carole's agent, Myron Selznick, and discovered that the story was false and only happened because Columbia's studio head, Harry Cohn, begged to be able to use her name (and other actors too) in the conference. The intention, presumably, was to make the studio's dealings look more powerful than they actually were.

Several days later, the next draft of Carole's contract was on her desk and her changes typed up and sent back to Selznick's office by 7 July. Her corrections and queries covered two pages and various topics, such as billing, compensation for retakes, etc. Most of her demands were marked 'OK', but once again her request to take the morals clause out met with a definite 'no'.

In spite of that, Carole tried very hard to impress and be of use to Selznick. When she heard that Warner Brothers were desperate to sign her for one picture, she hit upon a great notion. She would say yes to them if they allowed actor Errol Flynn to make a movie with Selznick. She shared her idea with the producer, who was absolutely ecstatic. He assured her that this would be remarkable and then sent a memo to Dan O'Shea, to tell him that they should take advantage of this, as stars being involved in trading other stars could be beneficial.

On 2 August 1937 *Nothing Sacred* officially wrapped. Carole saw the rushes, exclaimed her absolute joy and told Myron Selznick that she would do any retakes without financial compensation. She was anxious to take possession of the suede suit she wore in the movie, however. When David O. Selznick heard about this, he instructed his staff to not only gift her that particular outfit, but several others too.

While everything seemed to be going well, by the start of September everyone at Selznick International was concerned that Carole's three-movie contract had not yet been signed. Phone calls to the office of agent Myron Selznick were met with a standard reply from colleagues: 'Myron needs to talk to you about this', and then silence. Despite that, David O. Selznick went ahead with plans to try and get the actress for a role in *Twin Sisters*. Retakes for *Nothing Sacred* went ahead on 19 September, but still the contract was left unsigned. Finally Selznick had enough and demanded the issue be settled immediately.

On 2 October 1937 Sig Marcus from Myron's office and Dan O'Shea from David's office got together to try and thrash out some kind of solution. The result was recorded in a four-page telegram, sent to both Selznick brothers on the same day. Issues that Carole wanted resolved before signing concerned a variety of standard things such as timescales and pay, but there were more specific ones too. Firstly, the actress required living and travel expenses for a companion when on location, then she requested once again that Travis Banton design her clothes. In addition to that, she also wanted Ted Tetzloff as cameraman and Loretta Francell as hairdresser. Fan mail was to be taken care of by staff at the Selznick office and Lombard wanted a say in her own publicity. O'Shea assured Marcus that the last two, particularly, were a definite 'no'.

As things rumbled on, David O. Selznick became more and more agitated. On 21 October he sent a two-page memo to Dan O'Shea and Sig Marcus, going through each point previously brought up. He thought that paying for Carole's companion on location shoots was totally unacceptable, but agreed to it anyway on condition that it was not to be mentioned in any other contract. He totally poo-pooed any obligation to hire Banton, Tetzloff and Francell and, since he had previously made his feelings clear, refused to discuss it again. As for fan mail, yes he would agree to that, but publicity would stay in the hands of Russell Birdwell, part of the Selznick team. The telegram showed every ounce of anger that Selznick felt in the situation, and he ended by exclaiming that he was sick of the entire matter. If the contract couldn't be sorted out, then he would just rather forget the entire thing. In short, he had gone beyond caring.

Away from Selznick International, Carole had been making *True Confession* at Paramount, playing the part of Helen Bartlett, a pathological liar accused of murdering her boss. Carole described the character as 'a goof' and when asked what she thought of her, the actress answered, 'I could cut her throat'. In the film she was reunited with actors Fred MacMurray and John Barrymore, but it was actress Una Merkel who had the honour of sharing a house with Lombard during location shooting at Lake Arrowhead.

Merkel shared her memories with reporter Jerry Asher for *Silver Screen* magazine. During the interview, the actress described Carole as someone who brought out a mothering instinct in her. 'There is something special about Carole that makes people concern themselves over her,' she said. 'It's partly because she is always so interested in everyone else. She never spares herself for a moment. She loves to meet people and she loves to listen to what they have to say.' Una also recognised the tough side of Carole, noticing that she always said what she thought and that there was absolutely no pretence about her. 'When I first met her, I got the impression that she was frail,' she told Asher, 'but I soon found out who the "frail one" really was!'

The two actresses spent a week sharing a bungalow together; a time which Merkel described as 'wonderful'. Carole had arrived on location at Lake Arrowhead on 6 October, which was also her 29th birthday. She was in a jovial mood, carrying her battered suitcase filled with perfume stains and still sporting the initials C.P. (Carole Powell) on the side. Una was intrigued that the star had not brought any maids with her and instead hauled her luggage into the bedroom herself. There, she proceeded to unpack a variety of old but well-loved items: a cracked hand mirror (which she said was the first one she had ever used), a thick dressing gown that had clearly seen better days and a Chinese silk robe which was, by then, threadbare and virtually falling to pieces.

Someone else who had fond memories of Carole was screenwriter Claude Binyon, who accompanied the cast and crew to Lake Arrowhead. The pair had been introduced before shooting at Carole's home, where she shocked him by appearing in a satin robe trimmed with fur. 'She came downstairs in that robe,' he said:

> … and if there ever was a million dollars cash she was it – with her right hand just enough out in front to make you wonder whether to kiss it or shake it. Behind her was a Pekingese pup, snorting and croaking with asthma, and just as she came into the room the pup stepped on the back of the robe. I turned the colour of a healthy beet. The director [who was with me] smiled in appreciation, because he had spent six weeks in an art school. Miss Lombard took a sharp breath and then said, 'Haw!'

On location, Binyon and Carole got talking about guns and before long she had invited him to shoot clay targets with her. The actress was a keen shot. 'She instinctively knows what to do,' said her shooting teacher, Harry Fleischmann. 'She wanted a gun that fit her and she took it home and played around with it, got used to it, before she came for her first lesson. Now she uses a 41-gauge gun, the smallest gauge made [and] the hardest to shoot …'

During the time together, Binyon was only able to shoot two out of the ten targets. 'Binyon, you stink!' said the actress. 'The lady is frank,' the writer wrote, but he knew Carole was only having fun with him. One day, when working on the set was simply too noisy for the quiet writer, the actress decided to help. She found a small building on the very outskirts of the set, told others that she had a use for it and hung a sign – 'Binyon's Corner' – above the doorway.

The shooting of *True Confession* was generally a happy one and newspapers wasted no time in reporting on Carole's love of playing jokes on cast and crew. Whether any of the stories were true didn't seem to matter, and fan magazines told readers that the tables were being turned and the jokes were now on Carole herself. Exploding matches, trick cups, lightbulbs that flashed … you name it, the actress apparently fell for it and then replayed it. Then rumours abounded that when her servants arrived to deliver some gifts from Clark Gable, they presented her with a host of Chanel No. 5 perfumes and a ruby heart necklace. While the actress was busy unwrapping them, her staff quietly went into her bedroom and placed a giant rubber spider on her pillow.

While fans still got a kick out of hearing about Carole's love for jokes, the actress herself was getting a little tired of it, particularly when the reports were untrue or grossly exaggerated. 'A gag can be mean, it can be unfunny, it can be thoughtless,' she said:

It's not very nice to find myself blamed for all the gags in Hollywood and some that don't happen at all. Who thinks up the gags that don't happen and who puts my name on them? What do fans think? I have a reputation for giving crazy parties because I staged one or two a few years ago. I pull a few gags and I'm the queen of practical jokers.

Judging from some of my fan mail I must be a first-class nit-wit by the time the phoney stories reach good old Pawtuxet.

While she had thoroughly reached her limit where false rumours were concerned, the actress took everything else in her stride. Una Merkel remembered:

Carole sets a wonderful example on the set. She has a great capacity for work and she never lets down for a second. Carole's enthusiasm carries the whole troupe with a high morale. Before the second week was over, the picture we were working on was five days ahead of schedule. There was only one retake for the entire production. In Hollywood we call that a record!

Una learned a great deal from working with Lombard; particularly how to remain a complete professional while on set:

If Carole has anything to complain about, she does it before the picture starts. But once she is on set for a job, she allows nothing to interfere. In this way everyone on the set has a chance to do his own job to the best of his ability. Every day's work is a new experience for Carole. She gets so excited at each new thing and burns up so much energy doing it.

This comment would be repeated by various colleagues over the years. In an interview with *Modern Screen* in 1940, director Mitchell Leisen described just how hard Carole worked on set. 'She has marvellous intensity,' he said:

She works so hard, believes so in her roles that she lives them. She'll squawk and battle over a script she doesn't like, but once its decided upon she'll slave over it. She doesn't only learn her own part, she learns everyone's, so that she knows the story and feels it. She doesn't memorize words and dialogues, but tries to get the thoughts behind them. That's why she can't go wrong. It's this understanding that gives her performances an underlying current of plausibility.

Still, while Carole was very friendly to everyone on set, she wasn't so sure about the presence of interviewers and reporters. Edward Churchill found himself on the receiving end of her temper when he innocently repeated a rumour that she had been having fun on Venice Pier the night before. 'And where did you hear that?' she asked.

The calmness in her voice made the reporter uneasy, and he replied carefully, 'I really don't know. I just picked it up on the morning rounds. Somebody said ...'

Carole waved her arm in the air and demanded that Fieldsie be brought into the room. While she was waiting for her to arrive, the actress stared at Churchill coldly. It was confirmed by her secretary that no such event had taken place and she had actually been at home asleep, but Carole was not going to let it drop. 'Where did it start and who started it?' she demanded. 'Where do rumours come from? How could I be in bed and at the Venice Pier at the same time? It has me stopped. I tell you, I'm afraid to do anything and afraid that if I don't do anything somebody'll say I did.'

The reporter took the telling off and wrote, 'I nodded and wished I'd gone fishing instead. When Carole burns it's a four-alarm event. In comparison, the Chicago fire just smouldered.'

Her hatred for rumours and gossip was getting more and more profound. Through Churchill she asked fans to always consider the source and make sure the information had come from reputable channels:

> I think that should go for rumours concerning everyone in the industry, or out of it. The best way to spike a rumour is to ask the one who passes it along, 'Do you know that to be a fact? How can you be sure? Who told you?' Usually the rumour spreader will back down with the admission that he or she heard it from so-and-so, who knows so-and-so, who heard so-and-so say.

Once the filming of *True Confession* wrapped, Carole decided to take a little time off to be with Gable and potter around at home. 'I'm going to have a little [fun] now,' she said. 'I take a lot of pride in making my home a real home. I like to fool around in it, buy knick-knacks for it.

I'm going in for more riding and more tennis.' However, she was quick to add that in no way did this mean she was retiring:

> It might not work out. The word might get round that I was giving up my career and going in for the simple life. The gossips might have me all washed up. Poor Carole! No jobs, no future. So she has to build a ranch and retire to it.

In spite of taking a break, the actress did not forget her friends. Actress Una Merkel was surprised when a large bowl of daisies arrived at her home. Inside was a box that contained a beautiful daisy-shaped charm; a present from Carole to her fellow co-star and roommate. Merkel was completely taken aback by such a kind gesture and never forgot the enjoyment she had working with Lombard and how very much she wanted to do it again. Speaking to *Silver Screen* several years later the actress said, 'It's very hard to keep from worrying about Carole Lombard. And right now I'm going to do a little worrying and wondering if I will ever be lucky enough to be in a picture with her again.'

For co-star John Barrymore, whose hard drinking had been catching up with him in recent years, Carole decided that she should kick-start his return to stardom. After *True Confession*, she campaigned to get him into more A-movies and for a time her enthusiasm seemed to outweigh his problems. When asked by reporter Charles Darnton what he thought of Carole's work on his behalf, the actor barked, 'First I've heard about it. Miss Lombard said nothing to me.' Then a few minutes later, he seemed to mellow:

> So that's what he meant! Who? Gene Fowler. Not long ago he said to me, out of a clear sky, 'Jack, you'd be surprised if you knew what a good friend you've got in Carole Lombard.' And now you come along and spring this thing on me. I seem to be the only one who hasn't been let in on it ... Strange that Miss Lombard should do this for me when all I did for her in *Twentieth Century* was to bawl her out and drag her around by the hair on her head. But it's exactly like her. I have played with an uncommon number of charming ladies, but never with one more regular, loveable and gifted than Carole Lombard.

But this more than generous action of hers is quite another matter and, for my part, I don't know just what it means.

While everyone involved with *True Confession* was happy, one person left seething was David O. Selznick. The contract was still not finalised, and by this point Carole was refusing to have anything more to do with it until Myron Selznick returned from holiday. That fact alone had wound up the producer considerably, but when he heard that Carole's role in *True Confession* was that of a liar – similar in nature to the role she played in *Nothing Sacred* – he could not believe it. Writing to Lowell V. Calvert on 22 November 1937, he expressed the importance of releasing *Nothing Sacred* before Paramount released *True Confession*, stating that he had seen the latter film just several evenings before and thought the Selznick movie was infinitely better. Calvert wrote back straight away to tell David that everything was being taken care of, and that they imagined *Nothing Sacred* would certainly be released before *True Confession*.

In the end they managed to get their movie out four weeks before Paramount's. Despite all of the behind-the-scenes disagreements and discussion, *Nothing Sacred* was a hit with audiences and critics alike. It played for three weeks at New York's Radio City Music Hall and fans continually streamed in to see it. Publicity took on interesting forms, such as bookmarks in libraries, a search for Lombard lookalikes and an ice cream sundae named especially for her. The dedication of a plaque on her old childhood home in Fort Wayne was also good timing. Photos of Carole holding the sign were placed in fan magazines and the caption of course mentioned that the actress was currently starring in *Nothing Sacred*.

*Photoplay* really enjoyed the film:

Aided by colour, an extremely smart Ben Hecht script and the competent direction of William Wellman, Carole Lombard and Fredric March have turned in a wild comedy drama that for this reviewer tops *My Man Godfrey*. It may seem unbelievable to say that a plot featuring Carole and Fred punching each other on the chin has a delicate theme, but it really has. Seriously dramatized, the plot might be grim indeed; but, satirized; it is packed with irrepressible laughter, novelty and strange tenderness ... It's among the ranking laugh-films of all time.

*Motion Picture Herald* dedicated two columns to the film, most of which was a rambling mishmash on the merits of colour technology. The rest of the review, however, was first class:

Although an unusual offering from the studios of David O. Selznick, noted for turning out a more orthodox and staple type of entertainment in the grand manner, *Nothing Sacred* is as finely accoutred, technically, as his serious works. William A. Wellman's direction is a successful test of his versatility and W. Howard Greene enjoyed himself thoroughly in putting the colour through trick paces.

The article ended by stating that if the film pleased the rest of the country in the same way it pleased the preview audience of Glendale, it was sure to give a good box office performance.

When it was time for *True Confession* to be released, Paramount placed page-long adverts in fan magazines, telling readers how wonderful the movie was and that it was breaking box office records. They also included quotes from theatre managers themselves, such as Robert M. Weitman from New York. 'I confess that *True Confession* has brought the best pre-holiday trade to the Paramount Theatre in years. Audience reaction is terrific,' he said.

*Screenland* magazine printed a photo article about the movie which praised Carole considerably:

Carole Lombard has been acclaimed for beauty, for glamour, for style-sense. But she has never received the applause she so definitely deserves for her rare flair for comedy. Carole is the one stellar girl on our screens who deliberately deserts all glamour rules in the cause of comic effect: she never hesitates to blind us to her beauty to gain the necessary gusto. Sometimes Lombard ceases to be a beauty when she goes after laughs; at times in *True Confession* she achieves a real characterization, amazingly believable, of a loveable but rattlebrained wife mixed up in a murder. We hail Carole Lombard as the best trouper among Hollywood beauties.

Also in *Screenland*, editor Delight Evans did something which surely would have raised David O. Selznick's eyebrows – she reviewed both films in the same column. For her, *Nothing Sacred* was:

> … the most provocative picture to be seen these days, and not only once but bearable for return engagements. *Nothing Sacred* is by way of being a screen sensation … That fight scene, of course is still the high spot of the screen season. Carole Lombard and Fredric March mix it and the fair heroine, hangover and all, is knocked out by the gallant hero. Just try to sell us any more old-fashioned lovers' quarrels after this.

*True Confession*, she felt, was:

> Completely mad, and comparatively unimportant; but it is so much fun that I have no hesitation in advising you not to miss it. It is no small triumph for Miss Carole Lombard, who dashes through it with pretty superb charm and chic, hurdling implausibility and absurd dialogue with her own special brand of innocence. For the first time, it seems to me, la Lombard manages to sustain a true characterization. She is not the Lombard of *Nothing Sacred*. She is, if possible, even madder than that.

'I like fantastic comedy roles,' Carole told a reporter on the set of her new film, Warner Brothers' *Fools for Scandal*. 'I'm expecting to evolve into a comedy character actress as time goes on, not break my heart when star days are over.'

However, while Carole was all smiles on camera, off screen her health was not great. Jumping from one movie to another in quick succession had once again run her immune system into the ground and she spent much of *Fools for Scandal* entertaining a cold. 'Will you be signing the three picture deal with Selznick?' the reporter asked. 'I think I'll sign it,' she answered, 'when I've got rid of these sniffles.'

This declaration did nothing to ease the worries of the staff at Selznick International. In December 1937 it was noted that the actress was still refusing to budge until she had spoken to her agent. He was due back to town several days later, and David insisted that he wanted to hear from him two days after that at the latest. When he still hadn't heard anything just a week before Christmas, Selznick sent a memo to Dan O'Shea telling him that there was simply no excuse for not having things signed and suggesting that they change the terms to two films yearly for two years, instead of three films in three years.

# MA AND PA

I n January 1938 the contract with Selznick was still not signed, but that did not stop Lombard pressing forward with various ideas for their next movie. One option, which David O. Selznick thought might work, was a film called *Light Woman*, while another possibility was *American Sleeping Beauty*. On 11 January Carole was headed out of town, but called the Selznick office to let it be known that she thought *Light Woman* was far too dull to be a Lombard movie and she was not interested in acting in it. *American Sleeping Beauty*, however, was a different matter entirely. She was wild about the story and liked it so much that she promised to try and get William Powell to act in it with her. The idea of working on it even spurred Carole to ask Myron Selznick to clean the contract up so that she could finally sign it.

David O. Selznick was thinking about the contract too, and particularly the kind of roles Carole was going to act in before their next picture together. If *American Sleeping Beauty* was to be a success, he decided, then she needed to stay away from screwball roles in the interim and stick to straight parts instead. His thought process was that if the public saw her in too many more comedies they would grow tired of them (and her) very quickly. He spoke to Carole on the phone about the potential danger she faced in continually doing comedies, and she totally agreed. Just to put his point across even more firmly, Selznick then put his thoughts down in writing and sent letters to both Carole and Myron respectively. He urged both to warn potential directors and screenwriters that they must not develop her future characters into so-called screwball personalities.

Carole would talk about her transition from screwball to drama to reporter Gladys Hall. 'I had a lot of fun doing the screwy comedies,' she said, 'but I was getting tired of them. Hollywood has done too many of them. The old "sheep" angle, you know. Now, I'd like to do two dramatic pictures, then another comedy, and so vary the ingredients a bit.'

Eager to remain on good terms with both Carole and Clark Gable, David O. Selznick invited them to a special preview of his latest film, *The Adventures of Tom Sawyer*. The screening was to take place on 10 February at Grauman's Chinese Theatre, but at the very last minute Gable decided he had no wish to go. Claiming an attack of appendicitis, Carole telephoned Russell Birdwell and told the publicist that her partner would be going to bed early with ice packs to relieve the pain. Whether or not this was true is unknown (officially his appendix had been removed years before, though some say this could have been a cover for extreme dental work), and it certainly wasn't the last time the actress called in sick on Gable's behalf. The next day, having heard the event was a success, Carole sent a telegram to Selznick. She apologised for not being able to attend but gave her delight that it had been such a triumph.

The fact that the couple cried off going to the preview showed the kind of mood both were in during the first part of 1938. The two christened each other Ma and Pa and lived an incredibly peaceful life. When Carole wrote to friend Natalie Visart on 17 February, she explained that things had been extremely quiet and she hadn't seen anyone recently. This was a definite attempt on their part to keep a low profile, not just from the ever persistent press, but also from Gable's estranged wife Rhea, who was still refusing to grant him a divorce.

When Gladys Hall was sent to interview Gable on the subject of 'Temptations I've faced in Hollywood', she hoped to uncover some secrets. She was left disappointed, however. While the article was aimed at whether or not Clark was tempted by the salacious ways of Hollywood, he did not give much away. However, he did give a glimpse into the kind of quiet life he and Carole were currently leading. When asked if he went out to wild parties and night clubs, the actor shook his head:

> Nothing doing. You've never seen me anywhere, have you? Nor ever read of me being seen anywhere, except at the races. I never go to big parties and never give them. I haven't been to a night spot for two years. I never have any fun in those places, so why go to them?

'But Carole must like to go places now and then, to see if not be seen,' commented Hall.

> Nope. Carole doesn't care for that sort of thing any more than I do. We never go to the night spots. I think we've been to one night spot twice in the past year or so, that's all. We have a few good friends and we have dinner at one of our houses and play tennis or ping-pong or badminton or something. That's the extent of our social activities. We go to the movies quite a bit, Carole and I. And once or twice she's gone duck hunting with me. She's a good shot, knows how to handle a gun. That about says it all.

Negotiations for her Selznick contract continued to rumble on, and in March 1938 *Photoplay* published an entire article dedicated to Carole's past contracts and demands. Entitled 'She Gets Away Murder', special mention was made of her insistence that she choose her own directors, dress designer and cinematographers. It was also noted that she insisted on strict working hours and dates, and that she must be involved in publicity and the approval of publicity photos. Most of these points were the sorts of things still being thrashed out at Selznick International. 'No-one can justly accuse the fair-haired lady of being a troublemaker,' wrote article author Janet Bentley. 'She never quibbles.

She goes to the place where it will do the most good – straight to the front office.'

Bentley noted that Carole looked towards her films with the eyes of a producer, and she was respected for it. Indeed, when the reporter asked what pleased her most about *True Confession*, the actress said:

We brought the picture in under its budget .., It's important to be cooperative. I've never fought unless I honestly believed I was right, and that the thing I was fighting for was really important. You know the reason that more people don't get more things they feel they deserve, is because they're afraid to ask for them.

Lombard certainly wasn't afraid to ask for what she wanted. Back at Selznick, the actress had now negotiated a deal for two pictures to be made between 1938 and 1939. If they did not make a film in the current year, the studio would pay her $150,000 which would be repaid if Carole were to die or not be able to make a movie with them. The contract sounded fine to all parties, but just to make sure, Selznick sent a memo to Dan O'Shea asking him to confirm that there was nothing in there about hiring designer Travis Banton. Having been browbeaten about Banton's services in the past, he had no wish to go through it again. He was, therefore, relieved when O'Shea confirmed that there was nothing about the designer at all.

For now the plan was still that Carole would star in *American Sleeping Beauty* with ex-husband Bill Powell. However, Hal Roach was also looking to work with her, so things had to move quickly and a firm film lined up. In that regard, *Of Great Riches*, the film proposed to her sometime earlier, was now back on the table, though it would soon be retitled *Made for Each Other*. Carole was somewhat interested, though her newly relaxed approach to life and career was revealed in a letter to friend Natalie Visart. The dress designer had written to ask if the actress would be interested in her latest samples and sketches. Carole thanked her profusely but admitted that she no longer had any interest at all in hats or clothes. Instead, she insisted, she had just bought a lot of pyjamas, which she intended to wear at every possibility.

While this lack of interest in material items seemed somewhat out of character, actually it wasn't a new thing. 'Extravagance means so little to me,' she had told reporter Faith Service in 1933:

I've been through it both ways from the middle, and I know what I'm talking about. My family had money – and then they lost money. And long ago I knew the meaning and the value of being well cared for and of poverty. And I found that I was just as happy in a one-room apartment with one dress to my name as ever I was in a deluxe apartment with a brimming wardrobe. I can make a one-room apartment look as charming as I can make a mansion look and get just as much satisfaction out of it. I can just have as many laughs in a $3.95 gown as I can in a creation at seventy-five times that amount. I can find interests just as vital to me as the interests I have now and – they will cost me nothing. I wouldn't have a single pang of fear if I were told that I would be poor again tomorrow.

On 3 March 1938 Los Angeles suffered a great and astronomical flood. In the middle of the night, water came down from the mountain, swirled around the city and began to recede by dawn, leaving an unbelievable amount of damage. Thousands of people found themselves literally running for their lives and newspapers reported that the cost to replace everything would be at least $25 million. Carole and Clark wanted to help those affected by the disaster, just as Carole's mother had when floods hit Fort Wayne in 1913. Fieldsie watched the unfolding events, 'While Clark was throwing chains and blankets into the station wagon, Carole was loading it with food and thermos jugs of milk and coffee. When he started off to pull out neighbours who were in trouble, there she was sitting up beside him.'

In mid-April, the Warner Brothers' movie *Fools for Scandal* was released. Despite happy photographs of Carole being presented with a huge cake by president, Jack Warner, the film was something of a let-down.

The story was fairly simple. Actress Kay Winters (Lombard) is a famous film star who encounters a penniless society man called Rene (played by Fernand Gravet). Not knowing Rene's identity, Kay eventually offers him employment as a butler and cook, and by the end of the movie they predictably fall in love.

Critics gave it a lukewarm response at best, and it was as though Selznick's prediction of audiences growing tired of her roles was actually coming true. 'It's not a good metaphor to call several reels of film a straw,' said *Photoplay*, 'but anyway this is the one that probably will break the back of that slapstick camel Carole Lombard's been riding so long. Of all the inane, pointless, laboured comedies, this is it ... An honest criticism must insist that warmed-over film material is essentially tasteless.'

*Motion Picture Herald* asked various theatre managers what they thought. 'A clever little comedy that hit a new low in grosses for the year,' said A.J. Inks from Indiana. 'Perhaps if Lombard would have had another male lead, the picture would have gone over big. Very disappointing.' A.F. Hancock from Columbia City was even more negative:

> No dice. Supposed to be a comedy, but if there were any laughs, we did not hear them. The entire picture seems to be a labour. There is no action at all; it is all dialogue, and if you ask the audience, as we got it, not all of it was bright. The picture just has not got what it takes. That tells the story.

While the actress may have been disappointed with the tepid reviews, just a week after release her mind was taken off the critics when disaster struck. Carole arrived at her St Cloud Road home to find that she had been burgled and a great deal of her jewellery, furs and clothing had been taken. In fact, so severe was the event that she told police most of her possessions had disappeared. One of her neighbours – Harry Curland – arrived home to find that he too had been targeted, the thieves breaking into both homes in exactly the same way.

Later, a gentleman by the name of Ralph Graham would be charged and sentenced to life in prison for the robbery of Carole's and various

Jane Peters (aka Carole Lombard), aged 9, helping on Miss Morgan's chocolate booth to raise funds for fatherless children in France. (Courtesy of Carole Sampeck, the Carole Lombard Archive)

A teenage Carole Lombard, in around 1925. This photo was taken during the height of her flapper years and during her first film contract at Fox. (Courtesy of Carole Sampeck, the Carole Lombard Archive)

*Opposite*: One of Carole's earliest roles was in *Hearts and Spurs* with Charles Buck Jones. (The Douglas Cohen Collection)

*Right*: Carole married William Powell in 1931. The age gap, press intrusion and conflicting personalities eventually led to the marriage failing. The two remained friends, however, and acted together after their divorce. (Author's collection)

*Right*: Gary Cooper acted with Carole in the 1931 release, *I Take This Woman*. The two were later romantically linked. (The Douglas Cohen Collection)

*Opposite*: After recovering from a car accident, Carole embarked on a new career as a 'bathing beauty' for producer, Mack Sennett. Here she is (first on the back row) with fellow cast members. (The Robert S. Birchard Collection)

*Left*: Carole was a forward-thinking woman who took charge of every aspect of her career. Here she is looking decidedly modern in a publicity photo from the early 1930s. (Author's collection)

*Below left*: Pets played a big part in Carole's life. She is seen here with her dog, just one of dozens of animals in the Lombard menagerie. (Author's collection)

*Opposite and below right*: Carole was classed as a fashion icon; a tag that sometimes annoyed her. These Paramount publicity photos show the actress wearing a variety of outfits, perfectly. (Author's collection)

This publicity photo shows Carole reading a copy of *Photoplay*. In real life she quickly grew frustrated – and often furious – with fan magazines' intrusion into her personal life. (The Douglas Cohen Collection)

On set with the cast of her most famous film, *My Man Godfrey*. Ex-husband and co-star William Powell is second from the left. (The Kobal Collection)

Carole's status in Hollywood reached legendary proportions when she met and later married Clark Gable. The two enjoyed a long relationship. (The Kobal Collection)

This photograph shows Carole on the set of the 1939 film *Made for Each Other*, co-starring James Stewart. This was the second film the actress made with producer David O. Selznick. (Author's collection)

With Clark Gable, Vivien Leigh and David O. Selznick. Gable's strained relationship with the producer led to Carole cutting ties with his company. (The Kobal Collection)

Carole and Clark Gable at the *Gone with the Wind* premiere. The couple did not want to attend the event, although they seemed to enjoy it on the night. (The Kobal Collection)

Alfred Hitchcock directed Carole in *Mr and Mrs Smith*. The two are seen here on the set with fellow actor, Robert Montgomery. (The Kobal Collection)

Carole on the set of her last film, *To Be or Not To Be*, with actor Robert Stack and director Ernst Lubitsch. (The Kobal Collection)

*Above*: A happy, smiling Carole in a
publicity photo for *To Be or Not To Be*.
This pose perfectly demonstrates how
the actress wanted to be remembered.
(Courtesy of Carole Sampeck, the
Carole Lombard Archive)

*Right*: One of the most striking
photos ever taken of Carole Lombard.
Her beauty is everywhere apparent.
(The Kobal Collection)

Carole was every inch a superstar; respected and loved by everyone she knew. (Debbie Beno Collection)

other properties. Nicknamed 'The Phantom Bel-Air Burglar', Graham sold a number of items – including a platinum clip containing rubies and diamonds from Carole's house and a camera from Gary Cooper's – to Hollywood jeweller Morris Wasserman. When caught, he denied all knowledge of handling stolen property, but changed his plea at the last minute when the trial went to court in July 1939.

Strangely, Carole had actually predicted she would be targeted a year before, when stories about her star sapphire jewellery collection appeared in newspapers. She became so concerned with the publicity that she decided to sell every one of the precious stones. 'I used to love them' she said in 1937:

> But I've heard so many untrue stories that I've sold them all. Why? Because heavens only knows what might happen if the tales keep circulating. My collection was small, very modest. But word of mouth advertising had them growing like weeds in a California sub-division. Both in number and size. The last reports I heard – the ones which frightened me into getting rid of them – sounded as if I'd cornered the star sapphire market. You can't enjoy things and be afraid of the consequences of having them at the same time.

Carole was certainly not the first or last Hollywood celebrity to be burgled during the 1930s. In fact, in recent years more and more incidents seemed to be occurring, and this would not be the last time Carole heard of an intruder being in her home. For now, however, she got back to negotiations with Selznick. Six films were put forward for her to consider, with one of them being *Of Great Riches/Made for Each Other*, scheduled to begin shooting in summer 1938. *Variety* announced the project on 4 May 1938, and Selznick told colleague Lowell V. Calvert that everyone in the office liked the screenplay tremendously. One thing was still bothering Dan O'Shea, however, and that was the fact that despite Carole's excitement for the film, she had still not yet signed the contract.

On 10 May he sent a memo to David O. Selznick explaining that he had spoken to Myron about a percentage agreement, but the agent had no wish to bring up the subject with Carole. With that in mind,

O'Shea asked, should they bypass Myron and speak to Carole directly themselves? David wrote back immediately to advise that someone in the office had already spoken to the actress, and that the matter needed to be resolved without any further delay.

On 12 May Carole went into the Selznick office to discuss details of *Made for Each Other*. John Cromwell was proposed as the director, but Carole was not happy. He was all wrong for the film, she complained. Instead, she proposed director Frank Borzage, whom she said had a heart. Selznick turned the idea down and eventually John Cromwell was hired as director. Carole did have her way with one request, however, that of hiring Travis Banton as designer. Several days later, James Stewart was brought on board as co-star and the film began to take shape.

While negotiations for *Made for Each Other* were going on, Carole turned her thoughts to her future, and something which she hoped would be a complete change from acting in motion pictures. 'Clothes should be a business, a very serious business whether [a woman] likes it or not,' she said.

'Shopping is never a pleasure for me. Keeping one's mental balance in a sea of eager saleswomen calls for every ounce of sales resistance and poise' – so said Carole Lombard in 1931. She spoke frequently about fashion over the years, and in 1933 even imparted her own advice on how every woman could make the most of their clothes:

> Even if you can't learn to make an entire frock or coat, you can learn to turn up hems, rip out machine-sewing on cheap evening frocks and turn the edgings back with fine hand-stitches. By such tricks as these are little inexpensive dance frocks made to appear like hundred-dollar models. Just take a needle in your hand and make yourself well-dressed.

Travis Banton told reporters in 1935 that Carole would buy fabrics for her personal wardrobe and sit next to him as he designed the garments.

Throughout the whole process she would advise, suggest alterations and approve every little thing. She loved the process and in 1937 told reporter Jeannette Meehan that, after retiring from movies, she would either become a designer or interior decorator. In support of that, just a year later she seriously considered having her own fashion line.

The actress had been approached on various occasions to have her name associated with commercial projects such as dresses and perfume. Carole always turned the callers down for fear that it would cheapen her image to be associated with products she did not wholeheartedly believe in. However, in May 1938 she sat down with publicist Russell Birdwell to talk about an idea she had for creating a series of women's garments. In order to be able to do this, however, she would need to interest a costume company to make and supply the creations. New York's Cleo Costume Company was put forward as a possible partner.

On 24 May Russell Birdwell sent a letter to the company, outlining exactly what Carole would like to do. In it he explained that if negotiations were successful, they could use the actress's name on some garments, and in return she would be paid an advance as well as have a royalty percentage on future sales. He wondered how much of an advance and royalty they would be willing to pay if the contract went ahead, and assured the company that while Miss Lombard was interested in working with them, they should in no way consider his query letter as binding.

Two days later the Cleo Costume Company replied, but not quite in the way that Birdwell or Carole had wanted or expected. In the short, sharp note, the company told Birdwell that if his client wanted to have her name on their dresses, then she must pay *them* $500 for the privilege. They also wrote to a mutual friend to ask if he had recommended them to 'this fellow' and to apologise for any trouble that may be caused with their reply.

While this initial foray into the fashion business was fruitless, Carole would not be put off. Shortly after, she told columnist Hedda Hopper that a Lombard dress business was forthcoming, and that fans would shortly be able to buy her creations over the counter. Fieldsie, her ever faithful companion, was assigned to run it on a day-to-day basis while

Carole – for now – spent her days at the studio. 'If dresses come in her size,' squawked Hopper, 'you'll have to diet on juices before you can squeeze into 'em.'

However, while the actress was more than determined her designs could be turned into a business, nothing substantial ever came of the idea. The nearest fans now get to owning clothes created by Carole is by buying 1930s dress patterns published by Condé Nast. While these items were not designed by the actress, they were said to be inspired by her fashion style.

# MADE FOR EACH OTHER

Because of Carole and Clark's reluctance to say anything but a few lines about their relationship, the media decided to print their own story of their love life. In May 1938, the romance was being analysed in the pages of *Photoplay* magazine. 'Can the Gable-Lombard love story have a happy ending?' Edward Doherty asked. Much of the piece was typical Hollywood fluff, but with some very cutting remarks along the way:

Here is a typical moving-picture situation. It has been used over and over again. You have seen it developed hundreds of times. You have seen the problem solved in hundreds of different ways. But this is a situation in real life – a beautiful blonde girl, witty and winsome and wise, in love with a debonair actor who has been married a number of years and whose wife is unwilling to divorce him. What will happen? How will the characters react? How will the story end?

The article portrayed Rhea Gable as a poor, heartbroken wife who had been left on the sidelines for the younger and more glamorous replacement. 'Here is the wife,' it said, 'the charming, cultured, sophisticated Mrs. Rhea Gable, watching the two with what emotions no one knows. What will the autumn bring her? Restored serenity, or grey despair? Loneliness, or peace?' It then gave ample column inches to the failed romances of both Gable and Lombard, taking a swipe at both in the process. It was particularly scathing towards Clark, who it portrayed as a gold-digger, jumping from one older woman to another in order to enhance his career. The couple gave no public statement about the article, as corny and flowery as it was. However, it was not the last time *Photoplay* would take a swipe at the couple, only the next time would be even more biting.

Away from the trial by media, by early June everyone at Selznick International was happy to learn that Carole had finally accepted and signed the proposed film contract. Carole was pleased too, and on 4 June wrote to her friend, Natalie Visart, to tell her all about it. In the letter the actress said that she was very happy to be working for the company again. However, signs of unhappiness with her career leaked through when Carole admitted that she would much rather never work again. 'I so like just sitting around playing and doing nothing,' she said.

Carole was supposed to begin her employment on *Made for Each Other* on 5 July and end on 12 September 1938. However, after a few postponements, the official start date of filming was 26 August and it went through to mid-October, with several retakes shot after that. Before beginning, however, Carole took part in a publicity exercise that saw her take over the reins of the Selznick press office for a week.

Her place of work was decked out with a 'Danger, Lombard Now At Work' signpost, along with a desk, telephones, a siren to summon help and various other pieces of equipment. If her role involved any real publicity work (apart from that created by her being in the job), it didn't make the newspapers. Columnist Hedda Hopper stopped in for a chat, during which time she witnessed the actress trying to get Mahatma Gandhi and the King of Ethiopia on the telephone. Then she was tasked with finding survivors of the *Titanic* – apparent research for a new Selznick movie – and setting up lunch dates with the likes of mayors and governors.

Another reporter, *NEA Service* staff correspondent Paul Harrison, visited in time to see Carole tell various media outlets that a number of fake actors and actresses had been added to the cast list of *Made for Each Other*. During his time in the office, he also overheard the actress trying to make calls to First Lady Eleanor Roosevelt, and authors Margaret Mitchell and H.G. Wells in order to get their opinion on whether or not Clark Gable and Norma Shearer should appear in the movie *Gone with the Wind*. Other calls asking the same question went out to the Duke of Windsor and George Bernard Shaw, though not surprisingly no one was around to take her call.

Incidentally, Carole was a huge fan of both the duke and Shaw. She once described the latter as 'undependable, irascible, caustic and cute. But there's nobody with a greater power to deflate, with a phrase, those humans of things that need deflating.' Regards the duke, she exclaimed that his story (of giving up the throne to marry the woman he loved) would go down in history as an important chapter, 'Instead of recording the facts of affairs of stages, this chapter will be a study in human emotions.'

The idea to have Carole work in the bustling press office was a publicist's dream and resulted in major publicity not only for the star, but for *Made for Each Other*, too. Photographs were taken of her making calls, looking at photographs and speaking with reporters, and everything was mentioned in the magazines and newspapers shortly after. This reaction surprised Carole, who gave her thoughts on the experience to *Picturegoer* magazine:

> For the life of me, I can't see why my week as a press agent should have stirred up any unusual comment … The answer I suppose is that it hadn't ever been done before, or so I'm told. No reason why it shouldn't have been. Publicity and exploitation are just as important to a star as any other department, and, having always believed that, I took the time to do a little bit of press work myself.

For any actors who may believe their own publicity, Carole had this advice, 'For stars who feel ego creeping up on them, I recommend a week's trick in a studio news bureau. They'll find that city editors don't swoon at the sight or sound of so-called Hollywood names.'

Not everyone was impressed with her work, however. For a while the British press had been taking more than one swipe in her direction, citing her pranks, jokes and screwball behaviour as simply too much. Hubert Cole at *Picturegoer* described the problem:

> The trouble was that Miss Lombard had a lot of support in all this craziness. The publicity was good while it lasted, so the publicity men plugged it for all it was worth. And one morning, unawares, Carole awoke to find that the honest citizens of America had taken a sudden dislike to all her goings on. The inhabitants of the humourless British Isles had been more than fed up for a long time already.

'Lombard – Look Out!' screamed *Film Weekly* in February 1938. In the article, author W.H. Mooring told Carole that she should stop playing characters so typically 'Hollywoodian'. 'I had begged her to remember that we stolid old British people still like a good dash of sincerity in our movies,' he said in a follow-up article. According to the author, British film fans wrote in their droves to give their support, but a phone call from Carole's agent showed that not everyone agreed:

> My regrets were transient when they told me that Carole had read my remarks with much displeasure and thought I had merely been unkind to her in a way not even a Hollywood star is accustomed to expect of an English as distinct from an American, film writer.

A short time later, Carole herself phoned Mooring and invited him to come and see her in her new role as press representative. 'I want you to come over and treat me just as though you'd never seen or heard of me before. I'm not Carole Lombard a certain film girl you know, but Carole Lombard a young recruit to the Selznick press and publicity department.'

The author headed straight for Hollywood and on entering the office was greeted with sirens and a great deal of hilarity. Other authors had been met this way during the week and saw the funny side, but Mooring was confused. 'She looked embarrassed,' he said. 'When finally the din subsided and we were able to talk, I knew for certain that the only sane force at work in that office was Lombard.' Having spoken to Carole for a while, Mooring wondered why she could not have performed her job in a quieter fashion. 'She had to put over the stunt with typically Lombardian accompaniment, noise, wild imbecility and all the rest,' he said. 'When I left Carole Lombard that day, I knew that she was within just a shaving of kicking over the whole silly apple cart.'

Pompous reporters aside, the week was a grand success. According to Carole, by the end of her time in the press office she had handled around seventy news stories. Of course some, she admitted, were specifically for *Made for Each Other*. On her last day, a party was held in her honour and she was sent home with a 3ft cup inscribed, 'To Carole Lombard, who gave publicity legs upon which to stand – Russell Birdwell'.

Her week as a press rep wasn't the only good publicity the star received. During 1937, Carole had earned in excess of $450,000 and found herself one of the highest paid actors in Hollywood. However, she ended up paying around 85 per cent of it in taxes. Then from what she had left came expenses for her agent, manager and staff. 'Funny thing about all that money,' she said, 'was that I got only $20,000 of it for myself, directly I mean.' During a conversation with Russell Birdwell, the actress gave the extraordinary news that she really did not mind paying her taxes at all. Birdwell enjoyed the comment so much that he saw an opportunity.

He telephoned reporter Frederick C. Othman of *United Press* and asked Carole to repeat the quote to him. She did and the news spread far and wide. 'I'm glad to pay my country's taxes,' she told fans. 'For all the things this country has done for me, for the things it has made possible, for the things it is doing for its citizens, the price is not too high.' This small quote (and several others like it) went all around the country and even President Franklin D. Roosevelt sent a letter to the actress, thanking her for the support. He was not her only fan. People from all walks of life put pen to paper and told the actress just how wonderful she was for paying her taxes without fuss. Paramount reported that it was the largest and most intelligent pile of fan mail that they had received in the past fifteen years.

Some members of the media weren't so enthralled, however. *Photoplay* asked its readers, 'What on earth do you suppose made Carole Lombard give out that silly statement about loving to pay her taxes … What's the girl trying to do … Prove she isn't human?'

Away from publicity, there was a movie to be completed. *Made for Each Other* is about newlywed couple Jane and John (Lombard and James Stewart), who are struggling to hold things together financially and emotionally. This is thanks, in part, to John's overbearing boss, who does not think twice before cancelling the couple's plans and overlooking John for promotion. Things look up when Jane becomes pregnant, but not even parenthood can turn their fortunes around as their young baby becomes seriously ill and almost dies. It is only at this point that John's boss sees how important his employee is. He personally makes sure that the baby gets the medicine needed, despite a terrible snowstorm making it difficult. The film ends with things looking up and John becoming a partner in the firm.

One of the babies used in the film was 10-day-old Bonnie Belle Barber, whose tender age made her one of the youngest stars on screen. She was also one of the better paid, since government regulations meant that while she was given the equivalent of £15 per day, Bonnie could only work for twenty minutes and be in front of the cameras for no more than thirty seconds at a time.

On set, things were relaxed. Carole was given a scooter bike; a rather strange looking contraption that ensured she could get from her dressing room to the set in record time. Cast and crew soon got used to the actress speeding past on her bike, and it became such a feature that she was even photographed on it for publicity stills. On the set itself, her love of practical jokes was rife and she enjoyed playing them, not only on the cast and crew but the entire studio. One day she gave Russell Birdwell a gift of a brand new portable air conditioner. The machine was designed to run on water, but the actress had replaced that with the strongest perfume she could find. The moment the publicist turned it on, the whole office filled with headache inducing fumes which caused him to go running from the building.

The next gag came when Carole received an inscribed cigarette case from Selznick, with the words, 'Will you marry us please? SIP and DOS'. Carole loved the joke but went one better by asking a local newspaper to print up a special edition, announcing her wedding to Selznick, complete with photograph and a faked marriage certificate. The item was then distributed throughout the entire film lot and everyone enjoyed the joke.

Although most interviewers were still being turned away, one lady Carole frequently enjoyed speaking with was Gladys Hall. She visited the star in her dressing room, and interviewed her for a forthcoming issue of *Motion Picture* magazine. Hall found the actress in a fabulous mood. 'I love everything I do,' she exclaimed:

I'm intensely interested in and enthusiastic about everything I do. Everything. No matter what it is I'm doing, no matter how trivial, it isn't trivial to me. I give it all I got and I love it. I love living, I love life. Eating, sleeping, waking up again, skeet-shooting, sitting around an old barn doing nothing, my work, taking a bath, talking my ears off, the little things, the big things, the simplest things, the most complicated things – I get a kick out of everything I do while I'm doing it.

When the conversation turned to Carole's tax situation, she was adamant that it was not a problem:

I get 13 cents on the dollar and I know it. So I don't figure that I've earned a dollar, I figure that I've earned 13 cents. And that is all right with me, too. We still don't starve in the picture business after we've divided with the government. Taxes go to build schools, to maintain the public utilities we all use, so why not? But I live accordingly, that's all. I've had girls show me diamond bracelets, say, 'I bought this little thing the other day, such a bargain, only $20,000!' If I bought a little trinket for $20,000 – and I never have yet – I'd say, 'There goes my profit for the year, in a hunk of diamond!'

Carole appreciated the comradery on the set of *Made for Each Other*; so much so that when Selznick International wanted to extend filming time she agreed to do so without additional pay. Her agent was less happy about this, however, and warned executives that when the extra time was over they were absolutely not to ask the actress for any more. For Carole though, it was firmly a case of give and take. Having given some free time to Selznick, she now asked for time off on the afternoon of 27 September so that she could rehearse for a radio broadcast that evening.

Ultimately the show on that particular day did not go ahead, but around this time Carole became more and more involved in the radio medium. These productions were often based on film scripts, and Carole had made her debut earlier that year in an adaptation of her film *My Man Godfrey*. While many Hollywood stars appeared regularly, Carole was only ever an occasional guest on the Lux productions, though at $5,000 per time they certainly supplemented her income. She also appeared on various other shows including the *Lucky Strike*, and a skit with Edgar John Bergen and his puppet, Charlie McCarthy. The latter was said to be done as an apology to radio executives for not wanting to take on a full-time weekly wireless job.

Another radio project was *The Circle*, a Sunday night variety programme airing on NBC's Kellogg Radio Show. There she mingled with the likes of Cary Grant, Groucho Marx and Ronald Colman, to name a few. During Carole's appearances she garnered great mentions in the media and even won a cover photo on *Radio Mirror*, calling her 'The New Radio Queen'. George Fisher, from the same magazine, told his readers, 'Carole Lombard, on the Kellogg hour, has the distinction of being the first feminine film star to have a show tailored to fit her personality.'

During the time the programme ran, *Radio Mirror* had a virtual love affair with the actress, and reporter Marian Rhea summed it up perfectly when she said:

> The Kellogg show isn't very old and from what I hear it will offer all kinds of bigger and better surprises as times goes on. But even before it opened, those who know its future and its intent, gave solemn assurance which I now pass on to you … That the Carole Lombard you are now meeting on the air, is the *real* Carole Lombard!

On the set of *Made for Each Other*, Carole was given a surprise party. Told she would be shooting on a different soundstage than usual, she was instead taken into a room where everyone was hiding, ready to greet her. According to publicity from the Selznick Archive, the actress was then given hundreds of gifts and many stuffed animals. Some enterprising soul also decided that the cast and crew should take revenge for all the jokes she had played on set and presented Carole with a young mule. The actress reacted as everyone hoped she would; with a peel of laughter and much noise. 'I'm calling her Scarlett!' she shouted (after the female lead in *Gone with the Wind*).

The party represented a milestone event – Carole's 30th birthday, an age where many actresses worried about how much longer they had left on screen. For Carole, however, it was something she had long been preparing for and she decided to be completely comfortable with it. 'I'm looking forward to my thirties with delight instead of with loathing,' she said:

> I believe thirty the most wonderful age for a woman. All the best stage stars – all the famous women in history – have been at their best in their thirties. Then a woman has become mellow and dignified. In her clothes, her manner and even the way she walks, she has gained a certain importance. Her years of worry and self-doubt should be over – if she has gained experience and growth, during the dangerous twenties! Lots of women may question this, but I definitely regard the teens and twenties as a darned dull time, even if it is fashionable to look back regretfully on the days when you were sweet sixteen! I look back regretfully – because I'm ashamed of some of the fool things I did!

Another party was held on 14 October 1938 to celebrate the end of principal photography. Carole and David O. Selznick sent out an invitation to all 'Jitterbugs, 'gators, hep-cats and Swingaroos', to head to stage seven, and the cast and crew enjoyed a huge celebration. Then the Selznick publicity department went full steam into a huge publicity campaign for the film. Calling the movie 'one to stir your heart', they took out full-page adverts in many fan magazines and publications. Local theatres did their own publicity too, which, in Boston, involved dressing two marathon runners in vests emblazoned with the film title and the stars' names.

One bit of publicity of which Selznick was not too fond was when *Life* magazine ran a story about Carole in their 17 October 1938 issue. The executive was not pleased that it showed the actress as a 'screwball' comedienne, rather than a serious actress. He instructed his team to speak to the *Made for Each Other* distributor, United Artists, to make sure their team would emphasise Carole's transition from screwball into strong, dramatic roles.

David O. Selznick's belief in the movie led to him telling colleagues that *Made for Each Other* was the best he'd ever made, and also, a good four months before release, he was already planning a sequel. This, he fathomed, would be the next film they'd make with Carole and James Stewart. On 5 October 1938, a long memo was sent from David O. Selznick to Dan O'Shea revealing plans to write a script and set a start date for the second instalment. They also needed to contact MGM in order to loan Stewart once again. If they denied the request, it was decided, they would be told that *Made for Each Other* would do more for his career than anything he'd ever done at MGM.

In the end, despite Selznick's enthusiasm, no sequel took place and instead Carole moved on to star in RKO's movie, *In Name Only*. David O. Selznick was rather interested in what kind of deal the actress had made with RKO, and asked Dan O'Shea to find out for him. He came back with the report that she had agreed a part payment, part percentage deal. Several weeks later, newspapers reported on the percentage plans and columnist Edwin Schallert told readers that it would probably be worth $150,000, but may rise higher. Just a week later his column mentioned that while Carole may be about to begin work on her new movie for RKO, David O. Selznick would soon have her back in his studio for a new dramatic role.

Behind the scenes, the company was looking to change the conditions of their current contract with the actress, particularly because of the seemingly money-saving deal that RKO had been able to negotiate. David encouraged his colleagues to speak to her agent, Myron Selznick, about it; even telling them to make a special trip out to see him if phone calls did not work. However, Nat Deverich, from the agent's office, did not seem in any great rush to broach the subject with Carole. Unless Selznick International had any particular film in mind for the star, he saw no reason to hurry anything.

# MR AND MRS GABLE

At the end of December 1938, Gable's estranged wife Rhea was back in the news again when it was reported that a divorce would not be forthcoming due to 'legal technicalities'. The difficulties arose because of an ongoing property settlement, which was unlikely to be resolved by the beginning of 1939. This meant that if Rhea decided to divorce Clark in California it would take an entire year for it to go through and he would not be free to marry Carole until 1940.

Reporters rushed to Carole's house to get a comment, only to find the doors firmly closed to their questions. They managed to catch Gable leaving MGM, where he told them that he had no comment and would be leaving on a hunting trip imminently. Finally, they found Rhea at the home of friends. She told them that the news had 'come as a surprise to me' and she had nothing else to say.

While Carole may have had nothing to say to the press, privately she had had enough of the current Mrs Gable and was desperate to marry Clark as soon as possible. Nicknaming her 'the old lady', the actress deeply resented Rhea's presence in their lives and brooded on the fact that their own relationship could not be made official until Mrs Gable was out of the picture. The press were also beginning to question why Rhea would not go quietly. 'Perhaps she expects Clark to send her an engraved card asking for a divorce,' wrote acidic Louella Parsons. 'He has tried in every way that becomes a gentleman, to let her know that he loves Carole and is waiting for her to make the next move.' A staunch supporter and friend of the couple, Parsons then gave a giant vote of confidence to the actress and her generous personality, while taking a swipe at Rhea's age and questionable motives. Did she want even more money than she'd already been given, Parsons wondered? She ended the piece by stating that if Rhea Gable did not file for divorce soon, then Gable should head to Reno and do it himself.

While the couple would always have a friend in Louella, some reporters were not so keen on the couple. Carole was already suspicious of their intentions, but in the months ahead she became even more resentful and downright furious with the constant press intrusion. It had begun in June 1938, when Carole wrote to friend and fashion designer Natalie Visart. In the letter she shared the news that *Photoplay* wanted to shoot her for the cover of their January 1939 edition. She gave precise details of the outfit she was to wear: sable coat and wine-coloured dress by proclaimed designer, Irene. She also wanted a hat and had a firm design in mind – small with no brim because she was afraid it might cast shadows during the colour shoot – and she sent ideas and sample materials to hat designer, Lilly Dache.

The photo was taken by famed photographer George Hurrell, but when the issue finally hit newsstands Carole was not on the cover after all. Instead, her picture was used in a feature called '*Photoplay* Fashions', alongside other actresses such as Bette Davis and Myrna Loy. However, she was featured much more prominently in another article in the same issue, which offended not only Carole but many others in the Hollywood community. Entitled 'Hollywood's Unmarried Husbands and Wives' and written by Kirtley Baskette, the article was generated to cause scandal to those actors and actresses currently in love but not married to each other. Carole and Gable were of course featured, alongside several photographs. Their portion of the article spoke mainly about the interests the two had in each other's lives, and then went on with the following:

Clark, tiring of hotel life, moved out to a ranch in the San Fernando Valley. What did Lombard do? She bought a Valley ranch! Carole has practically abandoned all her Hollywood social contacts. She doesn't keep up with the girls in gossip as she used to. She doesn't throw parties that hit the headlines and the picture magazines. She and Clark are all wrapped up in each other's interests. While Gable did all the night work in *Too Hot To Handle*, Carole, though working, too, was on his set every night … Like any good spouse might do, Carole has ways and means of chastening Clark, too. When she's mad at him she wears a hat he particularly despises. Carole calls it her 'hate hat'. Their fun now, around the town, is almost entirely trips, football games, fights and shows. Their stepping-out nights usually end up at the home of Director Walter Lang and his new wife, Madalynne Fields, 'Fieldsie', Carole's bosom pal and long-time secretary. They sit and play games! Yes, Carole Lombard is a changed woman since she tied up with Clark Gable. But her name is still Carole Lombard.

Since their relationship was still a delicate subject, Carole was understandably appalled that *Photoplay* had written such an article. She was not the only one. All around town, gossip circulated about the reactions of the celebrities involved and the Hays office even put out a statement to say that the article was 'pretty bad' and the title even more so. They assured readers that something would be done about it, though it looks unlikely that anything actually was – *Photoplay* continued as normal and the reporter was still working several decades later.

The article caused a sensation, but it did hold some truth too. Since meeting Gable, Carole had become something of a changed woman. While once her life seemed to revolve around glamorous parties and work, now she revelled in outdoor activities such as fishing, camping and hunting. These were very much Gable's hobbies, but the actress had soon learned that, unless she wanted to spend weekends alone, she really had to become involved in his interests. He was extremely dedicated to his time off from the studio, as he explained to reporter Max Smith in late 1938:

> Few people realize the nerve strain and long hours entailed in film work. Actors are usually thought of as privileged persons who sleep late. The fact is we are obliged to arise very early, before most people's alarm clocks ring, and we are still working while they are enjoying extra leisure hours at home. These hunting trips give me complete relaxation for nerves worn ragged in the strain of motion picture production. To me it's the greatest tonic in the world ... But, I believe in letting animals live unless you actually need meat for nourishment, so I usually content myself by shooting them with a camera.

While Gable would return from the trips rejuvenated and ready for more film roles, Carole said more and more that she was getting ready to retire from acting. 'Do you think I'd stick around this racket until they start feeling sorry for me?' she asked one reporter. 'Not this dame. You've seen these poor devils hanging around, trying to get parts. I'm quitting on top.' She then announced that when her final part did arrive, she would get the studio to advertise it as such. 'It'll be the world's first real farewell appearance,' she said. 'When I'm set, they can say goodbye to Lombard.'

To another reporter she confessed that money had been put away for her retirement, and her car repainted instead of buying a new one. 'That sounds like I'm a miser,' she said. 'I'm really not. Truth is, I'm trying to save my money so eventually I can retire.' The idea was that by saving money she would soon have enough to give herself an income of $8,000 a year. 'That'll be plenty for me. There's no reason why I shouldn't keep on enjoying life – if I can just save up a little nest egg.'

However, while she was still an actress Carole desperately went after parts she felt were worthy of her attention. One such role was Scarlett O'Hara in Selznick International's epic, *Gone with the Wind*. She was desperate to win the role, but was up against stiff competition from the likes of Bette Davis, Paulette Goddard and Katharine Hepburn.

The question of who would play Scarlett was something nobody could agree on. Clark Gable was straight away touted to play her love interest, Rhett Butler, and dubbed 'the people's choice' to play the role. Not every movie fan agreed, however, and some even wrote into fan magazines to protest the plans. In December 1937, a young lady called Alice from Cincinnati Ohio gave her thoughts to *Picture-Play*. 'There is one thing I cannot understand,' she said:

… and that is why people would want Clark Gable in the role of Rhett Butler. Why anyone should look forward to seeing him as such a conceited, sarcastic, egotistical, dishonourable, and intolerable person is more than I can see. How anyone could feel flattered to portray such a degrading character is something I can't imagine.

Alice's feelings about the part of Scarlett were equally scathing:

Scarlett is the worst that I've ever had the misfortune to run across. In my opinion, Scarlett is the most contemptible, vain, self-centred, unaffectionate, self-indulgent, 'I'll think about it tomorrow' individual who ever sprang from a book. Any actress who was tested for this role and then rejected should breathe a sigh of relief to think that she escaped living in such an undesirable characterization.

While Alice may have disliked the characters, Carole loved them. She encouraged Gable to take the part of Rhett, but there were two big problems. The first was that MGM was extremely reluctant to loan him to Selznick for the amount of time required to shoot the movie, and secondly, the actor just had no interest in playing Rhett Butler at all. For him, the character was such a big personality, such a force in the story, that he felt nobody could ever live up to the public's expectations. He spoke about this to *Motion Picture* magazine:

I tried to duck that Rhett assignment, you know. I didn't want any part of it. I had my neck out far enough, acting characters that only script writers had ideas about in advance, without sticking it out where everybody could take a swipe at it. Everybody this side of Tibet had read the book and everybody had different ideas about Rhett, and it was a cinch I couldn't please everybody.

They tried to tell me I was 'everybody's choice for the role'. They showed me a carload of letters to 'prove' it. The only way that made me feel good was that, in case I did play the role and there were any complaints, I could always say, 'Folks, you asked for it!'

Then they tried to make out that Margaret Mitchell had had me in mind when she created the character. That didn't go down with me. The book came out in 1936. She had been writing it for three solid years before that, and planning it for years before that. According to my figuring, she thought of Rhett Butler long before anybody, anywhere, thought of me twice.

As time wore on and more fans and critics gave their blessing for him in the role, Gable became more determined not to do it. With MGM also against the idea, he was safely out of the picture – for a while. However, David O. Selznick was not someone who gave up easily, and behind the scenes he negotiated with MGM to release Gable from his contract in order to make *Gone with the Wind*. In return, they worked out a percentage deal and the right to distribute the film. Gable was aware that with MGM distributing, his involvement would do a lot of good for the home team. Furthermore, he would finally have enough money to get him out of the stagnant marriage to Rhea. Gable eventually signed up to the project, and behind him every step of the way was Carole Lombard.

Selznick now had to find the perfect woman to play Scarlett O'Hara. Carole made it clear that she was more than ready for the part, but the producer was unsure, citing her screwball past as the reason she couldn't be taken seriously as a contender. Instead, it looked as though Norma Shearer would win the part, but the public protested. Then – as if from nowhere – another contender arrived.

Vivien Leigh was a young British actress currently involved with actor Laurence Olivier. She was a relative unknown in the United States, which made her very appealing to everyone at Selznick International. Not only that, she had exactly the right look and temperament to play Scarlett. She was hired, and the film headed quickly into production.

While Carole may have been disappointed – possibly even gutted – that she did not get to act alongside Gable, any resentment she felt towards David O. Selznick was kept strictly private. Instead, in January 1939 she sent a heartfelt message to him saying how pleased she was to hear about the casting. Addressing him as 'David Darling', Carole exclaimed that Vivien Leigh was the most interesting girl to be discovered in the past five years and gave her the very best wishes. Selznick wrote back immediately to tell the actress that he was very grateful for her remarks and felt it characteristically thoughtful of her to send them. However, while he may have been sincere, he also saw a chance for some quick and free publicity. The very same day, he wrote to publicist Russell Birdwell and told him to get Carole to contact columnist Louella Parsons. The aim was for the actress to reiterate her good thoughts about Vivien to the famous reporter. While Lombard may not have been deemed worthy enough for the part of Scarlett, Selznick was still keen on using her for publicity.

Better news came just a few days later when it was announced that Clark's estranged wife would finally give up her title of Mrs Gable, and head to Nevada for a divorce. The property matter had at last been settled and there was now no reason for the woman to drag her feet. Within six weeks, Clark Gable and Carole Lombard would finally be free to marry. For the couple, and the world's press, the time could not come soon enough.

In early February 1939, *Made for Each Other* was released. Selznick hoped that Carole and Clark would appear at the preview, but he was out of luck. Telling the producer that she always brought bad luck to previews, the actress cried off going to see it. The film opened anyway, and to mainly positive reviews. The *Independent Exhibitors Film Bulletin* said that Carole 'does herself proud in the dramatic role'. Their view of the film was good, if not a touch sexist:

> This poignant, touching comedy-drama of young married love is very much a woman's picture and will derive the bulk of its support from that contingent. Most men will find it a bit slow and may be annoyed

at the slow-thinking, bashful Mr. Milquetoast character created by James Stewart. On the other hand, the story is believable and human, sentimental but definitely entertaining. There is novelty in the fact that this is Carole Lombard's first dramatic role in a long time.

*Photoplay* told readers:

For the first three-quarters of its running time this is one of the finest pictures made for years in Hollywood. It paints a magnificent portrait of two un-exceptional, real people in the details of their life together; their problems, their happiness, their small miseries. With kindly touch and deep understanding, but often with brutality, it tells their simple story. Then, quite suddenly, the touch is lost, the plot goes wild and so does the screen. You are confronted with melodrama. There is a dying child, a mercy flight through a storm, a parachute jump and Carole Lombard prays in a chapel. Heaven knows she does it well. But you must try and forget about this finale. Instead give all your energies to the section that is great.

The film caused something of an upturn in Carole's fortunes, and the journalists who had grown tired of her screwball reputation began seeing her in a different light. British reporter, Hubert Cole, said:

Personally I think she's making the comeback pretty well, which is a strange thing to say of an actress who has scored some of the biggest hits of recent years. Yet it is a comeback that Carole needs. A comeback to sanity. I don't think she's ever going to be a great dramatic actress. I hope she'll never get too inextricably mixed up in crazy comedy again. But I do believe she has a considerable future as an interpreter of American youth.

'Yeah, yeah, I know,' Carole told reporter May Mann:

You gotta give the public what it wants. When it wants you dippy, be dippy and when it wants you glamorous, then turn on the glamour. I've played all the dizzy-dame parts I'm going to. It was a cycle of comic roles, but believe me I can be dramatically serious when I want to be.

Thinking towards her next role, Selznick International had a small problem. Their schedule was mainly taken up with *Gone with the Wind*, and Dan O'Shea did not know how they would be able to fit in another project with Carole before the end of 1939. He expressed his concerns to David O. Selznick on 7 February and recommended they seek an extension on her contract. Knowing just how much trouble the last contract had been, renegotiating an extension was not high on Selznick's list of priorities. Instead, he told O'Shea that he was sure they could find a project for the actress and they should talk again in March.

One thing he would like to change, however, was the deal they had in terms of payment. Still obsessing about the RKO percentage deal, Selznick once again requested the finer details to be sent to him and told O'Shea that, under the circumstances, they should be able to get the same kind of deal. Meanwhile, Carole's agent was more than concerned about the next picture and Myron telephoned his brother to find out what was going on. David assured him – as he did with O'Shea – that the matter was in hand and a story would be found.

This was not enough for the agency, however, and on 15 February representative Dan Winkler sent a letter to Dan O'Shea, reminding him that they had a definite commitment to make a movie before the end of the year. A rather sarcastic letter was returned shortly after, thanking him for calling the matter to their attention and asking him to remind them again within thirty days; they would consider the matter then. Obviously sensing the sarcasm, Winkler returned a note instructing O'Shea to write a note in his diary reminding him to reread the letter on or around the 30 March 1939.

By this time *Gone with the Wind* had begun shooting and Selznick was desperate to see his stars support the movie in every way possible, including making a special appearance at the Academy Award dinner on 23 February. The idea made Carole and Clark nauseous and it was left to the actress to let Selznick know. Instead of telephoning him directly, on 17 February Carole wrote him a warm, friendly letter. Addressing him as 'My dear, dear David', the actress got straight to the point and said there was simply no way the couple would appear at the dinner. First of all, they were trying to remain out of the spotlight as much as they could 'because of the old lady', and secondly, they just did not wish to go.

Citing the fact that award shows only lead to bitterness and jealousy, Carole told Selznick that the couple now only did things that made them happy. Since there was so much negativity at award events, their being there would only lead to unhappiness. This, she said, was why Hollywood was such a messed up town. Carole then went on to give the producer some sage advice: relax, stop worrying, enjoy life and be happy. She ended by declaring her intention to always make Selznick happy, but once again warned him not to ask or expect that she and Gable go to the Academy Award dinner. 'We die if we have to go out for an evening,' she said. 'When there's something important going on – like an Academy dinner – we have scouts who call us up and tell us what is happening.'

The letter to Selznick was heartfelt and poetic, and what's more it prompted the producer to sit down and take stock. He wrote back several days later to tell Carole that he fully understood what she was saying, and in fact, her philosophy had impressed him so much that he was seriously wondering why he was going to the event himself. He signed off with a note to say that he hoped once *Gone with the Wind* was finished he would have learned something about happiness from the couple.

On 23 February 1939 Carole wrote a guest spot for the popular Ed Sullivan column, syndicated to newspapers around the United States. It was funny, it was sarcastic and it was full of news and observations on Hollywood and beyond. The article was good news for the Selznick studio. In the story she not only praised the acting talent of co-star Jimmy Stewart, but also gave some behind-the-scenes gossip about the construction of the main Selznick building. She told readers that it was one of the most beautiful of all the studios; a thought that lead an excited Russell Birdwell to share the article with Selznick himself.

While Carole was busying herself with home and career, her mother, Elizabeth, was keeping occupied too, but in quite a different way. Having always been a campaigner, she now decided to go to court to put right what she considered a huge wrong. When Elizabeth's grandfather, James Cheney, had passed away in 1903, he left an estate worth well over $1 million. It was then distributed between his three daughters (including Elizabeth's mother, Alice) and $15,000 was left to his son, Willard. However, the three daughters agreed that their brother should have an equal share of the estate, which was what ultimately happened. On Willard's death in 1923, it was decided that his widow, Nancy, could continue with the inheritance until her own death, but it was always understood that when she passed away the money would revert back to the estate. However, when Nancy eventually did die at the end of 1936 this did not become the case. Instead, her money was willed to a number of relatives and charitable organisations.

Because of her forceful nature, Elizabeth was elected to represent sixteen heirs; all convinced that the money should come to them. When she went to court in early March 1939, she did so with a great deal of guts and chutzpah. Wearing a large hat and a stern smile, she gave her version of events. The judge listened carefully, looked at vast amounts of property transfers and heard from a Cheney friend who claimed Nancy never mentioned leaving any money to her in-laws. It was a stressful situation, made more so because it became tied up in the courts for several years. The case eventually went in Elizabeth's favour, but not until 1941 – years after she had originally brought the suit.

While Carole was interested and concerned with her mother's case, she had more pressing things on her mind; namely the fact that Rhea Gable had finally returned from Nevada. This unprecedented event left Gable free to marry Carole at last. The actress desperately wanted a quiet wedding, just as she had when marrying William Powell. However, this time things were different. She was a huge star and her fiancé was the King of Hollywood, and Rhett Butler to boot. This caused problems because the press was determined to gate-crash proceedings and began camping outside both Carole and Gable's homes. Reporters said they saw Carole planting petunias in her garden, and Gable riding a tractor and working on his chicken coop. Neither would answer their shouts for a comment, and instead remained tight-lipped on where and when the ceremony would take place.

Finally, on 29 March 1939, the couple sneaked into Gable's car with MGM publicity man Otto Winkler and headed off to Kingman, Arizona. Once there, they applied for a marriage licence, almost rendering clerk Viola Olsen speechless as they did so. There then followed a small ceremony during which Carole omitted the word 'obey' from her vows; a small matter that garnered lots of media stories the next day.

When it was over, Carole telephoned her mother, Elizabeth, to share the news and during the call Gable happily introduced himself as the new son-in-law. Once the news had been relayed, Carole told their witness – local high school principal Howard Cate – that they were headed to Boulder City on honeymoon. This was actually a red herring designed to fool the press. In fact, the couple went straight back to California and arrived at Carole's home in the middle of the night. The next morning the newlyweds were greeted by the world's media, where they gave a small press conference.

The questions asked that day were of a highly personal nature, but the couple tried to answer with typical aplomb. A short time later the couple headed to the Encino ranch where they were to spend the rest of their married life. As they entered the property, they were surprised and delighted to find a wedding present from David O. Selznick and his wife, Irene. Describing themselves as 'completely overcome', Carole sent a short note to the couple, saying that the Selznicks always did the sweetest things. She then signed off with a 'We love you' declaration.

While Carole was speaking on behalf of both herself and her new husband, the reality of Gable telling David O. Selznick just how much he loved him was pretty remote. By now he was deeply engrossed in the filming of *Gone with the Wind* and his relationship with the producer was fairly strained. The film was a massive spectacle that required a huge amount of input from everyone involved. Long hours, stunts and media intrusion coupled with exhaustion and the firing of several key crew members only intensified matters.

While Gable was on set, Carole set up home in the Encino ranch. Although she had actually lived there unofficially for a little while – keeping her own house more or less for appearance sake only – now everything was different. This was now Carole's official residence and she revelled in spending time there. Gable felt the same way and whenever the couple had any time off from the studio both could be seen on the ranch. There, Carole would look after their animals and arrange the house while her husband tended to fences and rode his tractor. This down-to-basics lifestyle was exactly what the couple – particularly Gable – craved.

'I started fixing up the house,' he told reporter James Reid:

Then I went at the barn. I took a trip out to Adohr Milk Farms and looked the establishment over; then I built a replica of it, in every detail, for three cows. Then I started looking over the fields and the orchards. All the farm machinery out in this country is big stuff; too big for a place the size of mine. So I sent back to Indiana for a one-man harrow, and a reaper, and some other stuff – and a mule to haul it. Yeah, I've even got a mule. And chickens. When I eat a chicken, I know what went into the bird. And I know my scrambled eggs are fresh. And those vegetables – they taste like nothing you can get in town.

By May 1939 David O. Selznick was concerned that the studio should find another vehicle for Carole, or else risk having to pay her despite not doing any work. Selznick did not want things to get that far, but at the same time he had his hands full with *Gone with the Wind*. He wrote to colleagues asking them to find something for Carole, so long as it wasn't comedy. Several films were proposed, including *Anna Christie*, *The Letter* and *The Doll's House*. There was a problem though, and that was once again centred round contract issues.

For some time it had been suggested that the current contract be revised slightly, particularly regarding payment, dates and outside pictures. Everyone seemed to be in agreement and it was believed that the revised document would be signed in March 1939. This had not happened, however, and on 30 May a very stern letter was sent from David O. Selznick to Sig Marcus at the Myron Selznick Agency. In the note, he described their behaviour as 'inexcusable' and added that he believed this to be a perfect example of how difficult it was to get anything done with the agency office.

The very next day, he sent a memo to Dan O'Shea telling him that they should try and do a movie with Vivien Leigh and notify Carole that they would not be working with her until much later. Several days after, he told him that the previously discussed *Doll's House* would be a good vehicle for Leigh, not Lombard. The revised contract was eventually signed towards the end of summer 1939, but the experience left a bitter taste.

When Gable finished up principal photography on *Gone with the Wind*, life on the ranch became fairly quiet. Yet the couple's peace threatened to be shattered at the end of July 1939. On 30 July a young man by the name of Willard Broski somehow gained access to the Gable property and, without the couple's knowledge, managed to peak at some rifles and guns that the actor kept in his private gun room. Seeing an opportunity to make some money, the 18-year-old stayed on the property overnight with the intention of stealing the items the next day. He then made friends with the Gables' guard dog (prompting the couple to nickname him 'Old Dependable') and made himself comfortable in the garage.

The next morning, when Clark was in the orchard and Carole had left for the day, Broski managed to gain access to the property while the servants' backs were turned. Unaware that there was anything wrong, Gable went back to the house and straight upstairs for a shower. The next thing he knew, he was face to face with Broski, who had been hiding behind his door with the actor's gun sticking out of his jacket. Gable wasted no time. 'I let him have it behind the ear,' he told reporter Peter Martin of the *Saturday Evening Post*. Then he grabbed Broski, threw him to the floor and took the gun away from him, but a scuffle broke out when Gable insisted the intruder accompany him downstairs. After much shouting and drama they both eventually arrived in the kitchen, where Gable noticed how young the intruder was and started to lecture him about the perils of breaking into someone else's house. The talk did nothing to calm the young man, however, and the actor eventually ended up calling the police. 'If he had shown any remorse I wouldn't have called the cops,' the actor said.

Broski was taken to the local station and Gable was called to testify against him. In true form, Carole burst into laughter when she heard of her husband's heroics, but recovered in time to accompany her husband and their two servants to court. Sitting in the public gallery, they watched as Gable explained what had happened. The judge bound Broski over on a burglary charge and told him to come back to court on 19 August to be arraigned. The Gables never heard from the young man again, but did sympathise with him. 'I am sorry it happened,' Clark told reporters outside the courtroom. 'He's only a boy who got off on the wrong foot. I hope he gets off without too much trouble.'

Back on the ranch, Carole and Clark continued to enjoy their country living, but despite being out of Hollywood they were still occasionally bothered by fans and the curious. In the end they installed a large electric gate to keep people out. The reason for this was explained by Gable, to reporter James Reid:

> I understand the word's out that Gable's changed – he's keeping people at a distance because I put up an electric gate and a No Trespassing sign. Let me tell you how that happened. I was working out by the barn late one afternoon when a car with three men drove in. One of them was in uniform. He got out and came over to where the farmer and I were putting some pipe together. 'Mr. Gable,' he said. 'I drive for one of the bus companies that make regular tours of the Valley. We pass by your place every day. Mighty pretty place. We think folks would like to see it. Would you be willing to let us drive in? We wouldn't stop or anything. I've been looking over the layout – and the bus could turn around right over there.' He pointed.
>
> Before I could say anything, my farmer said, 'Why you —! Get!' And he got. How would you like it if strangers just opened your gate and wandered in, at odd hours? Wouldn't you want to get a gate they couldn't open? I'm no hermit. I'm an easy guy to meet during working hours, but when I get home, I want to be able to relax. You feel the same way. Anybody does.

While they craved privacy, the couple did temporarily let down their guard and invited photographer Clarence Bull and his assistant, Eric Carpenter, to spend the day with them. Their time was relaxed and happy, and the couple were dressed appropriately for time on the farm. 'I hope we'll look hearts and flowery,' Carole exclaimed, as she introduced Bull to Gable's horse, their chickens and various other members of the family.

At one point a dog called Toughy appeared, covered in mud, and shook himself all over Carole's trousers. 'He's a philosopher,' she told Bull. 'He likes to play all day and sit down at night and think. Sometimes he thinks out loud and his barking scares the owls for miles around. He has a terrific time trying to explain that he means no harm and is only thinking.' Bull found the couple to be totally relaxed in each other's company, and they even served the photographer and his assistant a homemade lunch on the porch.

Reporter Ruth Waterbury interviewed Gable while on set at MGM. She was there on the pretext of asking about his upcoming film, *Gone with the Wind*, but it was Gable's wife who dominated the conversation. 'Carole is the best business woman I know,' he said. 'Plus being the finest hostess, the cleverest manager and the best sport ever, all of which adds up to a lot of girl.'

One of the most memorable pieces of the interview was when Waterbury asked if the couple intended to have children. 'You bet,' said Gable:

There's been a story published to the effect that we expect to adopt some. That's not true. We'll have our own. When they come, of course, our present scheme of living will necessarily change and I'll bear all the financial burdens, but until then Carole and I live as free personalities. If that sounds as though we were, either of us, seeking too much freedom in marriage, I can honestly say we've found it works out just the opposite. When I want to do something Carole doesn't want to do – like going on a hunting trip, say – I've discovered, the few times I've tried it, that without her it's no fun. I want to do the things she wants to do, not alone to make her happy, but because sharing them with her actually makes me happier. Carole says it's that way with her, too. She is happiest doing what I want to do. Maybe that's what love really is: getting your greatest pleasure out of doing what the other desires and liking the fact that your thinking of the other guy's happiness just makes you happier than insisting upon your own. At any rate, that's the standard Carole and I have set for our marriage. What's more, you wait and see we'll make it stick.

It was interesting that Gable mentioned financial responsibilities. In another part of the interview, he told the reporter that he bought the Encino ranch himself but that he and Carole each paid their own way in terms of living expenses and pocket money. Any money left over from that was kept in their own separate accounts. 'There is nothing holding me and Carole together but love,' he told Waterbury. While this was a beautiful sentiment, it has been widely discussed in the years since that it was Carole who bought the ranch, not Gable.

The actress rarely discussed anything so personal with reporters, though she did provide a quote about finding the ranch to reporter Adele Whitley-Fletcher. This seems to point in the direction of the couple buying the property together:

> I'll never forget the day the real estate man called to tell me this place was for sale! It was just before we were married. I called Pa at the studios right away – even though we'd bought another place. 'How would you like the Raoul Walsh ranch?' I asked. He got choky. I could scarcely understand him. 'How would I like it?' he said. We closed the deal the same day – traded in the other property as part payment. It's wonderful here, and the taxes – they're nothing! We pay no more for these twenty acres than we'd pay for one elegant acre in town.

Carole's friend and assistant Madalynne Fields was there when the couple first looked around the place. 'I wish you could have seen Lombard the day she and Clark went to look over the ranch,' she said:

> I thought, 'Now! Now she's met her Waterloo! She can't possibly be up to this!' But she was up to it. She didn't stand in the middle of the living room and go into rhapsodies over a cute window. Not her! She investigated the plumbing. She found out all about the furnace. She instituted a thorough examination of all beams for signs of termites. And when they went into the kitchen she took a folding rule out of her bag, to measure the wall for an ice box.

# VIGIL IN THE NIGHT

*V*igil in the Night was due to film in summer 1939, for a release date of October 1939. Unfortunately, things did not go quite to plan when the actress was rushed to hospital with an acute attack of appendicitis. The infected organ was removed and she recovered at the Good Samaritan Hospital, with Gable at her side. On 4 August, newspapers around the country began reporting on the event, claiming that Carole had been admitted to hospital the day before, although an article in the 17 July edition of the *Winnipeg Free Press* seems to suggest otherwise.

Gable's friend and fellow actor, Andy Devine, was in Canada on a fishing trip and the press managed to track him down while he was there. They photographed him with a tiny fish, caught that morning, and asked about the trip. The actor told reporters that he was supposed to have been there with his hunting companion Gable, but at the last minute Carole had been rushed to hospital to have her appendix out. Clark cancelled the trip, but Devine hoped he would be able to go with him on another occasion.

This article was published over two weeks before the world's media caught on to the story. The 4 August announcement seems to be the result of RKO Radio Pictures – the studio behind *Vigil in the Night* – taking Carole off salary. At the same time that newspapers were telling the story of her illness, executives at the studio were writing to the stricken actress to tell her that, as from 2 August, she was suspended from her contract and would not be reinstated until she was ready, willing and able to go back to work.

On 17 August – a full month after the initial report – Carole sent a letter to her friend Nat, thanking her for a bouquet of flowers and telling her that she expected to be home the following week. At the same time, RKO created full-page adverts for the media, explaining that exhibitors would not be able to see *Vigil in the Night* in October as planned, due to Carole's illness. These were published on the back pages of many industry magazines on 22 August, and at the bottom of each one – almost as an afterthought – the studio wished the actress a speedy recovery. By early September Carole and Gable were in the High Sierras, where she was recuperating from her illness, then on 11 September 1939 the actress was back on set and taken off suspension.

While Carole was recovering, *In Name Only* was released. Co-starring Cary Grant and Kay Francis, the film told the story of a young widow (Lombard) who falls in love with a married man (Grant). Luckily for her, he is married in name only; his wife (Francis) being in it purely for the money. While this should have made the story fairly simple, of course nothing goes to plan and the scorned wife does everything in her power to delay the inevitable. Add a case of pneumonia and a hospital sick room to the mix, and the plot was pretty much complete.

Ticket sales for the film were good and RKO took out full-page adverts in fan magazines, telling readers that *In Name Only* enjoyed the biggest opening day of any of their pictures. For the most part, critics seemed to enjoy the story. *Motion Picture Daily* said:

With names as potent as Carole Lombard, Cary Grant and Kay Francis for the marquee and a title that strikes back into mellowed memory, it is hard to see how this up-to-date treatment of a theme already old when kerosene footlights gave way to incandescents can fail to bring the moderns, their parents, and even their parents, to the cinema in droves.

*Photoplay* told readers, 'If you're the pushover for Cary Grant and Carole Lombard we think you are, this will be worth every long minute you sit watching it – it is just such good acting.' Strangely, however, a number of vocal fans wrote to magazines to complain about Carole's appearance, saying that she should never have appeared in the movie with her hair scraped back from her high forehead, or tucked behind her ears. One fan wrote a scathing letter to *Photoplay*:

> The Kay Francis banner still waves on high and in the recent turn of events, Miss Francis has more fully established her position in motion pictures. Her performance in the RKO picture, *In Name Only*, left nothing for Carole Lombard in the way of credit for acting or personal appearance. Indeed, Miss Lombard, since she appeared with Kay Francis, has been greatly criticised by the press and public for her lack of chic in dress and make-up, and for her insufficient grasp of her role as the other woman. This case of a star taking a secondary role in a picture proves that sooner or later the work of a capable individual will speak for itself. Alone, Carole Lombard has held her own in many a picture, but, given every advantage in star privileges, she was a poor second to Kay Francis. She is not to be blamed either, because it is not her fault. It is just that the producers should never have exposed her to comparison with Miss Francis, who is an experienced actress with an innate sense of good showmanship.

Another person not keen on *In Name Only* was David O. Selznick. He wrote to colleagues to complain that the camera set-ups were very close to those used in *Made for Each Other*, and that the film also had Charles Coburn in a supporting role. Despite his reservations, however, he was very interested to see exactly how well it did at the box office, and asked colleagues for information not only on that, but on the audience reaction to Carole too.

The script for her next movie, *Vigil in the Night*, had been a problem from the very beginning. Originally the writer was to be Norman

Krasna, but he fell ill and withdrew from the project. Other writers were assigned, but the finished screenplay – at 145 pages – was just too long. Pandro S. Berman, the executive in charge of production, suggested they edit out 1,000 lines of dialogue and thirty pages, before going any further. The final film was officially ninety-four minutes long, though the addition of another scene in some international markets made it longer.

The story itself was based in England and revolved around a young nurse (Lombard) who has taken the blame for the death of a young child, due to the negligence of her sister, also a nurse. She goes to another hospital and falls in love with Dr Prescott (Brian Aherne), where a scandal and then a health epidemic threaten to derail not only their romance but her career.

It was a dark movie and, as a result, the atmosphere on set threatened to be depressive, though Carole was never known to brood for long. 'I don't feel depressed for more than five minutes at a time,' she told reporter Gladys Hall:

I'm very seldom depressed. Never morbid. I wouldn't let it get that far. And the only time I'm depressed is when I'm bored. And when I'm bored it's always with myself, no one and nothing else. And when I get bored with myself, find myself uninteresting, it's because my vitality is in low key. And when that happens I just strap on a sandal and do something about it. I never sit and brood.

Carole thought of ways to bring light to the set and began with director George Stevens. He was a quiet man; a deep thinker. Every day he would take a break and sit in silence, lost in his own thoughts. No matter how much she tried, or how many jokes she told, nothing would pull him out of his thinking time.

Finally Carole discovered that he was a keen duck hunter and so invited him to join Gable and herself on a weekend outing to Bakersfield. The director declined because he believed the best hunting spot was Imperial Valley. At the end of the working week, Stevens went there and found no ducks at all. When Carole got wind of this, she saw the perfect opportunity for a prank. She brought dozens of ducks – living and otherwise – to the set, put them all around the place and displayed a card. 'Personally, we didn't have any trouble finding ducks,' it said.

Stevens liked Carole a great deal. 'It's difficult to discuss Carole Lombard,' he said:

> She's so good that there's the danger of speaking only in superlatives, and having it sound like a lot of goo. The thing that strikes me about Carole's talent is her imagination, her creativeness … She is blessed, further, with a perfect degree of detachment. She can do a gripping scene, stop it, and a second later discuss what she'll eat for dinner. This sometimes upsets her co-players, who think she can't be very interested in the role. But they just don't understand her.
>
> The most marvellous thing about Carole is the way she can throw herself entirely into a scene. I'll never forget one bit in *Vigil in the Night*. In the script her sister had just died and Carole came into her room and wearily hung up her coat. It was a very tense scene. We shot it once and no soap. Tried again, and I still wasn't satisfied. The third time, Carole shuffled in, put up her coat, wavered and toppled over! I thought it was a gag – but she almost killed herself falling into the nearby sink, and I then learned she'd fainted. Sure, fainted from trying so hard, being so emotional, imagining she had a sister who had just died. Do I have to tell you more about Lombard, after that?

Production closed on 29 November 1939 (although she returned for a day's retakes in January 1940) and, shortly after, Carole's stand-in was rushed to hospital with a case of pneumonia. The actress heard about the misery that had befallen her and immediately arranged to pay her hospital bills. When the woman returned home, she found an envelope waiting for her. Inside was two weeks wages; enough to tide her over until she could get back to work.

The stand-in wasn't the only person Carole cared for while times were tough. Photographer John Engstead described a time when he was ill and she arranged for the Brown Derby restaurant to send him some food. 'And in through the door came that,' he remembered:

Then it was time for a laugh, and Carole could always figure out a gag. And then came what she called 'the important gift' – something that a person could keep after the hospital days were over. When Mitchell Leisen was ill, she sent him a handsome comforter, for instance, and one of the girls at Paramount was given a stunning bed jacket. And finally Carole made a personal call. She followed this routine on all occasions. No one knew how she found the time – but she did.

*Vigil in the Night* was not going to be released for a little while yet, but one film that was close to being premiered was *Gone with the Wind*. The couple were eager to see an advance print and contacted David O. Selznick's office to ask about the possibility of themselves and a few friends viewing it in private. Selznick was not terribly keen on the idea. First of all, he was about to do final edits, which meant that anything they saw may not be in the final picture. Secondly, he wanted them to be able to see it in a public theatre – somewhere out of the way, where they would not be recognised – so that they could experience the audience reaction.

The couple did end up seeing a print of the movie, and Carole told reporters that her husband was fabulous in it. However, the official premiere – a very grand affair – was planned in Atlanta, which would require the presence of all cast members and promised to be the event of the year. As soon as Gable received word that he would have to attend, he refused. For what it was worth, Carole did not want to go either. She was just finishing work on her latest picture and wanted nothing to do with the drama of a gala premiere. David O. Selznick pleaded with her but she stuck her heels in, determined that, while Gable needed to be there, she had no obligation to the picture at all. There was nothing Selznick could do but begrudgingly accept her decision.

The last week of November 1939 was a very stressful one for Selznick. Gable decided that he would come to the premiere after all, but made it clear that he was not there because he wanted to be. The same went for Vivien Leigh, and Selznick described them both as 'squawking their heads off' about having to attend. Not only that, Gable called executives at MGM and gave word that while he may have to attend the premiere, he most certainly had no plans to go to the Junior League

Ball, due to take place after the event. In the end he did go, but not without some coaxing.

Meanwhile, word spread of Carole Lombard's planned absence from the entire event, and colleague Katharine Brown contacted Selznick on 25 November to tell him what a mistake it would be if she didn't come. He was in no mood for any more drama and sent a reply demanding to know exactly who it would be a mistake for? He added that just because fans wanted her there was no reason to plead for her presence, particularly as she could normally earn $5,000 for her own publicity appearances. With the other stars in attendance, he could not understand why anyone would be in such dire need of her presence anyway. In the end, Lombard did decide to go to the premiere, but for no other reason than she was sure Gable would back out if left to his own devices.

The premiere, held at Loew's Grand on 15 December, was a spectacle like no other. The stars of the film, as well as Carole herself, were all driven through the crowded streets and greeted madly by media and fans alike. Each actor was expected to make a speech and Carole was surprised when she too was thrust towards the microphone. After standing for several seconds, a voice boomed, 'Say something Carole!' She smiled and then in a small voice announced, 'I'm so happy to be here with you all. I'm going to let Mr. Gable do the talking for all of us but I love all of you.'

Whatever reservations Clark had about the appearance were long gone by this time, and the actor gave a speech which was short and humble:

> Ladies and gentleman, tonight I'm here just as a spectator. I want to see *Gone with the Wind* the same as you do, and this is Margaret Mitchell's night and the people of Atlanta's night. Allow me please to see *Gone with the Wind* as a spectator. Thank you.

A young man then gate-crashed proceedings and gleefully had his photo taken with the Gables, before the party entered the theatre and watched the four-hour-long masterpiece.

The event was a magnificent success. Not only did fans enjoy seeing Gable and Lombard, but they also appreciated what one reader described as their 'down-to-earth good-fellowship'. This observation came as a result of the couple signing autographs and posing for a great many photographs during and after the event, and led columnist Jimmie Fidler to exclaim that all celebrities should behave in such a manner.

'I like the picture,' Gable said:

I think it's a good one, but that doesn't mean a thing. I got paid for making it. Besides, any ham likes any picture that gives him a meaty role. And what the critics say doesn't mean too much, either. They see shows on passes. The opinion I'm waiting for is the opinion of the fellow who plunks down thirty-five cents of his own hard-earned dough to see it.

With *Gone with the Wind* turning into a magnificent success both critically and at the box office (though Gable ultimately missed out on an Oscar for his role), people wondered if the glory would go to the actor's head. He pondered the thought with reporter James Reid:

Why in the name of common logic, should Rhett change my whole life? The picture was in production five months; the rest of the time it was in the cutting-room and the Technicolor works. I was in it about two and a half months. I worked longer in both *Mutiny on the Bounty* and *San Francisco*. And the only times I worked at being Rhett during those two and a half months, was when I was in front of a camera. Maybe you can picture me trying to be Rhett around home. You know the ribbing I'd get [from Carole] and no mercy whatsoever.

19

# REAL LIFE VERSUS FAIRY TALE

By the time 1940 rolled around, 31-year-old Carole was thinking seriously about her future and in particular what movie she should make next. In mid-January she telephoned Myron Selznick and made it clear to him that she would like to go ahead with the third picture promised to his brother, David.

For Carole, this was a controversial decision. Since working on *Gone with the Wind*, the tensions between Gable and the producer had come to breaking point. There was no love lost between the pair and Gable made it clear that he had no intention of working with him in the near future. However, Carole saw Selznick differently. She had enjoyed making *Nothing Sacred* and *Made for Each Other*, and despite a few hiccups the interaction between herself and the producer was always cordial. She saw absolutely no reason why she shouldn't fulfil her third picture deal, and wanted to do so as soon as possible.

David O. Selznick thought otherwise. A few months before, Dan O'Shea had wondered aloud if it might be best just to settle with the actress, instead of making another movie. His reasoning was that they already had Joan Fontaine, Ingrid Bergman and Vivien Leigh under contract, and they were not only exclusive but also cheaper. Added to that, the movies Carole had made with the studio had not been as successful as Selznick hoped and therefore he didn't have much confidence in another.

O'Shea took his concerns to Myron Selznick and promised that the studio would pay Carole $25,000 to forget the next movie for the moment, provided they could have the option to do another with the same conditions within a year. The payment would then be used against any future project, should the need arise. Myron laughed at O'Shea and told him he would be ignoring the request. Would he be prepared to just discuss it with the actress, he was asked? 'Absolutely not', came the reply.

Because Myron had not passed the message to Carole, she was in the dark and still eager to begin another picture. She asked Myron to pass on the message and then, when Selznick did not make a favourable move, another message came. Then another. Finally, on 19 January 1940 the producer sat down and wrote a letter to the actress that was so personal and honest, it took him three days to complete. In the two-page document, Selznick told Carole that he had always thought of working with her as one of the most pleasant experiences of his career, and acknowledged that whenever he had a problem as a producer on set, she would not only appreciate the dilemma, but help resolve it too. He knew she liked him as a work colleague and person, but understood only too well that Gable felt differently. This, he explained, was most certainly a problem and she was bound to receive repercussions in her personal life if she did decide to go through with another picture. Finally Selznick told the actress that, taking everything into account, he was more than willing to let her out of her obligation to make another movie with him, but the final decision would be hers.

The letter was sent on 22 January 1940, and then the very next day Selznick contacted his associate, Dan O'Shea, to talk about making yet another change to Carole's contract. This time, he wondered, if they went ahead with a third project perhaps she should take far less money than they had previously paid, or perhaps just a percentage of the profits?

While all this was going on, Carole and Gable left their home and headed south to Ensenada, a coastal city in Mexico, where they intended to take a month-long ranch vacation. The holiday was exactly what Gable needed after *Gone with the Wind*. The trip would have been perfect had the couple not decided to take a short visit to the Hattie Hamilton Ranch to do some hunting. Once there, they were disappointed with the results so left to go to another ranch, a short trip away. However, an almighty rainstorm hit, sending mud and clay cascading onto the road. Traffic came to a halt and a bus became stuck in the mud, making it impossible for them to drive round. They were stuck in their station wagon with no means of communication.

Meanwhile, MGM employees Otto Winkler and Eric Carpenter travelled to Ensenada to spend time with Gable on his birthday. On their arrival they were shocked to discover that the couple had not returned to their base. They grew increasingly worried and, in the end, Winkler arranged for a search party to be sent out to find them. On 2 February, various press reports were published about the disappearance, though MGM played down the drama and told waiting journalists that they were unconcerned. They were right not to worry as, by noon, Gable and Lombard managed to get to a phone in order to tell everyone that they were safe and well.

While everything was simmering down after the mysterious disappearance, *Vigil in the Night* was released. Some reviewers enjoyed the powerful drama and gave it good mention in their columns. Others did not appreciate the painful and gritty story about the English hospital system, and said so in their reviews. The *Showmen's Trade Review* called it:

> … a heavy, emotional drama reaching the highest standard in every department, whose only drawback is the lack of comedy relief. It has been presented in a very sombre manner, that makes no concessions for the average audience entertainment, and its box office draw, therefore, will depend largely upon the manner in which it is sold.

They were more positive about Carole's performance, and said that she 'proves her versatility as a splendid actress, by giving one of the finest dramatic performances ever to reach the screen'.

Back at Selznick, a film project had been offered to Carole; an adaptation of the play, *The Flashing Stream* by Charles Morgan. The idea was for Alfred Hitchcock to direct and also work on the script; a concept originally reported in newspapers during early 1939. At the time, Hitchcock had declined to offer Carole the role, as he felt nothing he'd seen her in could help determine whether she'd be any good. He did think she had a great sex appeal, but as for acting, he was undecided. The director was given more movies to watch, and executives presented the project to Carole as a possibility. She was not enthusiastic about it, and had also got wind that Hitchcock was not keen either. Nothing had come of the project, but now in 1940, faced with the possibility that she may like to work with him again, Selznick was keen to get things moving.

Myron Selznick approached the actress to see if she would sign up for the film, but she turned him down. There was no way she would act the part, she said. In fact she was absolutely dead set against having anything whatsoever to do with it. Myron took the news to Dan O'Shea, who was disappointed but wondered if her decision was just based on her remembrance of the play. He hoped that by the time Hitchcock was through with the script she would change her mind, and sent a memo to David O. Selznick to tell him this.

Before Selznick was able to reply, Myron telephoned O'Shea again. This time he had apparently told Carole about the $25,000 settlement and she was keen to take it. The surprised executive told Myron he would take the matter to Selznick and thirty minutes later he was back on the phone. This time, not only was Myron in the office, but Carole too. O'Shea told both that they would pay the $25,000, but only on the condition that the actress could give them the option on her services within the next year. She refused to put anything in writing, but told O'Shea that she would always be happy to work with David in the future, if and when he needed her.

Selznick then spoke to Myron himself, during which time they discussed future projects with three French producers and the possibility of buying *The Man who Came to Dinner*. After the call, it occurred to him that perhaps a role in this movie could be given to Lombard, but made it clear that this should only be an option if the company was unable to make a settlement. In the end the film was not offered to Carole, and both parties decided to go their separate ways. On 14 March a cheque was written for $25,000 and a letter drawn up to release the actress from her obligations for another film. Despite any hold-ups in the past, this agreement was signed by the actress straight away. Carole would never work with Selznick again and Dan O'Shea always held the suspicion that the actress and her agent only settled to make way for a better contract with RKO.

He could have been correct. On 29 May 1940, Carole began work on the RKO picture, *They Knew What They Wanted*, and welcomed heavyweight columnist Hedda Hopper into her dressing room. While the two were cordial over the years, the reporter was not particularly enamoured by her on this occasion, and gave a pretty blunt write-up in her newspaper column. Describing her as wearing a $2.50 wardrobe, Hopper told Carole that she was sick of seeing her onscreen in cheap dresses and uniforms. When director Garson Kanin came over to talk, he told Hopper that Carole was the best producer in Hollywood. This was fine praise for someone who had never officially been credited as producer, though Hopper was not impressed. 'They'd better hurry up and prove it,' she wrote in her column.

Kanin adored Lombard. 'She acts entirely with the heart,' he said:

She has a faultless instinct, a mystical feel, for right and wrong. She doesn't know how or why she does things, but she does them unerringly. I have worked with many people and seen many greats in action. Irene Dunne and Bette Davis both act with their heads. Charles Laughton, one big exposed nerve, acts with his stomach. That is, when he does a scene wrong, he gets a pang in his stomach. But with Carole Lombard, it's intuition. She feels a scene and plays it. She's remarkably good.

The most important thing I've learned about her is that she can completely get out of herself. Before I worked with her I wondered if she had that ability. You see, Hollywood has more personalities than actors. Most men and women who walk on the screen are themselves and nothing more. But take my word for it; in *They Knew What They Wanted*, Carole is different. She does not just repeat her real or reel personality. She's the character in the story, the waitress who falls in love by correspondence. The first scene we shot, her voice pitched differently, her very movements changed. All of this makes me feel that Carole Lombard has more talent than has ever been tapped. I want to make this prediction – that while other stars become dated and obsolete by additional calories or wrinkles, Carole Lombard will go on acting as long as she wants to. She's got that much on the ball.

Carole wrapped on *They Knew What They Wanted* on 3 August 1940, and was due to go to Universal by the 15th to start production on a movie entitled *Glamour*. However, the project was cancelled and instead she decided to spend a relaxing summer at home. Life on the farm grew more and more enticing and she longed for children.

Carole had never been secretive about her desire. Back in 1932, while she was still married to Bill Powell, she had made her intentions clear to reporter Laura Ellsworth Fitch:

Naturally [I want a family], but not until I'm entirely through with pictures. Never before that. It would be a rotten trick to play on a child, giving it a mother who called out, 'Good morning, dear,' as she left for the studio, got home in time to see it tucked into bed, and occasionally summoned it out to say, 'Curtsy for the ladies.' I think that is dreadful. When I was a child I had such fun with my mother I'd feel like a thief if I deprived my own children of that happiness. And too, from a purely selfish viewpoint, what is the sense of having a child if you can't constantly watch its subtle growth and development every day?

As Lombard became more interested in spending time away from the studio, her plans to become a mother were put into motion. Gable was keen too, but unfortunately, no matter how much the couple wished for it, no pregnancy was forthcoming. Over the coming year, both Carole and Gable would undergo a series of tests in order to find a solution to their conception problems, but the situation remained unresolved.

This sad matter was further complicated by the fact that Gable knew there was nothing wrong with him in that department, as he had already fathered a secret child with actress Loretta Young in 1935. The actress hid the pregnancy successfully from the press, and when the baby was born she sent the child away to an orphanage, only to 'adopt' her some time later. This 'heroic gesture' made sure the actress's career and good reputation stayed intact. For his part, Gable apparently only met his child on one or two occasions and never had a relationship with her.

Away from the difficulty of becoming pregnant, there was another obstacle in their relationship. There is absolutely no doubt at all that Clark Gable was madly in love with Carole Lombard, and vice versa. However, for many years he had lived the single life, even when he was previously married. He had flings with co-stars right under the nose of his two former wives and they seemed – to all intents and purposes – to just let it slide. Even though he had now won the love of his life, it is widely believed that Gable was never truly faithful or truthful with Carole, and rumours abound that he occasionally slept with co-stars throughout his married life.

While the two previous Mrs Gables may have turned the other cheek, Carole Lombard was never going to do that. She was an outspoken individual who demanded – and got – respect from everyone she was involved with. According to friends, the actress would often find out about Gable's dalliances and reprimand him severely. He would then tell her it wouldn't happen again, but would soon resort to his old ways.

The couple took their minds off personal issues by throwing themselves into work around the ranch. Journalist Adele Whitley-Fletcher was invited in for a tour when she was writing an article for *Photoplay*. As she arrived at the property, Fletcher saw Gable's tractor parked in the field and a station wagon on the driveway. Inside, in preparation for getting lost again, Carole had placed handmade cases with a first aid kit and thermos bottles. 'Carole found a man to make these cases just the way she wanted them,' Fletcher wrote. 'Before they were finished she had learned how to stitch leather and she was working on the bench beside him.'

Fletcher was impressed with the home, 'Their living room is far from elegant. It's better than elegant ... gay and comfortable and friendly. The furniture is maple. There are chintzes at the windows. The sofa is covered in bright yellow.' The journalist was even allowed access to Carole's bedroom and photographed a bedside table full of magazines, books and scripts. Despite slowing her acting career down, the actress told Fletcher that she had five films lined up that she could not wait to do.

Fletcher spoke about day-to-day life on the ranch with Carole's friend and tennis champion, Alice Marble. 'It's something to see Carole go into action,' she said:

> If someone particularly likes a Rum Collins that's what is served. If he makes a Run Collins especially, well he'll be put behind the bar. However, even when Jessie, the cook, is in the kitchen Carole takes nothing before dinner. She's too busy looking after things, talking to people. 'Come on in and help' she said to me one Sunday, on her way to the kitchen. I went. But I didn't help. She had the broilers under fire and two salads made before I could turn around. She didn't have to ask where things were, either. She knows her kitchen as intimately as any woman who does her own housework!

One group of fans who were very impressed with Carole and Clark's life on the farm was the California branch of the 4-H Club, a youth organisation for young people aged 10–21. The four Hs stood for head, heart, health and hand, and in 1940 their membership comprised boys and girls who had pledged clean living, clear thinking, good health and better farming. Because the Gables now seemed to do all of these things, it was felt that their involvement with the club would be highly beneficial.

On 16 July 1940, the leader of the California branch sent a heartfelt letter to the Gables, bypassing their agents and going straight to the ranch itself. In the note, the purpose of the 4-H Club was explained and the couple were asked to become members of the organisation. They were also invited to attend the club's regular meetings. Several days later, a large document was sent to publicist Russell Birdwell, explaining the various aspects of the society and telling the agent that an invitation to join the club had never been extended to any other motion picture personality. The purpose of joining would not be short-term publicity, it said, but a virtual Gable and Lombard fan club, with the opportunity to inspire with much more than just a signed photograph.

Birdwell was intrigued. He spoke to a representative on the telephone and was told that Carole would be invited to open the club's annual convention. During the day she would speak about farm versus city living, both on a personal and professional level. Birdwell jotted everything down and then put it to colleagues that they should approach Carole and Clark about the proposal. The team agreed that while the club's intentions mainly revolved around plans for Carole, Gable should definitely be included.

Birdwell told colleagues that the actor would probably love the prospect, and then made a big list of ideas for Carole's future involvement. Perhaps she could have a barbecue for club members at the ranch, he suggested. Or what about a dance, picnic or short play? She could even hold club meetings at her home and get to know the youths personally. The publicity, he felt, would extend to agricultural and farm magazines, as well as spilling over into the fan magazine market. The rep predicted that the publicity would be a great career move for the actress, show her to be real and down to earth and win her a crop of new fans.

While the couple's involvement would have been an amazing coup for the club, in the end real life got in the way. First of all, Gable was awaiting release of his next movie, *Boom Town*, and working on *Comrade X*. Carole, meanwhile, was about to see the release of *They Knew What They Wanted*, and by September 1940 was working on *Mr and Mrs Smith*.

The latter was an RKO comedy directed by Alfred Hitchcock and co-starring Robert Montgomery and Gene Raymond. It told the story of a young couple (Ann and David) who frequently quarrel but have vowed never to leave each other's company until each fight is resolved. At the end of one quarrel, Ann asks David if he would chose to marry her again if he had the option. He replies – a little light-heartedly – that no, he would not. That morning a gentleman pays David a visit, to tell him that because of a technicality his marriage is not legal. He then goes to tell Ann the same thing, confessing that he has just been to break the news to her husband. That evening, when David does not mention it to Ann, she comes to believe her husband no longer loves or wants to remarry her. She takes on her maiden name, throws David out and begins dating his business partner, Jeff. When the two go on a weekend trip to a winter resort, David follows them and by the end of the movie they are reunited.

The making of the film was relatively straightforward, though rumours surfaced that Alfred Hitchcock made Carole work under quite torturous conditions. One story was that the director put the actress into a bathtub for four hours in order to get one tiny shot, and then took five hours to film a particularly physical scene between Montgomery and Carole. Then, during a scene where Jane and Jeff get stuck on a fairground ride in the middle of a storm, Hitchcock apparently wanted to film it on the very last day so that if the actress caught pneumonia, it would not affect the schedule.

While her relationship with Hitchcock could be tense, Robert Montgomery and Carole had a relaxed friendship on set. When she found out that he was a Republican, cheering on their candidate Wendell Wilkie, she ordered in a box of Franklin D. Roosevelt stickers and plastered them all over the windscreen of Montgomery's car. He eventually got them off, only to find a new lot glued there again the next evening, and the evening after that …

The film gave Carole an opportunity to direct – if only for a few minutes – when Alfred Hitchcock did his infamous cameo appearance, walking down a street. The direction and accompanying photos were really only something of a publicity gimmick, but it worked, gaining many column inches in the weeks ahead. Hitchcock, it should be said, was apparently not overly happy with the finished film and would be quite dismissive of it in later years.

It seems he wasn't alone. While the film made a profit at the box office and garnered some positive reviews, other critics dismissed it. *Modern Screen* had the following to say:

> *Mr. and Mrs. Smith* is a comedy – and a pretty good one in spots – but it hasn't the pace or the timing which comedy (especially in American

films) must have. The story of *Mr. and Mrs. Smith* is the same comedy premise we've been kicking around in films for a year or so – two people are married, but they're not married, or are they? There have been about a dozen variations on this theme of late, and chances are that this is the picture which'll wash 'em all up. There can't be any more ways of twisting the theme around, we hope ... Thinking back on the film, it becomes obvious that there is a lot of good stuff in it; some of the business is screamingly funny. But a good deal of it is in shockingly bad taste – and almost all of it is paced in so lethargic and happy-go-lucky manner as to annoy. The only way this sort of thing can be sold is by playing it so fast that the audience doesn't get a chance to think. The audience will do a lot of thinking through this one.

*Screenland* was a little more optimistic, claiming that it would appeal:

... if you prefer style to substance, giggles to guffaws ... Maestro of movie melodrama, Alfred Hitchcock, turns to farce with satisfactory if not important results. His celebrated technique carries off inconsequential scenes with a certain dash and there are few dull moments in which to worry about wasted artistry. Carole Lombard is decorative and clever as the wife but before the film is finished her brittle charm wears a little thin.

# THE LAST HOORAH

As 1940 came to a close, Carole was embroiled in a major court case with Myron Selznick. It had all begun on 1 July when she took the shock decision to fire him as her agent, citing the fact that he had not given her career enough attention. He disagreed to such an extent that he took the matter to court; a decision that had hung over Carole's head for the second half of 1940.

The whole matter intrigued everyone at Selznick International. In November, David O. Selznick wrote to his lawyer, Barry Brannen, asking if he had any news or highlights he could share about the case. Then, on 4 December, he asked O'Shea if he ever remembered discussing Myron's share of ownership in the film company with Lombard. It could be guessed that the reason for the question stemmed from the belief that perhaps the actress had fired Myron in order to strip herself of any Selznick association whatsoever.

When it was discovered that Carole had cited Myron's drink problem for their lack of great work together, David was incensed. He asked O'Shea to discuss with Brannen why she hadn't thought about that before she signed with him twice and then recommended him to other actors, including her husband, Clark Gable. It was at this point that Carole's openness with David O. Selznick worked against her. He was willing to reveal that the actress had great suspicions about MGM and the late head of production, Irving Thalberg. She had told Selznick that she would never want Gable to sign another contract with MGM, and that Thalberg had basically pushed him into the last one. If Gable signed with Myron, she said, he would get a better deal because he was the only agent who had the nerve to stand his ground with producers. If all this was revealed, Selznick believed, it would show that Carole had believed in Myron and his abilities as an agent all along.

January 1941 got off to a stressful start. Not only was the arbitration looming, but also Carole's health was in question. With the couple still not being able to conceive, they travelled to John Hopkins Hospital in Baltimore for what they hoped would be a very quiet series of tests. The press soon discovered their whereabouts, however, forcing them to release a statement saying that Gable had been admitted on account of a shoulder injury. At the same time – according to the statement – Carole had received a check-up and it was decided she needed to be operated on.

The exact nature of the operation was not discussed, though the revelation that it would be performed by chief gynaecologist Richard W. TeLinde, made clear the kind of procedure it would be. When the couple left hospital, the story had changed slightly. This time the couple had both undergone check-ups but after a second opinion, Carole did not require an operation. The problem with Gable's shoulder was – according to the spokesperson – apparently caused by a tooth infection. No other details were released.

Despite what officials said, the couple did undertake tests to try to find a reason for their failure to conceive. There were no positive conclusions, however, and the couple headed back to California still not knowing what the problem was. Actress Patsy Ruth Miller wrote about this period in her autobiography. According to the actress, she and her husband, John Lee Mahin, went to visit the Gables one evening and found Carole in bed. Leaving the two men to talk downstairs, Miller went upstairs to see the actress. As the two women chatted, Lombard told Miller that she had just undertaken a procedure to increase her chances of becoming pregnant; something she said Gable was very excited about.

After having recovered from the trip to Baltimore, Carole's lawsuit loomed large. Two thousand pages of testimony had been prepared and in the last week of January it all went to court. There, a number of revelations were brought to light, including the fact that Carole was to be paid $900,000 for six pictures at RKO, with a potential $2 million in earnings over the next three years, taking into account other screen and radio appearances. Quite bizarrely, in defence of his ability to push forward Carole's career, Myron Selznick named in his testimony a film contract that he had been able to negotiate for her. That would have been fine, if not for the fact that when examined by Carole's lawyers it was discovered that she hadn't acted in the film – Ginger Rogers had.

After hearing all the testimony, the court went in Carole's favour and it was decided that her decision to discharge Myron was both justified and legal. However, she would be required to pay the agent commission on her earnings up until the date she had fired him, which would total $27,500. Myron was excited that he would still be entitled to his share of her past earnings, and contacted the press to announce himself as the winner of the suit. This confused matters greatly and led to the Screen Actors Guild issuing a statement to newspapers, film magazines and trade journals:

> It is not true, as reported, that Myron Selznick won the arbitration. Miss Lombard won. The SAG regrets that an agreement by the parties that the only announcement in this matter would be a joint statement has been violated. This makes it necessary for the Guild to state the facts in justice to its member, Miss Lombard ... The arbitration board held, in favour of Miss Lombard, that the discharge was justified and rightful; that Selznick's contract was annulled, and that he had no right to commissions negotiated after that date.

On 12 February 1941 contracts were drawn up to officially release each party from their original agency agreement. Myron had been previously ordered to return all of Carole's documents to her, and this was also confirmed on 12 February. These items included cancelled cheques, monthly summary statements, notes on paid bills and expenses, income tax returns, ledgers, insurance policies, deeds, maps, leases, endorsements, letters and savings books. Everything was released into the hands of the Gables' secretary, Jean Garceau, and taken back to the ranch.

After the stress of the first few months of 1941, Carole decided to spend much of the rest of the year quietly with Gable, on the ranch and touring the country when he had time off from the studio. In November 1941 Carole wrote a letter to her friends, Babs and Eric, and told them that her time off had been wonderful. Despite just beginning a new film (*To Be or Not To Be*), she had little interest in her career any more. She explained that her decision not to make many films seemed to please Gable, and that he was the only person she was interested in pleasing.

*To Be or Not To Be* was a comedic melodrama directed and produced by Ernst Lubitsch, and co-starred Jack Benny and young actor Robert Stack. The film was mainly a send-up of Hitler and the Nazis, told through the eyes of a Polish theatrical company, with Carole playing an actress called Maria. Jack Benny played her husband, and Stack played Lieutenant Stanislav Sobinski. Stack had known Carole ever since her divorce from William Powell, and to him she was the consummate professional and the most thoughtful performer he had ever worked with. If he happened to move out of the light, she would gently move him back in before the director noticed. She looked after him not only on set but during the publicity photos, directing the shoot, incorporating a wind machine and showing him exactly what to do. The results, according to Stack, were the best publicity photos he had ever seen.

Once the film was completed, Carole got back to what she considered her real vocation: supporting her husband, spending time with friends and family and pottering around the ranch. Christmas was spent quietly and, as usual, she was kind and thoughtful to friends and colleagues. When she learned that her stand-in, Betty Hall, was ill after a serious accident, Carole decided not to give her the piece of furniture she had previously decided on. Instead, she found a large box and filled it with perfumes, a dressing gown, nightwear, pillows and a beautiful blanket. The note attached read, 'The least you can do, is get well in style'.

Carole started the year 1942 by working on her scrapbooks and took a real interest in gathering copies of her movies for personal use. The actress realised that she did not have a copy of *Made for Each Other* and asked publicist Russell Birdwell to contact Selznick on her behalf. On 2 January 1942 the producer wrote back to say that he would not be able to oblige the request, feeling that if he did it for one star, he'd be obliged to do it for others. He recommended that Birdwell tell Carole she should come back to him in August and he'd see what could be done then.

Away from hobbies, the Second World War was heavily underway and professional activities beckoned. As chairman of the Defence Co-ordinating Board for Actors, Clark Gable had been asked if he would tour the country in order to sell defence bonds, sold by the Treasury Department to raise money for the war effort. Being a terrible public speaker and busy with work, his first response was to decline. Carole thought this was a terrible decision and told him she would be honoured to be asked. Gable apparently turned to his wife and said, 'In that case, consider yourself asked', and with that, the actress was enrolled in the project.

At first reporters told readers that the couple would be doing the tour together. Hedda Hopper interviewed Carole on the subject, and asked what she would do if the Japanese invaded the ranch. In true Lombard style, she replied that the couple had already put themselves on a wartime status, selling some of their horses and growing vegetables to sustain the family. As for the Japanese, the actress declared that they were welcome to drop in. 'We haven't been banging away at ducks and skeets all these years for nothing,' she joked. Actually, the subject of the war was something she and Gable took very seriously. They had loaned some horses to the local air raid wardens and while Carole joked to reporters that she would chain her husband to the barn door if he tried to enlist, privately she did encourage her husband to do something for his country.

The war had not made much of a difference to the way she worked at the studio, though in an interview the actress explained that working hours had been changed from eight to five instead of nine to six, to ensure everyone was home during any blackouts. Another thing that had changed to an extent was the kind of movies the studios were putting out. Carole herself was planning to make a series of short movies to show patrons what to do in the event of a blackout or other war-related conditions.

Once it was decided that Carole should sell war bonds, plans were put into action straight away and the tour organised quickly. On 11 January 1942, a representative from Russell Birdwell's office arrived at Carole's home to help her write the speech she would make while in Indiana. Together they spent three hours talking about the kind of things she would like to say, and what information she wanted to impart. They came up with an impassioned speech, which Carole was very pleased with. The representative then added more points when he returned home, phoning the actress on Monday 12 January to give her the updates.

Once the speech and all necessary arrangements were completed, it was time to leave for Indiana. Carole hoped that her husband would accompany her, but his work on *Somewhere I'll Find You* prohibited that. In the film Gable would be working with young actress Lana Turner and, according to various friends, this knowledge irritated Lombard no end. The idea of him working with the blonde actress while his wife was out of town terrified her and the two had words shortly before she left. What transpired during the conversation can never be confirmed but, according to various sources, the two did not part on the best of terms. However, any arguments they may have had did not stop Carole placing a blonde dummy in his bed and giving a series of letters to her secretary with the intention they be given to Gable throughout her trip.

Before she left, Carole's long-term hairdresser, Loretta Francell, came to the house to work on the actress's hair. She noted that Carole looked tired and asked why she just didn't stop working and stay at home instead. 'I have my little people to take care of,' she said, 'and I don't want to put that burden on Pappy [Gable]. He has his little people too.' The two then talked about good deeds they had performed in the past, and how some people never stopped to thank them. Loretta exclaimed that from now on she would just be looking after herself, to which Carole replied, 'Listen, you'll end your life doing for the other fellow, and I will too.'

Because her husband could not attend the events, Carole asked her mother, Elizabeth, if she would like to go. She agreed and, together with MGM publicity man Otto Winkler, they set off. Gable was not at the train station to say goodbye; a decision that would ulitmately the actor would regret for the rest of his life. The train headed off to Indiana, but the journey was long and made stops at different towns and cities on the way.

As the group arrived in Utah, reporters clamoured to speak with the actress. She told them that she would be selling war bonds in Indiana, but added that this would not be the only destination. Comparing herself to a barker at a carnival, Carole announced her intention to get as many people as possible to 'realize what a good show we have in these United States'. She planned to travel around the country throughout the year, promoting the war bond scheme and taking part in United Service Organizations benefit programs on the east coast, similar to one she had recently done in the west.

While signing autographs for the fans who ran up during the stop, Carole explained the benefit of selling war bonds. 'I think the wonderful thing is that people are buying them so fast they can hardly keep going,' she said. She then gave a brief but passionate radio address, 'The morale of the country is the main thing. We've got to get out and get the boys pepped up.' Carole told the crowds how sad she was not to have enough time to sign everybody's books, and then posed happily for photographs for the next few minutes. Some of the lucky fans were soldiers and a small girl called Barbara K. Wadsworth, who had travelled to the station in the hope of buying a bond from the lady herself.

By the time Carole arrived in Indiana, the actress had sent Gable a telegram and spoken to him on the telephone. Any disagreement they may have had was now seemingly forgotten. Carole, wearing a black dress, fur cape and black hat, was welcomed back to her home state like a queen, and she was both humbled and ecstatic. Itinerary documents show that the actress, her mother and publicist were expected at 1.35 p.m., from Chicago. There, she would be met by Will H. Hays and other representatives, and escorted by police escort to the statehouse.

Everything was planned to the minute, but the demand for photographs was so great that she was delayed for some time while posing for the cameras. Up to 30,000 fans and local folk braved freezing temperatures, while Carole, Governor Henry F. Schricker and president of the Motion Picture Producers and Distributors of America, Will H. Hays, took part in a flag raising ceremony on the state capitol lawn.

After the thirty-minute ceremony, it came time to sell bonds at the statehouse. It was announced that at least $1 million worth of bonds were expected to be sold, but Carole incited so much passion that the money kept coming to the point where she had actually sold $2,017,513 worth. Purchasers were told to write their name, address and bank details on a piece of paper and give it to one of Lombard's assistants. In exchange, everyone received a receipt showing a photo of Carole, her autograph and a message, 'Thank you for joining me in this vital crusade to make America strong. My sincere good wishes go with this receipt, which shows that you have purchased from me a United States Defence Bond.'

The first purchaser was Cecilia Wenz, who bought $50,000 worth of bonds on behalf of the American Legion Auxiliary. Then a gentleman spent $1,000 from his own personal fund. The crowds loved meeting Lombard, and the feeling was mutual. When an elderly lady thanked her for coming to Indiana, Carole replied, 'My life would be insignificant if I didn't give my time to such causes'. To the crowd in general, she said:

> I feel that it is the duty of all of us to concentrate every ounce of energy and every dollar we possibly can spare for the purchase of defence savings bonds. This will not only help to carry us to victory in this war, but will fortify us in the future against a recurrence of this kind of attack.

After the bond selling, there was a reception for Carole at the governor's mansion, reserved for women only. Then, by 6.30 Carole and the rest of her team were in the Empire Room at the Claypool, where she relaxed and had dinner before the Pageant of Patriotism began, bringing drummers, soldiers, sailors, bands and singers together. The magnificent event reached its climax when Carole stepped up to the microphone to give her rehearsed speech.

It was a fairly short talk – just a page and a half of double-spaced type – but it was very personal in nature. 'Nothing could have made me happier than the kind of invitation to be here with you tonight,' she began, and then revealed that her invitation to the bond rally had been extended to her entire family, too. She joked that while that was in keeping with the spirit of Indiana hospitality, there would have been no room left for anyone else, had her clan attended.

The original speech was supposed to read, 'I've come home as Jane Peters, of Fort Wayne, Indiana'. However, this was changed because the governor intended to introduce her as such. Instead, Carole went straight into the reasons she had attended the event. The war needed to be won, she said, but more importantly, it needed to be fought to bring peace back into everyone's lives and to provide aeroplanes, guns and ships to those fighting for freedom. 'That is our job,' she said. 'To give our fighting men the instruments for winning this war and insuring the peace.'

Carole ended the impassioned speech by declaring it was everybody's duty to buy more and more stamps over the weeks, months and years ahead. 'With your help, we will win this war!' she shouted, before asking everyone to join her and the accompanying band and choir in a rendition of the 'Star Spangled Banner'. The effect the actress had on everybody who attended could be felt for miles around. Carole Lombard had come home, not only a success but a heroine of magnificent proportions.

# THE DARK MOUNTAIN

Carole was supposed to return to California by train, the day after the Indiana celebrations. However, quite suddenly she decided that the party should take a plane back instead. The reason was never fully made clear, but the general consensus is that she was fearful of giving Gable any more time alone with young actress Lana Turner and wanted to get home immediately.

Elizabeth Peters did not trust planes and had no wish to fly. A keen numerologist, she felt that travelling that way would be a terrible mistake and begged Carole to change her mind. The actress loved and respected her mother, but she refused to alter her plans. The three headed for the airport, where Elizabeth asked Otto Winkler for the name of the plane. Two witnesses – Mr and Mrs James C. Todd – recalled a conversation between the parties, where Winkler told Elizabeth that it was Flight 3 and called the Douglas Sky Club. Apparently she shook her head, told the publicist that they could not fly on that plane, and begged Carole to charter a private jet instead. The actress stubbornly refused and, after a decision based on the flip of a coin, the party of three eventually boarded Flight 3, bound for Los Angeles.

The Douglas DC-3 carrying Carole, Elizabeth and Otto had originated in New York and was also carrying a number of service personnel on board. During the trip back west, the plane made a variety of stops and passengers proceeded to get on and off. At one point Carole was asked if she would be prepared to give up her party's seats for some soldiers who wanted to board. She refused, citing the fact that she had been on the bond tour as a reason why she be allowed to stay. Carole had said no to countless things over the years. Sadly, this time it would cost her life.

The plane stopped in Las Vegas to refuel, and then at 7.07 p.m. on 16 January 1942 it took off again, destined for Los Angeles. The weather was clear, with high clouds and unlimited visibility. However, just fifteen minutes after take-off, the Douglas DC-3 crashed into the side of nearby Table Rock Mountain, killing the pilot and all passengers instantly.

Carole Lombard was dead. She was just 33 years old.

In Los Angeles, Clark Gable was impatiently awaiting the return of his wife. In retaliation for the blonde dummy she had placed in his bed when she left, he had placed a male one in hers. He told his secretary that he was desperate to see Carole again, and exclaimed that nothing was the same without her on the ranch. A limousine was sent to the airport to pick up Carole, Elizabeth and Otto, and Gable waited for a call from a friend at MGM to tell him when they had landed. By the time the telephone did ring, however, it was another friend, Eddie Mannix, on the line. He was not calling to announce Carole's arrival. Instead he gave Clark the desperate news that her plane would not be coming home.

Gable, Carole's brother, Stuart, and Otto's wife, Jill, all headed immediately to Las Vegas. Once there, all they could do was wait, though Clark himself tried desperately to climb the mountain to reach his wife. Support crews had to persuade the man to turn back. Thankfully, any photographs of Gable trying to climb were not captured as the press had previously been forced to hand over their cameras to the authorities. The only footage taken of the site was from official representatives of the Sheriff's Office. 'These photographs show the wreckage from various angles,' stated the FBI records, 'and also a number of the photographs show the bodies of the victims of the crash as they were strewn about the mountainside.'

For rescuers, the climb up Table Rock was atrocious. There were no roads, no clear footpaths, only a great deal of lose rock and shill. To make things worse, the mountain was also covered in snow, making the climb even more treacherous. The rescuers had no idea what – if anything – they would actually find once they'd reached the top. On the afternoon of the 17 January, the group was finally able to reach the wreckage and, as expected, the sight that greeted them was horrendous. One of the party gave his opinion of the crash to the FBI:

> The plane hit the mountain in a normal flying position, hitting with the left wing first on the sheer granite wall. This wing hitting had swung the plane enough that the right wing and the cabin of the ship had hit next, and the passengers had been literally thrown through the side of the cabin, which had practically disintegrated after the crash. It appeared to [Redacted] that the nose of the ship had gone up on the ledge after the crash, but the rest of the ship had fallen back down several hundred feet after the crash into a small ravine. The force of the impact had thrown gasoline further up on the ledge, which had burned on the ledge and also burned the nose of the ship.

The rescuers noted that the bodies of three army personnel had been thrown from the wreckage and were lying in the snow. They were described as 'badly mangled but identifiable'. All around the mountain were body parts, pieces of the plane wreckage, packages, mail, personal items and luggage. It was a truly disturbing site, made more so when some of the rescuers were chosen to stay on the mountain overnight while the others went down to gather more resources and people. One of the men told the FBI that he watched a number of planes fly over the site during the evening. To him, they all appeared to be around 3½ miles south of the wreckage, leading him to believe that Carole's plane must have been off course to hit the mountain the way it had. Furthermore, he could see the tops of the mountains all covered with snow, clearly visible for some distance:

> He could not understand how the pilot of the wrecked plane could not see the outlines of the mountains in sufficient time to turn either to the left or right and miss the peaks, even without gaining any altitude. It appeared to him as though the plane had made no effort to turn away from the mountain but had flown directly into the peak, and there was nothing to show that the plane had been in a dive.

At the hotel, Clark Gable heard the news that there were no survivors on the mountain and his beloved 'Ma' had gone. 'Oh God,' he moaned, and hung his head in his hands. He had given Carole a decorative clip for Christmas, and part of this – along with a few strands of hair – were found and returned to the actor. Body parts said to be those of Carole, Elizabeth and Otto were eventually brought down from the mountain and Gable took them back to Los Angeles by train. Because of Carole's work for the war effort, she was offered a full military funeral, but knowing how much she would have hated such a fuss Clark turned the offer down and instead had a very private funeral with just a few friends and family in attendance. She was then interred in a wall crypt at Forest Lawn with her mother on one side, and the other reserved for Gable.

On 21 January 1942, David O. Selznick wrote a note to Clark to express his deep sorrow at the loss of Carole. He told the actor that, in all his years in the business, he had never met such an inspiring person as Lombard, and promised that she would be missed by all who knew her for the rest of their lives. He also arranged for Clark to have a print of *Made for Each Other*; the film Carole had so desperately wanted for her collection just a couple of months before.

Her death had a profound effect on the producer, and on the very day he wrote to Clark he also sent a letter to the people in charge of defence bonds. In it he encouraged them to name the sale 'The Carole Lombard Memorial Drive'. Then he wrote to the Academy of Motion Picture Arts and Sciences, begging them to consider giving the actress a posthumous award. Unfortunately, the idea never came to pass.

From Washington, President Roosevelt and his wife sent a warm and caring telegram to Clark Gable. They had met and liked Carole very much and her loss was felt around the White House:

Mrs. Roosevelt and I are deeply distressed. Carole was our friend and our guest in happier days. She brought great joy to all who knew her and to the millions who knew her only as a great artist. She gave unselfishly of her time and talent to serve her Government in peace and in war. She loved her country. She is and always will be a star, one we shall never forget or cease to be grateful to. Deepest sympathy.

MGM released a photo to the press, showing their lion mascot bowing his head sorrowfully before a photograph of Carole. Then her final film, *To Be or Not To Be* was released just a month later and it was viewed rather poignantly by most. *Photoplay* summed up everybody's feelings:

The last picture made by Carole Lombard remains a fitting tribute to the vital, arresting beauty and personality of the star. There is no sense of shock at her posthumous appearance, so natural it seems that she should speak to us in this way.

# POSTSCRIPT

Because of the service personnel on board the plane, the FBI opened an investigation into what caused the crash. The initial notes disclosed the specifics that the plane had left New York at 10.00 p.m. on 15 January 1942 and stopped in Albuquerque, New Mexico, where it picked up several passengers. Because of air conditions at Boulder City, Nevada, the plane then landed at Las Vegas, taking off and crashing into the mountain just a short time later.

However, among the facts there were also notes about passenger Joseph Szigeti, a world-famous Hungarian violinist. Because he had given up his seat shortly before the crash, some members of the public falsely believed that he could have had something to do with it. This led to many letters being sent to the FBI with various accounts of how or why he could be involved.

Szigeti wasn't the only suspicious person, according to amateur sleuths. One anonymous, handwritten and garbled letter was postmarked Cincinnati, Ohio, 27 January 1942, and informed the FBI that the plane was destroyed by a German agent who had fought with the official pilots in the cockpit:

Enemy subs are still around Cape Cod. Their supplies are dwindling. A ship to shore communication is going on. The Island is between 40 or 60 miles all rock from Cape Cod. Hard to reach. The water surrounding is blueish, green. White capped. Subs in Sav., Ga., is same, heading for home [Japan] hugging the coast line.

There were also witnesses who claimed to see strange lights in the sky, both on the evening of 16 January and a few days before. One anonymous witness worked for the Civil Aeronautics Administration and described what he saw on 12 or 13 January 1942. In the report he stated that his duties were to observe the functioning of beacon lights, and on the night in question he was travelling south with a colleague approximately 4 miles north of Baker, California. During the trip they glanced west and saw a light above the mountains, about 15 miles from where they were:

> This light was a white bright light similar to an 18 inch course light, stationary and suspended against the sky as a background, and never moved or varied as long as we could see. It looked like it was suspended in the sky with nothing to show how it could be supported there.

Neither man had ever seen such a light before and they did not know what it could possibly be. On driving back to the station an hour later, the light had gone. They both decided that it could not be a star since it was much bigger in size but, because they could not give an answer to what the strange light could be, it was dismissed from their minds.

On 17 January, as the anonymous man was helping authorities with Carole's plane crash, he came into contact with rancher Willard George. He described that he had witnessed a strange light in the sky during the evening of the 16th, which is what prompted the first witness to give his story to authorities. A few days later, Mr George gave his version to the US Senate Subcommittee of the Commerce Committee on Safety in Air. In his report, George described how he had entertained guests at the El Rancho Hotel in Las Vegas. After leaving the hotel they were on the road and noticed a strange light above the mountains. 'A reddish-yellow glowing light which seemed suspended in the air … We noticed no flickering to it – it seemed just a glowing light which might be a light that was covered with a parchment.' Both George and his wife commented on the strange observation and decided first that it must be a bonfire in the mountains but then decided it could not be, due to the fact that there appeared to be no flicker.

When the couple arrived back at their ranch, Mr George went outside to drain the radiator on his car. As he did so, he was shocked to hear a roar in the sky above him. On looking up he observed a large plane which 'seemed to be revolving from left to right in a "flat spin" and appeared like a disc revolving in the air and gradually losing altitude'. He watched as the vessel did what he described as 'dives and climbs' before steadying itself, going into another spin and then disappearing behind a mountain.

He noted that there was no fire coming from the engines and 'at no time were the landing lights or any other lights lit on the plane'. He thought the sight strange enough to mention to his wife, though he admitted to authorities that his first thought was that it was probably a dive bomber from the school in Las Vegas, doing a few stunts.

While the FBI took an interest in the stories about Szigeti, as well as those coming from the witnesses in Las Vegas, in the end nothing came of the reports. Instead, they were all listed on the department notes as being 'undeveloped leads', with no visible follow-ups. The report of the Civil Aeronautics Board decided that there was no malicious intent involved with the crash; it was all a tragic and heartbreaking accident. Furthermore, there was no evidence of any failure of the plane's mechanics before the impact. It did not seem to have been in descent and the tops of the trees immediately below the crash site were not broken, meaning the plane had not been trying to climb steeply either. Instead, everything looked as though it had gone straight into the rock face, with the left wing impacting first with a protruding ledge.

Captain Wayne C. Williams and First Officer Morgan A. Gillette were both physically fit and qualified to fly the plane, and the radio was in perfect working order. With everything taken into account, the board decided that the crash was simply a case of pilot error, made when he did not follow the proper course nor use the navigational facilities available. In addition to that, most of the beacons in the area were turned out as a result of the war, meaning additional care and attention was needed, but not undertaken during the flight.

Williams was known to his employers as being someone who sometimes rejected instructions. The FBI concluded that while other pilots flew to the south side of the remaining beacon, Williams seemed to have flown to the north, 'consequently, it appeared that the pilot might have been off his course and believed that he had sufficient altitude, although actually he did not have. [Redacted] merely cited the above as an opinion.'

Clark Gable took some time off after the death of his wife and embarked on a period of mourning. He went hunting, but told friends it was not the same without Carole so he went home to the ranch and pottered around aimlessly. To preserve his wife's memory, Clark instructed his staff to keep her bedroom exactly as she had left it. Everything about him changed. Gone was the man who had the world at his feet, and in his place was a broken individual who raced his motorbike around the Hollywood Hills in the middle of the night and drank and smoked heavily.

The actor eventually returned to the studio in order to complete *Somewhere I'll Find You*, but his heart was no longer in his job. Instead, he thought endlessly about Carole's insistence he do something for the war effort. In August 1942 he signed up, attended courses in Florida and then headed overseas for combat. He insisted to friends that he had no interest in whether he came home dead or alive.

Clark did come home alive, and on 15 January 1944 attended a dedication ceremony to christen the SS *Carole Lombard*, named for his wife in celebration of her war effort. The event was also attended by best friend Fieldsie, MGM executive Louis B. Mayer and actress and friend, Irene Dunne. It was Dunne who had the honour of smashing the champagne over the bow of the ship. Gable did not flinch or alter his stoic facial expression as the bottle broke, but as the ship slipped peacefully out of the dock, he raised his arm and gave a final, sad salute.

# POSTSCRIPT

I'd like never to do anything in my whole life but laugh! The only thing of which you can be sure is today. Tomorrow is purely problematical. Make today as lovely as you can, laugh as much as you can – this day is your only sure possession!

Carole Lombard

# SOURCES

Hundreds of newspapers, magazine articles, documents and other materials have been accessed in order to write this book. Many of these items are listed below in specific chapters, but due to the huge amount of research done, it should be noted that the list is not exhaustive. In addition to the list below, I have also referred to items from:

The Selznick International Archive (Harry Ransom Center, the University of Texas at Austin).
The Russell Birdwell Papers (University of California, Los Angeles).
The Myron Selznick Papers (Harry Ransom Center, the University of Texas at Austin).
The Douglas Cohen Collection.
The Vincent Paterno Collection.
The Carole Sampeck Collection.
FBI records from the National Security Archive (Carole Lombard File, Box 18 – 'Federal Bureau of Investigation (FBI) Personality Files', a Michael Ravnitzky donation).
Files from the Sennett, Pathé, RKO and Paramount archives (Academy of Motion Picture Arts and Sciences).
Census, travel and other records from www.ancestry.com.

# SOURCES

## 1 – The Hoosiers

The life and death of James Cheney – *Fort Wayne Weekly Gazette*, 4 July 1895; *Fort Wayne Journal Gazette*, 14 December 1903; *The New York Times*, 14 December 1903.

Details of Fred C. Peters' accident – *Fort Wayne News*, 2 July 1898, 8 July 1898; *Fort Wayne Sunday Gazette*, 3 July 1898.

Fred C. Peters' career at J.C. Peters & Co. and Horton Manufacturing – *Fort Wayne Sentinel*, 30 June 1899, 2 Jan 1900, 5 June 1901.

The marriage of Fred C. Peters and Elizabeth Knight – unknown newspaper, 31 March 1902 and *Fort Wayne Weekly Sentinel*, 9 April 1902.

Other sources for this chapter– *Fort Wayne Journal Gazette*, 28 September 1903; *Movie Mirror*, July 1934; *Picture-Play*, June 1934; *The New Movie Magazine*, September 1931; *Screenland*, June 1931; *Washington Post*, 20 September 1931.

## 2 – Heading West

The trip to California – *Fort Wayne Sentinel*, 4 October 1915; *Fort Wayne Journal Gazette*, 5 October 1915; *New England News*, 14 April 1932.

Information about growing up in California – *Photoplay*, October 1933; *Oakland Tribune*, 12 April 1936; *Hollywood*, August 1934; also Los Angeles street directories and census records.

School plays, auditions and Carole's appearance in *A Perfect Crime* – *Fort Wayne Sentinel*, 6 July 1935; *Oakland Tribune*, 27 March 1932; *The Decatur Review*, 3 February 1929; *Silver Screen*, January 1937.

Trips to the Cocoanut Grove – *Hollywood*, November 1935; *Movie Mirror*, December 1936; *Motion Picture*, November 1938.

## 3 – Up, Up and Away

Carole's discovery – *Picture-Play*, June 1925; *Oakland Tribune*,
  27 March 1932; *Fort Wayne News Sentinel*, 6 July 1935;
  *Hollywood*, November 1935; *Movie Mirror*, December 1936.
*Marriage in Transit, Hearts and Spurs* and other very early career
  details – *The Galveston Daily News*, 11 October 1925, 21
  October 1925; *Movie Mirror*, December 1936; *Motion Picture
  News*, 20 June 1925, 4 July 1925; *Photoplay*, June 1925,
  September 1931; *Exhibitors Trade Review*, 25 April 1925;
  *Picture-Play*, December 1930; *Fort Wayne News Sentinel*, 6 July
  1935; *Variety*, 15 July 1925; *Titusville Herald*, 8 August 1925;
  *Hamilton Evening Journal*, 19 December 1925.

## 4 – Catastrophe

Carole's car crash and recovery – *Variety*, 19 October 1927; *Picture-
  Play*, August 1929, June 1934; *Los Angeles Examiner*, 20 May
  1934; *Motion Picture*, September 1934; *Hollywood*, November
  1935; *Ogden Standard Examiner*, 15 January 1939; *Radio
  Mirror*, April 1939; *American Cinematographer*, February 1927;
  *Film Daily*, 20 February 1927; *Modern Screen*, October 1940.
Carole's time with Mack Sennett – *Picture-Play*, December 1930,
  June 1934; *Hollywood Vagabond*, 3 November 1927, 1 December
  1927; *Motion Picture News*, 18 November 1927, 14 January
  1928, 24 November 1928, 30 March 1929; *Film Daily*, 24 June
  1927, 11 March 1928; *Oakland Tribune*, 12 April 1936; *Radio
  Mirror*, April 1939; *Exhibitors Herald and Moving Picture World*,
  3 November 1928.
Information from the Mack Sennett and Pathé Archive, housed in the
  Margaret Herrick Library, was accessed by Vincent Paterno on
  4 September 2015.
Contract with Pathé – *Variety*, 21 November 1928; *Exhibitors
  Daily Review*, 2 October 1928, 22 November 1928; *Exhibitors
  Herald and Moving Picture World*, 13 October 1928; *Motion*

*Picture News*, 29 September 1928, 6 October 1928, 10 November 1928, 16 March 1929, *Hollywood*, February 1935, *Picture-Play*, August 1929.

Quote about perfume – *Screenland*, June 1931.

## 5 – Looking Forward

Some of the items used in Chapter 4 in connection with Pathé, were also used in Chapter 5.

Carole's interest in fashion – *Motion Picture*, December 1933.

Transition from silent movies to talkies – *Motion Picture News*, 16 March 1929; *Hollywood Filmograph*, 1 June 1929; *Picture-Play*, August 1929; *Exhibitors Herald and Moving Picture World*, 15 December 1928.

*Show Folks* and *Ned McCobb's Daughter* – *The Film Spectator*, 10 November 1928; *Picture-Play*, March 1929; *Variety*, 8 August 1928, 15 August 1928.

*Dynamite* – *Photoplay*, March 1929; *Motion Picture News*, 2 February 1929; *Los Angeles Times*, 4 December 1928; *The Decatur Review*, 3 February 1929; *Picture-Play*, March 1929, August 1929; *Hamilton Evening Journal*, 25 July 1929; *Screenland*, February 1929, September 1929; *Exhibitors Herald and Moving Picture World*, 8 December 1928; *Motion Picture*, May 1929; *Oakland Tribune*, 12 April 1936; *Picturegoer*, 28 January 1939. Also, please see http://carole-and-co.livejournal.com/11206.html.

Howard Hughes – http://carole-and-co.livejournal.com/573215.html; *Hollywood*, February 1935.

*High Voltage* – *Picture-Play*, May 1929, June 1929; *Motion Picture News*, 25 May 1929.

*Big News* – *Los Angeles Times*, 12 April 1929; *Variety*, 9 October 1929; *Screenland*, December 1929; *Los Angeles Evening Herald*, 25 May 1929.

*Racketeer* – *Variety*, 6 November 1929; *Film Daily*, 12 January 1930; *Picture-Play* April 1930; *Motion Picture News*, 2 November 1929.

## 6 – Breakthrough

Termination of Pathé contract – *Variety*, 4 December 1929.

*The Arizona Kid* – *Screenland*, July 1930, August 1930; *Film Daily*, 18 May 1930.

*Safety in Numbers* – *Screenland*, September 1930; *The New Movie Magazine*, September 1930; *Educational Screen*, October 1930; *Screen Mirror*, November 1930.

Contract at Paramount – *Film Daily*, 9 September 1930.

Death of Alice Knight – *Fort Wayne Journal Gazette*, 26 January 1930; *Photoplay*, May 1931; *Nevada State Journal*, 30 November 1930. Also, travel records from www.ancestry.com show that she sailed from New York on 24 October 1929 and arrived in Los Angeles on 10 November 1929. She was travelling with Fred and Mary Hoffman (her daughter and son-in-law).

Trip to Fort Wayne and New York – *Film Daily*, 18 June 1930, 22 June 1930, 25 June 1930, 3 August 1930, 12 October 1930; *The New Movie Magazine*, September 1931; *Picture-Play*, December 1930.

Horace Liveright – *Photoplay*, October 1933. Also, http://carole-and-co.livejournal.com/50074.html.

## 7 – Mr and Mrs Powell

Relationship with William Powell (including marriage and divorce) – *Screenland*, April 1931, June 1931, November 1931; *Photoplay*, May 1931, September 1931; *Picture-Play*, April 1931, June 1932; *Silver Screen*, August 1931, September 1931, January 1932; *Modern Screen*, January 1932, October 1932, November 1932; *Motion Picture*, December 1931; *New York Times*, 8 July 1933, 19 August 1933; *Washington Post*, 27 April 1932, 8 July 1933, 11 August 1933; *Los Angeles Times*, 16 July 1933; *Movie Classic*, September 1931. Also, 'Carole Lombard's Carson City Divorce' by Guy Rocha, Nevada State Library and Archives, and interview conducted via letter from Robert Stack to Douglas Cohen, 20 February 1994.

*Man of the World – Screenland*, June 1931; *Variety*, March 1931.
*Ladies' Man Silver Screen*, August 1931.
Carole's illnesses after her honeymoon and *The Greeks had a Word
for It – Washington Post*, 28 August 1931; *Los Angeles Times*,
31 August 1931; *Film Daily*, 25 August 1931, 30 August 1931,
3 September 1931; *Modern Screen*, December 1931; *Movie
Classic*, November 1932.
Interest in tennis – *Photoplay*, June 1940.
*No One Man – Photoplay*, March 1932; *Motion Picture Herald*,
30 January 1932; *Film Daily*, 24 January 1932; *Silver Screen*, May
1932; *Variety*, 26 January 1932.

## 8 – Rebellion

*Sinners in the Sun – Los Angeles Times*, 11 June 1932; *Oakland
Tribune*, 31 July 1932.
Problems with Paramount – *Oakland Tribune*, 31 July 1932;
*Los Angeles Times*, 15 October 1932, 18 October 1932, 30
October 1932; *Picture-Play*, June 1932, June 1934; *Film Daily*,
2 September 1932, 19 October 1932; *Variety*, 18 October 1932.
*Virtue – Film Daily*, 26 October 1932; *National Board of Review
Magazine*, November 1932; *Variety*, 1 November 1932; *Motion
Picture Herald*, 5 November 1932.
*No Man of Her Own – Variety*, 22 November 1932; *Film Daily*,
31 December 1932; *Motion Picture Herald*, 24 December 1932.
The Depression – *Movie Classic*, May 1933.

## 9 & 10– Divorcee & Sudden Heartbreak

Items related to the divorce of William Powell and Carole Lombard
are listed in Chapter 7, under the general heading of 'Relationship
with William Powell'.
Rumours of love affairs and freedom after divorce – *Hollywood*,
September 1934; *Movie Mirror*, July 1934; *Screenland*,
December 1931.

*White Woman* – *Picture-Play*, June 1934; *Photoplay*, January 1934; *Film Daily*, 18 November 1933.

*Twentieth Century* – *Movie Mirror*, July 1934, December 1936; *Hollywood*, February 1935, February 1938; *Motion Picture*, undated.

The Film Stars' Frolic – *Los Angeles Examiner*, 20 May 1934. Also, http://www.sagaftra.org/sag-timeline and Morgan, Michelle, *The Ice Cream Blonde: The Whirlwind Life and Mysterious Death of Screwball Comedienne Thelma Todd*.

New house – *Silver Screen*, June 1935.

New Paramount contract – *Washington Post*, 2 September 1934.

Russ Columbo – *Photoplay*, October 1933; *Screenland*, December 1934; *Chester Times*, 3 September 1934; *Los Angeles Times*, 3 September 1934, 4 September 1934, 5 September 1934, 6 September 1934, 7 September 1934; *Waterloo Daily Courier*, 3 September 1934; *Lima News*, 3 September 1934; *Mansfield News*, 19 October 1934; *Washington Post*, 30 September 1934; *Movie Classic*, November 1934, December 1934; *Modern Screen*, November 1934; *Motion Picture*, September 1934, December 1934. Also, emails from Gregory Moore and Evonne Quinn.

## 11 – *Hands Across the Table*

Reunion with Powell rumours – *Los Angeles Times*, 24 September 1934.

*The Gay Bride* – *Film Pictorial*, 23 February 1935; *Screenland*, August 1936; *Los Angeles Times*, 26 September 1934; *Washington Post*, 7 November 1934, 18 November 1934; *Oakland Tribune*, 27 March 1932; *Movie Classic*, September 1935; *Film Daily*, 30 January 1935.

Proposed trip to Europe and time off – *Washington Post*, 5 January 1935; *Film Daily*, 7 January 1935, 8 January 1935, 10 January 1935, 12 January 1935, 22 January 1935, 28 January 1935, 8 February 1935; *Los Angeles Times*, 6 January 1935, 17 January 1935; *Variety*, 29 January 1935; *Fort Wayne News Sentinel*,

6 July 1935; *Hollywood*, August 1935; *Motion Picture Magazine*, August 1935.

*Rumba* – *Variety*, 27 February 1935; *Film Daily*, 12 February 1935.

Death of father – *Variety*, 27 February 1935.

*The New Divorce* – *Variety*, 10 April 1935; *San Antonio Light*, 30 April 1935; *Hollywood*, August 1935; *Film Daily*, 8 August 1935; *Motion Picture Daily*, 18 March 1935, 20 March 1935.

June 1935 party – *Picturegoer*, 28 January 1939; *Los Angeles Times*, 23 June 1935; *Washington Post*, 4 August 1935; *St Petersburg Evening Independent* (undated), found on http://carole-and-co. livejournal.com/621812.html.

Parties in general – *Photoplay*, February 1935, December 1936; *Washington Post*, 4 August 1935.

Road accident of servant – *Los Angeles Times*, 24 July 1935.

*Hands Across the Table* – *Radio Mirror*, June 1937; *Film Daily*, 25 October 1935.

## 12 – The King and Queen of Hollywood

Robert Riskin, Selznick International's interest in signing Carole and other details related to the film company were found in the Selznick International Archive. Also, *Screenland*, June 1936; *Modern Screen*, March 1936.

Early Gable romance in general – *Photoplay*, September 1936, October 1936; *Silver Screen*, July 1936; *Movie Classic*, December 1936; *Hollywood*, December 1937.

Mayfair Party – *Screenland*, April 1936; *Los Angeles Times*, 26 January 1936.

Breakdown Party – *Modern Screen*, May 1936, January 1937; *Silver Screen*, June 1936; *Los Angeles Times*, 9 February 1936; *Photoplay*, September 1936. Also, www.DearMrGable.com.

Valentine's Day car gag – *Los Angeles Times*, 21 May 1936; *Film Daily*, 6 April 1937; *Silver Screen*, June 1936. Also, http:// DearMrGable.com/?p=6254.

*Love Before Breakfast* – *Screenland*, May 1936, June 1936; *Los Angeles Times*, 2 April 1936.

Editor at *Screen Book* – *Screen Book*, April 1936.

*The Princess Comes Across* – *Screenland*, July 1936.

## 13 – *My Man Godfrey*

*My Man Godfrey* – *Screenland*, July 1936, September 1936; *Los Angeles Times*, 2 September 1936; *Photoplay*, August 1936; *Movie Classic*, September 1936; *Movie Mirror*, December 1936; *Film Daily*, 16 June 1936; *Motion Picture*, November 1938.

The continuing romance between Gable and Lombard was covered in many publications, including those listed in the Chapter 12 sources.

Change of name – *Los Angeles Times*, 30 September 1936.

1936 illness, good deeds and confidence – *Screenland*, October 1936; *Oakland Tribune*, 20 December 1936; *Movie Mirror*, December 1936; *Film Daily*, 26 June 1936; *Hollywood*, January 1937; *Modern Screen*, June 1942; *Picture-Play*, January 1937; *Motion Picture*, November 1938; *Radio Mirror*, April 1939; *Photoplay*, June 1940. Also, http://carole-and-co.livejournal.com/612283.html and www.DearMrGable.com.

Turf ball rumours – *Screenland*, May 1936; *Los Angeles Times*, 23 February 1936; *Hollywood*, December 1937; *Silver Screen*, June 1936.

New house – *Motion Picture*, February 1937; *Los Angeles Times*, 15 March 1937.

Selznick deal in general and contracts – Documents, memos and telegrams were found in the Selznick Archive.

*Dark Victory* – Memo from David O. Selznick to Dan O'Shea, 25 January 1937.

New contract and *Swing High, Swing Low* – Unknown newspaper, 7 February 1937; *Film Daily*, 15 March 1937; *Modern Screen*, June 1937; *Sandusky Register*, 31 March 1937; *Hollywood*,

December 1937. Also, http://carole-and-co.livejournal.com/11870.html.

## 14 – *Nothing Sacred Versus True Confession*

*Of Great Riches* – Letter from David O. Selznick to Frank Capra, 20 February 1937; memo from Selznick to Dan O'Shea, 19 March 1937.

*Nothing Sacred* and other information related to Selznick International – Documents, memos and telegrams were found in the Selznick Archive.

Jean Harlow's death – *Motion Picture*, March 1938.

Columbia Sales Convention – *Film Daily*, 1 July 1937. Also, memo from David O. Selznick to Dan O'Shea, 1 July 1937 and O'Shea's reply, 2 July 1937, found in the Selznick Archive.

Reviews of *Nothing Sacred* and celebratory plaque in Fort Wayne – *Motion Picture Herald*, 27 November 1937, 15 January 1938; *Screenland*, February 1938; *Photoplay*, February 1938.

*True Confession* – *Screenland*, February 1938; *Motion Picture Daily*, 21 December 1937; *Hollywood*, December 1937; *Photoplay*, January 1940, June 1940. Also, documents, memos and telegrams were found in the Selznick Archive.

*Fools for Scandal* – *Los Angeles Times*, 28 November 1937; *Film Daily*, 28 January 1938; *Photoplay*, June 1938; *Motion Picture Herald*, 18 June 1938.

## 15 – Ma and Pa

*American Sleeping Beauty* and break from screwball roles – Memo from David O. Selznick to Dan O'Shea, 10 January 1938; memo from David O. Selznick to Katharine Brown, 10 January 1938; message from Mrs Rabwin to David O. Selznick, 11 January 1938; *Motion Picture*, November 1938.

*Tom Sawyer* and low profile – *Los Angeles Times*, 10 February 1938; *Motion Picture*, March 1938; memo from Russell Birdwell to David O. Selznick, 10 February 1938; telegram from Carole to David O. Selznick, 11 February 1938.

More contract negotiations and general Selznick information – *Photoplay*, March 1938. Documents, memos and telegrams were found in the Selznick Archive.

Floods: *Photoplay*, June 1940.

*Fools for Scandal* – Please see sources for Chapter 14.

Burglary – *Hollywood*, December 1937; *Los Angeles Times*, 23 April 1938, 13 July 1939.

Possible fashion line – *Screenland*, June 1931; *Motion Picture*, December 1933; *Movie Classic*, May 1935; *Fort Wayne News Sentinel*, 6 July 1935; *Los Angeles Times*, 12 July 1938. Also, letter from Russell Birdwell to Cleo Costume Co., 24 May 1938; letter from Cleo Costume Co. to Mitchel Hamilburg, 26 May 1938; letter from Cleo Costume Co. to Russell Birdwell, 26 May 1938.

Gable/Lombard life in general – *Photoplay*, May 1938.


## 16 – *Made for Each Other*


Information about Carole's private life was gleaned from letters from Carole Lombard to Natalie Visart, including one written on 4 June 1938. These letters were accessed during other chapters too.

Publicity work at Selznick – *Los Angeles Times*, 12 July 1938; *Olean Times Herald*, 12 July 1938; *Hope Star*, 22 July 1938; *Picturegoer*, 20 August 1938, 23 December 1939; *Look*, 22 November 1938; *Film Weekly*, 5 February 1938, 17 December 1938.

*Made for Each Other* – Unknown newspaper article and press release from the Russell Birdwell Collection. Other documents, memos and telegrams were found in the Selznick Archive.

Also, *Photoplay*, January 1939, April 1939; *Motion Picture*, November 1938.

Paying taxes – *Picturegoer*, 28 January 1939; *Fort Wayne News
    Sentinel*, 25 August 1938; *San Antonio Light*, 9 October
    1938; *Motion Picture*, November 1938; *Photoplay*, November
    1938; memo from Russell Birdwell to David O. Selznick,
    20 October 1938.
30th Birthday – *Hollywood*, November 1935.
Radio appearances – *Radio Mirror*, March 1939, April 1939.


## 17 – Mr and Mrs Gable

'Hollywood's Unmarried Husbands and Wives' and other bad press –
    *Photoplay*, January 1939; *Los Angeles Times*, 15 December 1938;
    *Charleston Gazette*, 8 January 1939. Also, http://carole-and-co.
    livejournal.com/104986.html.
*Made for Each Other* reviews and positive press – *Photoplay*, April
    1939; *Independent Exhibitors Film Bulletin*, 11 February 1939;
    *Picturegoer*, 23 December 1939; *Ogden Standard Examiner*,
    15 January 1939.
*In Name Only* – Memos between Selznick and O'Shea; *Los Angeles
    Times*, 2 December 1938, 12 December 1938; *Photoplay*, October
    1939, December 1939; *Motion Picture Herald*, 4 November 1939;
    *Motion Picture Daily*, 3 August 1939.
Gable's hobbies and Carole's retirement – *Picturegoer*, 28 January
    1939; *Zanesville Signal*, 7 August 1938; *Fort Wayne News
    Sentinel*, 25 August 1938.
Gable's divorce – *Los Angeles Times*, 19 January 1939.
*Gone with the Wind* – Messages between David O. Selznick and
    Carole Lombard, January 1939, and other memos, telegrams and
    documents from the Selznick Archive. Also, *Los Angeles Times*,
    28 December 1939; *Showmen's Trade Review*, 23 December 1939;
    *Motion Picture*, March 1940; *Picture-Play*, December 1937.
Cheney will contest – *Los Angeles Times*, 26 January 1939, 9 March
    1939, 10 March 1939, 11 March 1939, 19 March 1939, 31
    May 1941.

Marriage – Letter from Carole to Natalie Visart, March 1939; *Fort Wayne Gazette*, 30 March 1939; *Los Angeles Times*, 30 March 1939; *Oelwein Daily Register*, 30 March 1939; *Waterloo Daily Courier*, 30 March 1939; *Bakersfield Californian*, 30 March 1939.

Intruder – Morgan, Michelle, *The Mammoth Book of Hollywood Scandals* (London: Robinson, 2013).

Home on the ranch – *Port Arthur News*, 15 October 1939; *Movie Mirror*, November 1939; *Motion Picture*, March 1940; *Photoplay*, March 1940, June 1940.

## 18 – *Vigil in the Night*

*In Name Only* – *Photoplay*, October 1939, November 1939, December 1939; *Motion Picture Herald*, 4 November 1939; *Motion Picture Daily*, 3 August 1939.

*Vigil in the Night* and appendix operation – Notes from the RKO Archive, accessed at Academy of Motion Picture Arts and Sciences by Vincent Paterno. Also, *Motion Picture Daily*, 22 August 1939, 28 August 1939, 11 September 1939; *Winnipeg Free Press*, 17 July 1939; *Showmen's Trade Review*, 10 February 1940; *Lock Haven Express*, 8 August 1939; *Modern Screen*, October 1940, June 1942; *Motion Picture*, November 1938.

Information related to Selznick International was found in the Selznick Archive.

For *Gone with the Wind* information, see sources in Chapter 17.

## 19 – Real Life Versus Fairy Tale

Problems with the next Selznick collaboration (and other information related to the company) found in a letter from David O. Selznick to Carole Lombard, dated 19 and 22 January 1940. Also the memos discussing her contract and *The Flashing Stream* were found in the Selznick Archive, dated 10 February 1940.

SOURCES

*The Flashing Stream* announcement – Various newspapers including
*Independent Exhibitors Film Bulletin*, 25 March 1939.
The disappearance of Gable and Lombard – *Los Angeles Times*,
2 February 1940, 3 February 1940.
*They Knew What They Wanted* and Hedda Hopper – *Los Angeles
Times*, 13 May 1940, 19 May 1940; *Hollywood*, October 1940;
*Modern Screen*, October 1940.
Life on the farm – *Photoplay*, June 1940.
4-H Club – Details were found in the Russell Birdwell Archive.
*Mr and Mrs Smith* – *Screenland*, April 1941; *Modern Screen*, April
1941; *Los Angeles Times*, 6 November 1940; *Middlesboro Daily
News*, 5 November 1940.
Christmas kindness – *Hollywood*, April 1942; *Modern Screen*,
June 1942.


## 20 – The Last Hoorah

Firing of Myron Selznick – *Los Angeles Times*, 25 January 1941;
*Motion Picture Herald*, 1 February 1941; *Film Daily*, 27 January
1941. Also, letters, documents and telegrams found in the Myron
Selznick Archive and David O. Selznick Archive.
Operation – *Los Angeles Times*, 2 January 1941; *Abilene Reporter*,
3 January 1941; *Picture-Play*, June 1932. Also, Miller, Patsy Ruth,
*My Hollywood: When Both of Us Were Young*.
*To Be or Not To Be* – Interview with Robert Stack by Douglas Cohen,
via letter; *Photoplay*, May 1942.
Not interested in her career – Letter to friends Babs and Eric, dated
29 November 1941.
War bonds – *Los Angeles Times*, 20 December 1941, 16 January
1942; unknown newspaper, 18 January 1942; *Hammond Times*,
14 January 1942, 15 January 1942, 16 January 1942; *Salt Lake
Tribune*, 14 January 1942; *Ogden Standard Examiner*, 13 January
1942; *Hollywood*, April 1942. Also, Carole's itinerary provided
by Douglas Cohen; memos from the Russell Birdwell Collection
and speech from the Russell Birdwell Collection.

## 21 The Dark Mountain & Postscript

Carole's death was recorded in hundreds of newspaper and magazine articles. In addition to those, I have also used FBI records from the National Security Archive – Carole Lombard File, Box 18, Federal Bureau of Investigation (FBI) Personality Files (Michael Ravnitzky Donation).

Roosevelt telegram – *Film Daily*, 20 January 1942.

Other information was found in documents, telegrams and memos from the Selznick International Archive.

Final quote – *Picture-Play*, June 1934.

NOTE: Many vintage magazine articles are available from an extraordinary website called the Media History Digital Library. This remarkable non-profit organisation is looking for donations and sponsors so they can continue making public domain magazines available to researchers and the general public. To find out more and support their cause, please visit their website: http// mediahistoryproject.org/

# SELECT BIBLIOGRAPHY

Bankhead, Tallulah, *My Autobiography* (Jackson: University Press of Mississippi, 2004).

Betts, Ernest, *Daily Express Film Book* (London: *Daily Express*, 1935).

Blum, Daniel, *A Pictorial History of the Silent Screen* (London: Spring Books, 1953).

Burk, Margaret Tante, *Are the Stars Out Tonight? The Story of the Famous Ambassador and Cocoanut Grove, 'Hollywood's Hotel'* (Los Angeles: Round Table West, 1980).

Cowie, Peter, *Louise Brooks: Lulu Forever*, edited by Eva Prinz (New York: Rizzoli, 2006).

Davis, Lon, *Silent Lives: 100 Biographies of the Silent Film Era* (Albany, GA: BearManor Media, 2008).

Fiell, Charlotte, and Emmanuelle Dirix (eds), *Fashion Sourcebook 1920s* (London: Fiell Publishing, 2011).

—— *1930s Fashion: The Definitive Sourcebook* (London: Goodman/Fiell, 2012).

Garceau, Jean, with Inez Cocke, *Dear Mr G: The Biography of Clark Gable* (London: Four Square, 1961).

Gehring, Wes D., *Carole Lombard: The Hoosier Tornado* (Indianapolis: Indiana Historical Society Press, 2003).

Golden, Eve, *John Gilbert: The Last of the Silent Film Stars* (Lexington: University Press of Kentucky, 2013).

—— *Platinum Girl: The Life and Legends of Jean Harlow* (New York: Abbeville Press, 1991).

Hampton, Benjamin B., *A History of the Movies* (New York: Covici Friede, 1931).

Harris, Warren G., *Clark Gable* (London: Aurum Press Ltd, 2003).

—— *Gable and Lombard* (London: Corgi, 1977).

Kanin, Garson, *Hollywood* (New York: Viking, 1974).

Kobal, John, *People Will Talk* (London: Aurum, 1986).

Marble, Alice and Dale Leatherman, *Courting Danger: My Adventures in World-Class Tennis, Golden-Age Hollywood and High-Stakes Spying* (New York: St Martin's Press, 1991).

Matzen, Robert, *Fireball: Carole Lombard and the Mystery of Flight 3* (Pittsburgh: GoodKnight Books, 2014).

Miller, Patsy Ruth, *My Hollywood: When Both of Us Were Young,* (Albany, GA: BearManor Media, 2012).

Morella, Joe and Edward Z. Epstein, *Gable and Lombard and Powell and Harlow* (London: WH Allen, 1976).

Morgan, Michelle, *Marilyn Monroe: Private and Undisclosed* (London: Robinson, 2012).

—— *The Mammoth Book of Hollywood Scandals* (London: Robinson, 2013).

Ott, Frederick, *The Films of Carole Lombard* (New Jersey: The Citadel Press, 1972).

Paris, Barry, *Louise Brooks: A Biography* (London: Mandarin Paperbacks, 1990).

Rice, Christina, *Ann Dvorak: Hollywood's Forgotten Rebel* (Lexington: University Press of Kentucky, 2013).

Rooney, Darrell, and Mark A. Vieira, *Harlow in Hollywood: The Blonde Bombshell in the Glamour Capital, 1928–1937* (Santa Monica, CA: Angel City, 2011).

Schessler, Ken, *This is Hollywood: An Unusual Movieland Guide* (Redlands, CA: Ken Schessler, 11th Edition, 1993).

Schickel, Richard, and George Perry, *Bette Davis: Larger than Life* (Philadelphia: Running Press, 2009).

Shearer, Stephen Michael, *Gloria Swanson: The Ultimate Star* (New York: Thomas Dunne, 2013).

Stenn, David, *Bombshell: The Life and Death of Jean Harlow* (New York: Doubleday, 1993).

——*Clara Bow: Runnin' Wild* (London: Ebury, 1989).

Swindell, Larry, *The Last Hero: A Biography of Gary Cooper* (London: Robson, 1981).

——*Screwball: The Life of Carole Lombard* (New York: William Morrow, 1975).

Tornabene, Lyn, *Long Live the King: A Biography of Clark Gable* (New York: Pocket Books, 1976).

Torrence, Bruce, *Hollywood: The First 100 Years* (Hollywood: Hollywood Chamber of Commerce and Fiske Enterprises, 1979).

Webb, Michael (ed.), *Hollywood: Legend and Reality* (London: Pavilion, 1986).

Wilkerson, Tichi, and Marcia Borie, *The Hollywood Reporter: The Golden Years* (New York: Coward-McCann, 1984).

Wills, David, and Stephen Schmidt, *Hollywood in Kodachrome* (New York: It Books, 2013).

# INDEX

You may also be interested in …

978 0 7509 6117 2

Exploring an aspect of Monroe's life that
has never been fully revealed  charting
every modellng job she did, and illustrated
with rare and unpublished photographs.

You may also be interested in ...

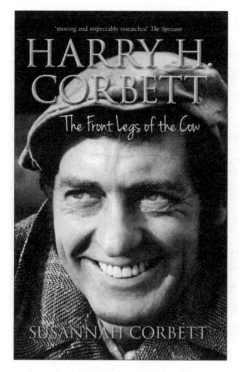

978 0 7524 8787 8

'moving and impeccably researched ...' –
*The Spectator*

You may also be interested in ...

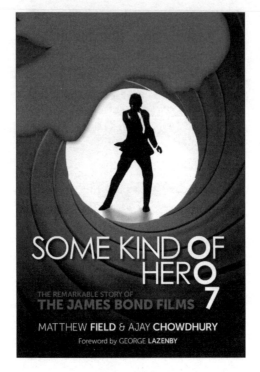

978 0 7509 6421 0

Some Kind of Hero recounts the remarkable story of the Bond films, from its
origins in the early '60s right through to
the present day, and draws on hundreds of
unpublished interviews with the cast and
crew of this iconic series.